Don't Think, Dear

Also by Alice Robb

Why We Dream

Don't Think, Dear

On Loving

Leaving Ballet

Alice Robb

MARINER BOOKS *New York   Boston*

HarperCollins books may be purchased for educational, business, or sales promotional use. For information, please email the Special Markets Department at SPsales@harpercollins.com.

FIRST EDITION

Designed by Chloe Foster

Library of Congress Cataloging-in-Publication Data

Names: Robb, Alice, author.
Title: Don't think, dear : on loving & leaving ballet / Alice Robb.
Other titles: Do not think, dear
Description: First edition. | New York : Mariner Books, [2023]. | Includes bibliographical references and index. |
Identifiers: LCCN 2022040833 (print) | LCCN 2022040834 (ebook) | ISBN 9780358653332 (hardback) | ISBN 9780358653318 (ebook)
Subjects: LCSH: School of American Ballet—History. | Ballerinas—United States—Biography. | Robb, Alice. | Ballerinas—United States—Social conditions. | Ballet—History—United States.
Classification: LCC GV1788.6.S36 R63 2023 (print) | LCC GV1788.6.S36 (ebook) | DDC 792.8/0973—dc23/eng/20220917
LC record available at https://lccn.loc.gov/2022040833
LC ebook record available at https://lccn.loc.gov/2022040834

ISBN 978-0-358-65333-2

22 23 24 25 26 LBC 5 4 3 2 1

To my parents

Author's Note

My memories of the School of American Ballet are occasionally intermingled with memories of other ballet schools and summer programs I attended in the early to mid-2000s. I am not exploring just one institution, but the culture of preprofessional ballet training during that time period.

"Rachel" and "Michelle" are, at their request, composites. All other names and stories are unchanged.

Contents

Introduction

We are eleven or twelve years old, but most of us look younger; we have been chosen, in part, because we are small for our age. Our smiles are tense, our necks stretched, our backs erect. Perhaps we are pretending, as we've been taught, that a puppeteer is pulling up our heads by a string. We have been told that our ballet school is the best in the world; we have been told that we are lucky. There are twenty of us in the photo, and we all want the same thing: to dance with the New York City Ballet.

My cheek is tilted up toward the light, but my eyes are pointed down. This year, my body has begun to defy me: the curve of my hip is peeking out from my torso, disrupting the once-smooth line of my leg. I can control my muscles and my weight, but, I am learning, I cannot control my bones.

For picture day, at least, I have managed to subdue my frizzy hair. It lies flat against my head, slicked into a bun so tight I can almost feel it tugging at my scalp. I don't want to add any volume to my head: our founder, George Balanchine, said that a dancer's head should be small, and this will always be his school, even if he has been dead for twenty years.

I am kneeling. My wrists are crossed in front of my heart—a gesture that, in classical ballets like *Giselle*, signifies love. Of course, I didn't choose this pose; I was only doing what I was told. Our teacher has arranged us in three rows and told us what to do with our hands and arms and legs. They don't have to tell us to smile.

I hadn't thought about this photo in over a decade when it popped up on my laptop one afternoon a few years ago. My primary social media vice is Twitter, and I was late to joining Instagram. My feed consisted of only a few types of content: skillets of hearty pasta and aspirational loaves of bread from the *New York Times* Cooking account; flowers hand-painted on fancy hotel walls, from a childhood friend who is now a wallpaper influencer; and all the mundane updates, selfies, and vacation snaps from a handful of women I hadn't spoken to since we were kids at the School of American Ballet.

I've forgotten who was in my fifth-grade class at school, and I stopped caring about the high school hot girls long ago. But these women—I follow them like they're characters on my own private reality TV show. I feel like a voyeur, a creep, but I can't help it: I need to know what happened to the girls I once spent hours with each week; the girls I once knew so well that I could recognize them by the curve of their fingers or the shape of their pointed toes.

When I see the picture, I feel, suddenly, less like a voyeur. I see my own face, and I feel like I have permission to be looking. I copy and paste the picture into a group chat and tell my friends to guess which little dancer is me. No one has any trouble. One says I look sad. Another says it makes him uncomfortable; it reminds him of the poster for *Cuties*, the French film about preteen dancers that drew comparisons to child porn and inspired a campaign to #CancelNetflix.

I zoom in on the picture. On the wall behind us are three Hopperesque paintings, scenes of our own studios: leggy women in leotards, and in the middle—engaged in what looks like a standoff with a dancer in pink—New York City Ballet's artistic director, Peter Martins, the man who could one day determine our fate. His hands are planted confrontationally on his hips, his chiseled jaw jutting forward. The painter has, in a few brushstrokes, captured his aura—his aggression. He looks angry. He looks like someone who would drag a woman down a flight of stairs. Like someone who would bully women about their weight and trade sex for roles. Fifteen years later, in the midst of #MeToo, dancers would allege—in an anonymous letter and in interviews with the *New York Times* and the *Washington Post*—that he did all those things.

But perhaps Martins learned from his predecessor, George Balanchine, pictured beside him, who in 1965 said that he chose dancers for the New York City Ballet "as you would choose horses." The older teachers, the ones who danced for him, still called him Mr. B, and we were in awe of their link to our hero. Dancers "are obedient animals," Mr. B told *Life* magazine. "They are trained to wait and wait and wait until you say do this and they do, stop and they stop. . . . Then you say thank you, now go home."

I didn't care if dancers were obedient animals or ethereal fairies or powerful athletes: whatever they were, I wanted to be one, had wanted to as far back as I could remember. From the earliest toddler "ballet" lessons I was enrolled in, I lobbied my parents for more. My favorite part of those classes was not the reward at the end—when we were finally allowed to freestyle, to flap our arms and make believe we were butterflies or birds—but when we stood at the barre: when we were told what to do, and when it was hard. When I arranged my feet in the neat little V of first position and earned the pretty teacher's praise.

At home, my shelves were lined with ballet-themed picture books—*Angelina Ballerina, Ballet Stories for Children*—and I turned the pages, staring at the pink tutus and white swans before I knew how to make out the words beside them. I rescued a tiny plastic ballerina from the top of a cupcake and developed an unnatural attachment to her, taking the figurine with me everywhere I went. When she slipped through my fingers, fell onto the sidewalk, and was crushed beneath the wheels of my stroller, I was devastated.

At night, after class, I would sit cross-legged on my bedroom floor, take one foot in both hands, and mold it, pressing my instep into a perfect arch and curling my toes into little Cs. *What would my life be like if my feet looked like this?* I would admire the shape, then release my hands and try to hold it, clenching my muscles as hard as I could. When I got frustrated, I would mash my foot into the floor, faking a higher arch by letting the full weight of my body fall on my metatarsals. I would stay that way until I couldn't stand it anymore.

If success is some combination of talent and hard work, then, in my case, the scale was tilted almost entirely toward work. "I auditioned to get into a famous ballet school called the School of American Ballet, abbreviated as SAB," I explained to my diary in the fall of 2001. I kept diaries sporadically throughout my childhood, writing regularly for a few weeks or months before losing interest, but every time I started a new one, I dutifully relayed the whole story: How I had auditioned for SAB twice and been rejected. How, when I was nine, my mom had said I could try one more time. How it was raining on the day of my third audition. I knew what to expect by then, and I forced my arches off the ground and sucked in my stomach as the ballet mistresses looked me up and down, making notes on a clipboard and whispering behind their hands. Afterward, I lingered in the dressing room, thrilled to breathe the same air and touch the same lockers as real students at the school. I unpinned the audition number—2—from the front of my leotard and stashed it in my bag with my slippers and tights.

When my mom told me that someone from SAB had called, that I had finally gotten in, I jumped up and down in the street, screaming. It was a few days after 9/11 and the sidewalks were nearly empty. A handful of dejected people, sitting aimlessly on their stoops, stared at me as if I had violated the code of silence. The city was in mourning, but it was the best day of my life. At home, I uncrumpled my audition paper, stapled it to my bulletin board, and decided that 2 would be my lucky number, rain my lucky weather.

Most afternoons from then on, I would hurry out of school as soon as the bell rang and hightail it across Central Park in a cab. The thrill of jogging up the escalator at Lincoln Center, pushing open the glass doors like I belonged, never wore off. I learned to pour all my energy, mental and physical, into microscopic adjustments to the way I moved. I loved that when I entered the studio, I didn't have to worry about saying the right thing; I didn't have to talk at all.

"I say that I don't want to become a ballerina, because my parents think it is a bad job, and maybe they're right," I wrote in my diary—whose cover was embossed with a picture of pointe shoes—when I was eleven. "It is true that it might be hard to find a new job because you can't go to college because of ballet classes. But it is true, too, that it is my dream to become a ballerina. I love ballet."

I was born in 1992: the Year of the Woman. It was a time of girl power and optimism, feminist zines and riot grrrls. My friends dismembered Barbies and cut off their hair. Teenage girls on TV slew vampires and confidently cast magic spells. My mom wore flannel shirts and no makeup. My teachers urged me to speak up, challenge authority, and think for myself. Still, I couldn't help noticing that it was usually boys who raised their hands (or, more often, called out the answers without bothering). I wondered whether my teachers had misled me—whether speaking up was unseemly after all. I wondered how many times I could roll up the waistband of my skirt before crossing some ill-defined line into indecency. How much makeup I could wear without looking high-maintenance. As a girl—according to T-shirt slogans, pop music, my parents—I could be anything I wanted. My options were endless, I was told, and overwhelming. Should I study Spanish or French? Wear jeans or a dress? Did I want to become a doctor, a writer, a stay-at-home mom?

But after school, I retreated into a world in which these responsibilities evaporated. My daily four p.m. code-switch gave me whiplash, but once I recovered, it was a relief. At ballet, no one asked me what I wanted to be when I grew up; it went without saying. Of course I wanted to be a dancer. The dress code was strict and hadn't changed in decades. Making an effort on my appearance was mandatory, and hiding this effort was unnecessary. I took lessons in stage makeup, learned to layer powder and bronzer and blush, to paint on a face that was, by the end, only loosely based on my actual face. But focusing on my looks wasn't vain; it was part of my art.

At ballet, girls followed the rules and did as we were told. "Don't think, dear," one teacher liked to say, affecting a faint Russian accent as she repeated George Balanchine's famous dictum. We couldn't go to the water fountain or the bathroom without permission. At the end of class, we curtsied to our teachers and thanked them—the only time we were allowed to speak.

I loved the hyperfeminine trappings of it all, the unapologetic girlishness. Every year, when I graduated to a new level and a new leotard—sky blue, bubblegum pink, hunter green—I went shopping for a new hair wreath to match, a gaudy mass of ribbons, beads, and satin flowers to wrap around my bun. I idolized the older girls around me, and the women in the company were like gods.

Outside the studio, I latched onto ballet as my identity. I wore my hair to school in a tight bun, and when I started needing a bra, I instead wore a leotard under my clothes. I relished my classmates' gasps when I faux casually eased into a straddle split during gym class warm-ups, or when I bent all the way backward playing limbo at bar mitzvahs. Anyone who entered my bedroom at home would be confronted by a veritable shrine to ballet. I collected pairs of pointe shoes autographed by NYCB dancers and nailed them to the wall above my bed. (We would leave notes at the stage door, complimenting our favorite dancers and asking for their worn-out shoes.) Inside the dresser were drawers of oversized T-shirts emblazoned with the logos of various summer programs I'd passed through. The wall above it was dominated by a giant poster of Degas's *La classe de danse*, and I would fall asleep studying it: the girl posing in an eternal arabesque, the girl pouting on the sidelines, the girl primping in the back.

✻   ✻   ✻

The twelve-year-olds in the class photo would be disappointed to learn that we did not all become dancers in the New York City Ballet; today, only one of us is a professional ballerina. The others are personal trainers or ballet teachers or makeup artists or college graduates. Just a few years after the photo was taken, I looked at my adolescent body—at my hips, which had continued to widen; at my feet, their underdeveloped arches— and conceded that my dreams were becoming far-fetched.

But even though I could stop going to class, avoid Lincoln Center, and cancel my subscription to *Pointe* magazine, I couldn't unlearn the values of ballet. Sometimes, in social settings or at school, I felt like I was still reading from a different script. And even as I finished high school and college and built a writing career I loved, I couldn't stop stalking my old ballet classmates on Facebook or dreaming about dancing at night.

"Ballet is woman," Balanchine famously said. Every day on my way to class, I walked by a banner bearing that quote. Ballet had given me a way to be a girl—a specific template of femininity. What did it mean to be a woman without ballet? As an adult, I struggled with contradictions that had plagued me since middle school: how to be ambitious but unthreatening, feminine but strong. I sold a book, and the man I was dating said it made him feel bad. I promoted the book, and men online critiqued my appearance. "This girl is too bubbly!" wrote a man who saw me on TV. "I found it very difficult to listen to you on account of your vocal fry," wrote another. I wondered how the values I had internalized at ballet continued to influence my psyche and behavior. I wondered why I still felt susceptible to feminine tropes that many of my peers had recognized as outdated, and shaken off. (I did not ditch the man who resented my book; I told him how much I liked his articles, how important I thought they were.)

I found myself missing ballet—the only environment where I had been able to throw myself into my work without worrying about the sound of my voice. Where hard work made me not just stronger and more successful but more feminine, too. Where I fully inhabited my physical being while also engaging my brain—solving, for myself, the mind-body problem.

And then I felt guilty about harboring affection for a system that clearly harmed women. If I'd had any doubt, the flood of allegations that came out during #MeToo—including NYCB "ballet master" Peter Martins's long history of sexual bullying—made it impossible to deny. Everyone, it seemed, was reevaluating their relationship to the art of "monstrous men." The once-canonical movies of Woody Allen and Roman Polanski were downgraded to guilty pleasures; DJs stopped playing R. Kelly. "Certain pieces of art seem to have been rendered inconsumable by their maker's transgressions—how can one watch *The Cosby Show* after the rape allegations against Bill Cosby?" asked Claire Dederer in a viral *Paris Review* essay. "Do we believe genius gets special dispensation, a behavioral hall pass?" Her words haunted me as I got on the subway to go see *Jewels*, my favorite Balanchine ballet. Balanchine, the brilliant choreographer whose work still took my breath away; Balanchine, the tyrant who punished his dancers for getting pregnant and required them to wear his favorite perfume. Balanchine, my problematic fave.

As I wrestled with my feelings about ballet and femininity and my body, I wondered how my old friends were faring. What had become of the ambitious girls in my SAB class? How had they coped with the disappointment of not making it?

How had growing up in a world where our looks were constantly critiqued, where abusive men were in charge, where we learned to talk with our bodies instead of our voices, affected our lives? How had it shaped our ideas about how a woman should be and how the sexes interact? How did we reconcile our past, and our residual love for ballet, with the feminist consciousness we eventually developed?

These questions matter not just for elite ballet students—according to a *Teen Vogue* web series, three hundred thousand students train at the professional level every year, undeterred by the fact that just two percent will make it into a company—or for the many more recreational ballet students, or even for the millions who have taken their children to *The Nutcracker* or signed up for a barre class or admired Misty Copeland on Instagram. Even those who have never been to Lincoln Center have inevitably been influenced by the aesthetics of ballet. Over the past few years, ballerinas have been featured in major ad campaigns for cars, sneakers, watches, and jeans; they have appeared on runways at New York Fashion Week and in music videos for Kanye West and Taylor Swift. Clothing inspired by dancers' costumes—leotards, ballet flats, tutus à la Carrie Bradshaw—cycle in and out of fashion. An *Allure* video chronicling "A Ballerina's Entire Routine" has been viewed almost ten million times. *Marie Claire*, *Cosmopolitan*, and *Vogue* regularly interview dancers about their makeup tricks and eating habits. Fashionable women, hoping to achieve a "ballet body," sign up for pricey barre classes based on traditional warm-ups or stream workouts from *Ballet Beautiful*—a series founded by the dancer who helped Natalie Portman achieve her skeletal *Black Swan* figure.

For many young girls, wanting to be a ballerina is practically as much a stage of development as holding a crayon or riding a bike. When the journalist Peggy Orenstein looked through a stack of exercises by the children in her daughter's preschool class—they had been prompted to fill in the clause "If I were a [blank]"—she noticed that the girls had imagined themselves in only four occupations: princess, fairy, butterfly—and balle-rina. (The boys, meanwhile, filled in a broad range of make-believe roles, including superhero, fireman, athlete, and raisin.) Ballerinas are as much a part of the lexicon of little-girlhood as Barbie: Mattel, in fact, began selling a Ballerina Barbie in the 1970s, and entered into a sponsorship deal with the English National Ballet in 2001.

Ballet does not exist in a vacuum. It is a laboratory of femaleness—a test-tube world in the middle of modern New York or London or Paris in which traditional femininity is exaggerated. The traits ballet takes to an extreme—the beauty, the thinness, the stoicism and silence and submission—are valued in girls and women everywhere. By excavating the psyche of a dancer, we can understand the contradictions and challenges of being a woman today.

Mr. B

I don't know when I first became aware of George Balanchine; it may have been before I started forming long-term memories. As far as I can remember, he was always a part of my consciousness—a ghost or a god looming over my childhood. By the time I entered the School of American Ballet in 2001, Balanchine—who founded the school in 1934, and the New York City Ballet in 1948—had been dead for almost two decades. But it didn't feel that way to us. He grinned at us from larger-than-life photos lining the hallways and watched over us as a bust beside the elevator. "Mr. B said," one of the older teachers would begin—a note of pride in her voice—and we listened, rapt; we were the chosen ones, the special recipients of secret knowledge. We stood up a little taller and took those corrections extra seriously, striving to please the master we would never meet. My classmate Rachel has similar memories. "Our teachers would speak about him as if he was still alive," she said, "as if he were some sort of savior."

Like an evangelist always trying to proclaim my faith, I found ways to incorporate Balanchine into my life outside the studio. When I had to write a "biography" of an American figure for my fourth-grade history class, I chose him. A few years later, assigned to write an essay about my role model for an

English class, I chose Darci Kistler—Balanchine's last muse, and the only one still dancing.

From beyond the grave, Balanchine had given us the best Christmas gift a kid could want: when he choreographed his version of the Russian *Nutcracker* ballet in 1954, he had created roles for more than a hundred children. Before I started at SAB, I had been a wide-eyed member of the *Nutcracker* audience, one among the throngs of children for whom the ballet was a holiday tradition. (Ballet companies all over the country rely on families' annual pilgrimages to *The Nutcracker*; NYCB's five-week, forty-seven-show run accounts for almost half of the company's annual ticket sales. Nearly every regional troupe has its own rendition, from the burlesque *Nutcracker* in Seattle to the *Cracked Nutz* parody in Columbus, Ohio.)

In October 2001, a handwritten casting sheet was posted outside the dressing room. We crowded around, scanning for our names, and I jumped when I saw mine; I didn't care that I had been given one of the smallest parts. As a toy soldier in the ballet's battle scene, I would spend only about three minutes onstage each night, but I took my responsibilities—sashaying in a line, aiming a fake rifle at men in mouse costumes—very seriously. "I'm rehearsing for *The Nutcracker*. Yes, the 'real' *Nutcracker* at Lincoln Center," I bragged to my own diary.

Backstage, older girls helped us get ready, dipping bottle caps in paint and tracing bright red circles on our cheeks. My favorite part of the night was just before I went on: I would huddle with my friends in the wings, giddy with the anticipation of going onstage and the thrill of sharing the space with real company dancers. I watched the grown-up snowflakes warm up for Act II, casually glamorous in their tutus and sweatshirts, and breathed in the musky stew of makeup, hairspray, and sweat. I'd hear my cue and run onstage, and the giddiness—which had escalated, briefly, into nerves—disappeared, leaving only a pleasurable alertness in its wake.

Beside me in the phalanx of red-cheeked soldiers was my friend Lily. I don't remember how, exactly, Lily and I became friends. We had been assigned to stand next to each other at the barre—forgotten residents of tall-girl Siberia—but talking in class was forbidden, and we were as obedient as everyone else; our alliance must have been forged in the dressing room, or in the stolen moments before the teacher arrived. I know that by the time we were cast as battle scene comrades, we had the kind of all-consuming teenage friendship that feels like a love affair. We groomed each other like cats—sticking bobby pins in each other's buns and helping each other stretch—and played jacks on the floor, a *Nutcracker* tradition that had been passed down for decades. (I would start practicing jacks around the same time we began rehearsing in October, sitting in a straddle and bouncing a palm-sized rubber ball on the living-room floor; proficiency at jacks was as much a social currency as packing the right lipstick in our plastic Caboodles.) Lanky and studious, Lily had a longer commute to Lincoln Center than most of us; she came in every day from Queens, where she lived with her Hungarian immigrant parents. A competitive, tomboyish kid, ballet for Lily was not about the dream of wearing a tutu but about the physical challenge and the drive to succeed. I don't remember whether Lily and I commiserated openly about our height—whether we admitted to wishing we could join our shorter classmates in the Stahlbaums' stately living room in Act I, or under Mother Ginger's skirt in the Land of Sweets—but I'm sure a sense of indignation was part of the glue that bound us together.

After our army was trounced, and the mice—played by company men in puffy fat suits—hauled us, flailing and kicking, into the wings, I would join my friends backstage to watch the second act on the basement monitor or, if I spotted a free seat in the theater, sneak into the audience. After I got home, I would pick dirty scraps of paper "snow"—which fell from the ceiling in a magical Act I blizzard—out of my clothes or my hair, like grains of sand after a day at the beach. But I didn't mind; I gathered them up and kept them as souvenirs, stashing them in an antique matchbox in my dresser. (They're still there, next to a yellowed wedge of the Styrofoam cheese we soldiers used to distract the mice.)

Some nights, I went to bed without washing the red circles off my cheeks, and wore them proudly to school the next morning. I wanted everyone to know I was special.

I was thrilled to be a part of it all, but I envied my classmates who got to wear frilly dresses and curl their hair for the party scene in Act I. While they were onstage at a lavish Christmas Eve soirée, I was in the basement, finishing my homework and zipping up my own boyish costume of boxy blue trousers and a mustard-yellow jacket. I listened to the muffled strains of the festive music streaming in from the orchestra pit and felt like I was peering through the keyhole at the nightly party I was never invited to.

Emily, the tiniest girl in our class, looked like a living doll in her long blue dress with its lace smock and white sleeves. Quiet and unassuming in the classroom, she came alive onstage; by the time she first danced in *The Nutcracker* at age eight, she was already a veteran performer, having grown up singing in the Metropolitan Opera's Children's Chorus on the other side of Lincoln Center Plaza. Backstage at *The Nutcracker*, Emily's mom—a distinguished ballet dancer herself—knew just how to hot-iron her glossy dark hair, how to contour her cheeks and outline her enormous eyes. Emily was so shy that her classmates at school sometimes wondered if she was mute; it was only at ballet that she felt like she could be herself. Every night onstage, she danced and played with her friends, flirted and bickered with the boys, without ever having to open her mouth.

The Nutcracker was extra special for Emily that year: her older brother was in the party scene, and her best friend, Meiying, had been cast as Marie—the host of the party and the young star of the show. The winner, in the words of a *New York Times* reporter who trailed us backstage, of "the most sought-after role in Little Girldom." As the two shortest girls in the class, Meiying and Emily were often pitted against each other for roles, but instead of succumbing to cattiness or competition, they forged a bond that transcended their circumstances. Meiying was as outgoing as Emily was shy, at ease chatting with adults and vamping for the cameras. But she drew inspiration from Emily's technical prowess—she knew that standing beside Emily at the barre made her a better dancer.

Meiying and I attended the same middle school, and it was a relief to have someone at school I could talk to about rehearsals and ballet gossip; who understood why I had bags under my eyes during *Nutcracker* season. Our mothers took turns taking us from school to ballet in the afternoons, and Meiying and I were allies for that half hour, united in our frantic pursuit of a single goal: to reach Lincoln Center before the clock struck four. There was never enough time. We became experts at brushing our hair into neat buns without looking in the mirror, and even—if we ran into traffic—changing into our leotards and tights without (we hoped) flashing the taxi driver. But once we arrived, we had a tacit understanding that we would go our separate ways: I to my gangly crew on the tall side of the barre, and Meiying to her friends on the other side of the room—to the girls who, like her, were tiny and favored.

Meiying shared the role of Marie with dark-haired, dark-eyed Rachel. A natural performer and a girly-girl, Rachel was only three when she resolved to become a ballet dancer. Rachel's grandmother had taken her to *Coppélia*, and the curtain rose for Act III on the most beautiful sight she had ever seen: twenty-four girls, students at SAB, in shiny pink bodices and puffy tutus the color of cotton candy. Rachel knew then, with absolute certainty, that she wanted to be up there with them. Like Emily, Rachel hailed from a showbiz family: her mom was a TV actress and her dad was a stagehand at Lincoln Center. Now, at age nine, she seemed well on her way to achieving her dream. There was a moment each night when Rachel was alone onstage—staring in awe as the twinkling Christmas tree began to grow into the ceiling—and her father, who was crouching behind the tree, would throw her a wink.

Half the magic of *The Nutcracker* was the pride we took in carrying on a tradition that stretched all the way back to 1954. In knowing that we wore the same, slightly smelly costumes that had been passed down for years. And in knowing we were dancing steps that had been choreographed by the great George Balanchine himself.

But it was bittersweet, too. We would never meet Balanchine; we would never know what he thought of our production. Everyone around us—the dancers and choreographers, the company as a whole—was struggling to find a way forward without their founder, their father, their raison d'être. The New York City Ballet had been so deeply entwined with Balanchine's genius, with his particular preferences and personality, that when he died, some said the company should just shut down. Even star dancers felt adrift. In 2006, fifteen years into her tenure as a principal dancer, Wendy Whelan told the *Times* that she sometimes doubted whether she deserved to be at NYCB at all. "Balanchine never knew me, so do I actually belong here?"

George Balanchine wasn't just a giant of the insular world of ballet; he transcended it, giving ballet—at least for a while—a place at the heart of American culture. In the 1970s and '80s, Irving Howe and Susan Sontag debated the finer points of Balanchine's latest work in the pages of *Harper's* and the *London Review of Books*; the editor of *The New Yorker* served on the board of the New York City Ballet. The writer Gore Vidal took adult ballet classes, and the artist Edward Gorey was a daily fixture at Lincoln Center. And it wasn't just intellectuals who cared about ballet; Balanchine had worked in film and theater and knew how to draw a crowd. Tickets cost a couple bucks, and ordinary New Yorkers would line up around the block to get the best seats for a Balanchine premiere or a new dancer's debut. "Longtime friends once fell out for good disagreeing over the degrees of goddess stature of their favorite dancers, over a specific ballet interpretation," James Wolcott wrote in his memoir of 1970s New York. Balanchine's ballerinas—Maria Tallchief, Gelsey Kirkland, Suzanne Farrell—were bona fide celebrities, feted not just for their beauty or their makeup tricks, but for their artistry and technique.

Born Georgi Balanchivadze in 1904 into an artistic, financially precarious family in Saint Petersburg, the man who would one day revolutionize ballet was not, at first, interested in it at all. His father was a musician and his little brother would grow up to become a composer; his first love was piano. In 1913, his mother—hoping to set her children on a path toward a stable career and, one day, a pension—brought Georgi along to his sister Tamara's audition for the prestigious, state-sponsored Imperial Ballet School. Tamara, who dreamed of becoming a dancer, failed the exam, but an official noticed her little brother and suggested he apply, too. Nine-year-old Georgi had never taken a ballet class, but based on the way he carried himself as he walked back and forth before a panel of judges, he was offered a place on the spot.

Georgi would have preferred to stay home and focus on his music lessons, but he didn't have a choice. His mother went home without him that day, leaving Georgi "alone in an alien circumstance, committed to studying an art he had no interest in," Robert Gottlieb wrote in *George Balanchine: The Ballet Maker*.

After one botched attempt to run away—his aunt, who he hoped would take him in, instead marched him back to the school—Georgi resigned himself to the ascetic life of the academy, standing at the barre every day and performing repetitive exercises whose purpose he didn't understand. It wasn't until his second year, when he got his first taste of performing—as a tiny cupid in *The Sleeping Beauty*—that he fell in love with ballet; with the beautiful orchestra music and the opulence of the Mariinsky Theatre. He started working harder in class and experimenting with his own choreography. By his early teens, he had earned a reputation for pushing the boundaries, and scandalized his teachers by writing an intimate partnering scene into a student piece.

But as he was refining his technique as a dancer and finding his voice as a choreographer, the world outside the gates was crumbling. In 1917, civil war broke out and the school shut down. Georgi's family fled to Tbilisi, leaving him to fend for himself. He managed to find some work playing piano for silent films—he asked to be paid in scraps of food, since cash had lost its value—but as the war raged on, he and his friends took to scouring the countryside for anything edible, including horse feed and even stray cats. "By the middle of 1918 few cats or dogs were to be seen in St. Petersburg," wrote Bernard Taper in his 1963 book *Balanchine: A Biography*. "Most pets had gone into the stew pot."

In 1924, Balanchine and three of his classmates wrangled permission to dance in Germany for two months, and from there fled to Paris, defecting from the Soviet Union. It was an easy decision for Balanchine; the Russia he had known as a child and an Imperial ballet student was gone. "I never doubted, I always knew," he told the writer Solomon Volkov, "if there were ever an opportunity—I'd leave!" The Paris-based impresario Serge Diaghilev, who needed a new choreographer for his Ballets Russes, caught wind of the young Russians' arrival and arranged a meeting. After assuring Diaghilev that he could make ballets "*very* fast," according to Taper, the twenty-one-year-old émigré "Georgi Melotonovitch Balanchivadze—or George Balanchine, as he would henceforth be known—found himself ballet master of the most famous and remarkable ballet company in the world." Balanchine stayed at the Ballets Russes until Diaghilev died, and then took temporary positions in London, Copenhagen, and Monte Carlo. But he couldn't do his best work this way. He wanted a company of his own.

Meanwhile, in New York, Lincoln Kirstein—the young, Harvard-educated heir to the Filene's Department Store fortune—dreamed of setting up an American ballet company on par with the great troupes of Russia and France. A restless entrepreneur and serial patron of the arts, Kirstein—still in his twenties—had already founded a literary journal, *Hound &*

Horn, and curated an exhibit of American murals for the Museum of Modern Art. He discovered Balanchine while scouting for choreographers in Europe and in 1933 brought the twenty-nine-year-old to New York to start a new company. "But first, a school," Balanchine said, according to SAB lore. The School of American Ballet was founded just months after Balanchine landed at Ellis Island. The first crop of students arrived with haphazard training but with other qualities that excited the founders. Kirstein compared the girls to "basketball champions and queens of the tennis court"; with these strong, healthy Americans, he hoped, "the purity and regal behavior of the elder ballerina were to be replaced by a raciness, an alert celerity" like that of "the champion athlete."

It would be another fourteen turbulent years before Kirstein cobbled together the money to give the New York City Ballet a permanent home, but in 1948, NYCB had its first season at City Center on West Fifty-Fifth Street. With stability at last, and a roster of SAB-trained dancers, Balanchine flourished. The hits came one after another: from crowd-pleasing narrative ballets (the Russian folklore-inspired *Firebird* in 1949; the blockbuster *Nutcracker* five years later) to patriotic tributes (the exuberant *Western Symphony* in 1954, with dancing cowboys and American folk tunes; the tongue-in-cheek *Stars and Stripes* in 1958, in which dancers march and salute in front of an enormous American flag). But it was the abstract pieces—*Allegro Brillante* (1956), *Agon* (1957), *Tchaikovsky Pas de Deux* (1960), *Raymonda Variations* (1961)—for which Balanchine became best known, for which Susan Sontag called him "the greatest choreographer who ever lived," and for which the critic James Wolcott wrote that he "was regarded not simply as a creative genius but as God's junior partner."

Ballets like this had never been seen before. The ballets of

Balanchine's childhood—*Sleeping Beauty*, *Coppélia*, *Swan Lake*—told sentimental stories about doomed princesses and jolly peasants; dancers acted them out with an esoteric system of mimed gestures. (Pantomime is impossible for the uninitiated to understand: a first-time ballet-goer would have no idea that a dancer raising her fists, for example, is talking about a wicked magician, or that a dancer tapping her forehead is explaining that she is a queen.)

Balanchine wanted a night at the ballet to be something you didn't have to study for. He wanted to express adult emotions and relationships, and he wanted to do it not through sign language but through steps alone. In two-person pas de deux and in bigger group dances, he explored love and romance, God and death, tension and release; coming together and falling apart, reaching and striving and pulling away. Everyone onstage had a role to play: whereas the corps—or "body"—of the ballet traditionally spent most of their time posing on the sidelines, the dozens of dancers in Balanchine's corps were in constant motion, weaving in and out of intricate formations, echoing the leads and enacting their own dynamics. The effect was to give his work an aliveness, an energy that was new to ballet.

Another of Balanchine's innovations was to strip away the fussy tutus and elaborate sets of the Mariinsky: in ballets like *The Four Temperaments* and *Episodes*, he dressed his dancers in simple black practice clothes. His pared-down "leotard ballets" helped the audience focus on the dancers' bodies, the steps, and—crucially—the score. "When too much goes on, on stage, you don't hear the music," he said. And as much as he believed that ballet was a calling, a serious endeavor, he considered the music even more important. "If you don't want to see what's on the stage," he suggested in the 1965 interview with *Life* magazine, "close your eyes and for two dollars you get a beautiful concert."

Balanchine scoffed at critics' attempts to "understand" his ballets, insisting that they were meant only to be appreciated for their beauty. "When you have a garden full of pretty flowers, you don't demand of them, 'What do you mean? What is your significance?'" he said. "A flower doesn't tell you a story. It's in itself a beautiful thing."

His ambitious choreography challenged the dancers, and Balanchine coached them and the students at SAB in an extreme, dynamic style of movement. The "Balanchine technique" emphasized speed and energy, training dancers to perform the off-balance steps and jazzy distortions that became his trademark. "It was literally impossible to do what he wanted as he wanted it," one student, Joan Brady, wrote in her memoir *The Unmaking of a Dancer*. But that was fine: spontaneity and attack were more important to him than perfection, and he never got angry if a dancer fell down; it proved that she was taking risks. The only crime was to be boring.

Balanchine wanted to keep his audience in suspense, unable to guess what would happen next. Russian dancers might be able to do enormous tricks—huge leaps and endless turns—but the time in between could drag. Even the pièces de résistance were predictable: if you saw a dancer bend her knees and lower herself into a deep plié,* you could be sure that a big jump was coming.

So Balanchine taught his dancers to short-circuit the preparatory steps—taking off for a jump, for example, from only a shallow plié. The viewer wouldn't know if a dancer with slightly bent knees was planning to hurl herself into the air for

---

* A simple bend of the knees

a jump or to launch into a pirouette or a fouetté* turn—or if she was going to do something as simple as a tendu,† or just straighten her knees and stand back up.

This succeeded in preserving an element of surprise, but it also had a catastrophic impact on dancers' knees. Balanchine pushed his dancers to their limits—and sometimes beyond. And they were so eager to impress him that they rarely protested. Edward Villella, who was a principal dancer in the 1960s and '70s, recalled in his memoir *Prodigal Son* how Balanchine would sometimes skimp on warm-ups not just in choreography, but even in class—spending only a few minutes at the barre before rushing the dancers into center. "Everybody was aching, sore, barely able to move, but they'd be saying, 'Oh yes, Mr. B. Of course, Mr. B.'" The studio was Balanchine's lab, and the dancers were his guinea pigs. "Balanchine . . . just forced turnout," Villella wrote. "He'd grab a leg and twist it in the socket." He wanted to find out how far the human body could go.

Some blame Balanchine and the spread of his technique for the shortening of dancers' careers: the average age of a professional ballerina's retirement declined, according to an analysis by *The Telegraph*, from forty in the 1980s to twenty-nine in the 1990s. And while stars of England's Royal Ballet and Russia's Bolshoi performed into old age—Margot Fonteyn gave her last performance at the age of sixty-six; Maya Plisetskaya debuted a new role on her seventieth—such longevity was unheard of at Balanchine's company.

---

* From the French word for "whipped"—a turn in which the dancer rotates on one leg while the other leg bends and straightens, swiveling back and forth between the knee and the air without ever touching the ground.
† From the French word for "stretch"—a step in which the leg slides out from the body while remaining on the floor.

Still, Balanchine was beloved. He had the charisma of a preacher and the unpretentiousness of a folk hero. He was gracious with his collaborators, always acknowledging the work of the musicians, the conductor, the costume designer, the stagehands. He resisted the "genius" label foisted on him by the press, insisting that he was only a craftsman—comparing himself to a gardener, a cabinetmaker, a chef. (Inventing new steps is "like making salad, you know?" he told Barbara Fisher, who danced for New York City Ballet in the 1940s and '50s and later published a memoir. "Just mix up same old vegetables a little different.") He peppered his speech with quotable, enigmatic aphorisms, many of them borrowed from the likes of Pushkin and Hegel, Tchaikovsky ("My muse must come to me on union time") and the Russian poet Mayakovsky ("I am not a man, but a cloud in trousers"). But his high-mindedness came with a practical streak. He didn't consider himself above commercial projects; in 1941, he even accepted a commission from the Ringling Brothers Circus to make a ballet for elephants. He had no tolerance for diva behavior among his dancers, either. In contrast to the star system and strict hierarchies of the Mariinsky and the Paris Opera, the dancers of the New York City Ballet were listed in alphabetical order.

Though he was a stickler for technical details—the precise angle of the foot in tendu, the degree of rotation in the hip socket—he wasn't precious about his own choreography. If a dancer couldn't do a certain step, he thought little of changing it; if she felt inspired to improvise, then that was fine, too. He worked with the confidence of someone who had no fear of running out of ideas.

Perhaps it helped that he had an endlessly replenishing stream of beautiful eighteen-year-old women to work with. Balanchine's ballets are inextricably linked to the dancers who inspired them—his "muses." "Almost no one refers without irony to a living muse except in the world of ballet," Francine Prose writes in *The Lives of the Muses*, her study of nine (mostly historical) women who have inspired and sometimes slept with famous artists. It was an observation that surprised me, even as I realized that it was true; I was so accustomed to hearing renowned dancers described as the muses of great choreographers that I had come to think of it as an aspirational title. I hadn't considered how outdated the term is, how sexist and objectifying—how it implies that a woman's role is not to create art but to passively inspire it. Yet to be a muse for Balanchine was the highest honor, a label worn with pride. All the girls tried to catch his eye; Villella summed up the atmosphere at Balanchine's school: "I had the feeling all the ballet mothers sitting in the hall would have gladly thrown their twelve-year-old daughters at him on the chance he'd become entranced with one of them and make her a star."

Balanchine racked up a total of five wives, all of whom he choreographed on, from his seventeen-year-old Russian classmate Tamara Geva in 1923 to twenty-one-year-old Maria Tallchief in 1946, and twenty-three-year-old SAB graduate Tanaquil Le Clercq in 1952. (Balanchine had known "Tanny" since she was a child; it is unsettling to read, in Barbara Fisher's memoir, of Balanchine correcting his "prize pupil" and mocking her in front of her peers, warning her that if she didn't straighten her knees, her long legs looked like "cooked asparagus.")

For Balanchine, romance was the natural next step in a good working relationship. "When we were married, it was almost really like I was the material he wanted to use," Balanchine's third wife, Maria Tallchief—then in her sixties—reflected in the 1989 documentary *Dancing for Mr. B*. She looks pained; she hesitates, stumbling over the word "material." "I think he had

become really interested in me as a talent." Was he interested
in her as a woman? Was there even a difference? "I was a very
immature young girl," she says. She was taken aback when he
suggested they marry. "He suddenly one night proposed. . . .
I said to Balanchine, 'Well, George, you know, I don't know
what to say.' He said, 'That doesn't make any difference.'"

Tallchief quickly succumbed, but one of Balanchine's last
muses—and perhaps his greatest—refused the promotion from
principal dancer to wife. In one light, the story of Suzanne
Farrell is a clear-cut case of sexual harassment. The older man,
the all-powerful boss, becomes obsessed with a naïve young
woman in his employ; when she rejects him, he retaliates by
wrecking her career. In another, it is a tragic romance: two
people, drawn inexorably to each other, doomed to express
their love only through art.

The first encounter between Suzanne Farrell and George
Balanchine occurred in the same place where, over the next
twenty years, the relationship would unfold—where it would
heat up, spiral out of control, explode, and then heal: in the
studio. It was 1960, and it was Suzanne's fifteenth birthday. Balanchine was fifty-six. Suzanne's family had sacrificed
everything to prepare her for her SAB audition. Back in Cincinnati, her mother had cleaned houses and worked overnight
shifts as a nurse's aide to pay for Suzanne's ballet lessons. Now,
she had left her husband behind and moved the family to New
York to further her daughter's career.

Suzanne counted twenty-nine steps as she and her mother
ascended the long staircase to the school at the top of 2291
Broadway. They waited in the hallway until Balanchine sum-
moned Suzanne into an empty studio and asked if she had a
routine. She hadn't prepared one, but she offered to show him
the piece she had learned for her recital in Ohio. There was no

pianist in the corner, so she hummed along to fill the silence as she danced. After a few minutes, he told her to stop and remove her pointe shoes so he could inspect her feet. The next day, the phone rang: Balanchine not only had admitted her to SAB, but had granted her a full scholarship. For the rest of her career, Suzanne would always sew the ribbons on her pointe shoes with twenty-nine stitches.

Desperate to show that she was worthy of the opportunity Balanchine had bestowed, Suzanne worked obsessively—writing down every correction and grading her own daily performance in class. Balanchine occasionally dropped in to observe the students, and his every passing comment had all the weight of Holy Scripture. "I seemed to grow extrasensory receptors to his every step, nod, word, and glance," she wrote in her 1990 memoir, *Holding On to the Air*. "I kept a count in my diary of any and all Balanchine sightings."

Before long, her hard work began to pay off. Balanchine took her into the company when she was just sixteen. In pictures from this time, she looks even younger; with round cheeks and a dimple in her chin, wisps of hair escaping her bun, she could pass for a child. But Balanchine had noticed her: for her precocious technique and languid musicality, and for her unselfconscious beauty. Her hair was long and frayed at the ends, as if she hadn't had it cut since leaving Ohio. She thought of herself as plain.

In her very first season, Suzanne was asked to learn soloist roles. In rehearsals, Balanchine took every opportunity to touch her, demonstrating the role of her partner in pas de deux. On pointe, she towered over him by several inches, but he liked to look in the mirror and say, "Look how well we fit together." It was only later that she realized what he meant; she was a cloistered teen whose entire romantic experience consisted of a single chaste kiss. "Aside from some vague knowledge about 'consequences,' my education and interest in sex were almost nonexistent," she wrote. But Balanchine didn't care. His 1963 *Meditation*—an intense pas de deux between Suzanne, looking virginal in a white chiffon dress, and an older man, danced by Jacques d'Amboise—was seen as a public declaration of his love.

Over the next few years, Balanchine showered her with attention, giving her lead roles in almost all of his ballets. It wasn't just her youth or her beauty or her talent that made her his new favorite. As he explained to Diana Adams, the muse Suzanne replaced: "Well, you see, dear, Suzanne never resisted." No matter what steps he threw at her—no matter if they seemed dangerous or impossible, or if they hurt—she didn't question him. "If he thought I could do something, I would believe him," she wrote, "often against my own reasoning."

They spent almost every waking minute together. After Suzanne's final curtsy, Balanchine would take her out to dinner and walk her back to the apartment she still shared with her mother. If he was busy, he sent his assistant to escort her home; he always seemed to know where she was. When the company went on tour to Paris, he delighted in taking her to the Louvre, buying her shoes, and teaching her how to drink wine. These dates left her feeling insecure: "I was still an unsophisticated girl from the Midwest with little conversation aside from ballet, while he was a man of enormous culture and education." And his blatant favoritism made her a pariah among her peers; she was isolated, with no one to ask for advice.

Balanchine was forty years Suzanne's senior, but, as his advances intensified, she was even more perturbed by the fact that he was still married to a previous muse, Tanaquil Le Clercq. (Le Clercq had been stricken with polio three years after their wedding, and now, confined to a wheelchair, was unable to walk, let alone dance.) When Suzanne started declining his dinner invitations, his mood plummeted, and others in Balanchine's circle blamed her. Administrators and her fellow dancers added to the pressure: "Why don't you just sleep with him?" one of her (male) peers demanded. When she finally rebelled and married City Ballet dancer Paul Mejia—in a hasty ceremony, when Balanchine was out of the country—Balanchine stopped speaking to her. He then punished her by firing her husband and finally—although she was by then one of the most beloved ballerinas in New York—dismissing her, too. Suzanne was in her dressing room, sewing her pointe shoes for the evening's performance, when the wardrobe mistress knocked on the door: she would not be dancing that night. What Balanchine had given, he could take away. Her name was wiped from the programs, the security guards warned not to let her into the theater. Balanchine was so powerful that this public break made Farrell and Mejia unemployable: no director in the country would risk offending him. "I was twenty-three, and I had good reason to think my career had ended," Suzanne wrote. "I was a dancer without a job, and I felt as homeless as any bag lady."

It wasn't only the dancers he pined for whom he wanted to possess. "Balanchine considered his dancers his own," wrote Villella. "He wanted to control whether or not a man had a relationship with one of his women." In his memoir, Villella recalls asking out a young woman in the company—and how she accepted his invitation but balked at his choice of an Upper West Side bar. Someone might see them, she explained: Mr. B could find out. "That incident replayed itself over and over."

"Mr. B was like your conscience," said Darci Kistler, who joined City Ballet in 1980. (Kistler had the distinction of being the last dancer handpicked by Balanchine before his death in 1983.) "You'd walk into the studio and he used to say, 'I know where people have been the night before. I know what they've eaten. I know where they slept. I know . . . everything.' And you know, I really believe he did."

Balanchine tried to control not just the way his dancers behaved, but the way they looked—rewarding women who maintained an extremely low body weight, no matter what it took to get there. In her memoir, *Broadway, Balanchine and Beyond*, Bettijane Sills—a member of Balanchine's corps from 1961 to 1972—recalls how he approached her in company class, stood in front of her, and patted her all over. "You look pregnant, dear," he said, and walked away. Another time, he told her: "You are like inside a cocoon; your true personality will only be revealed when all the fat is gone, and you are down to your bones."

For months, Suzanne and Paul danced only in cheap studios they rented by the hour. To make ends meet, she modeled hairstyles for Vidal Sassoon and appeared on a celebrity game show in which contestants had to guess which of three men was her husband. Finally, Maurice Béjart, an avant-garde European choreographer, threw her a lifeline, offering her and Paul jobs with his Belgian troupe. In Brussels, they had to learn an entirely different style of dance. Béjart's work was brash and erotic, often set to electronic scores. For Balanchine, ballet was about women; from both a personal and artistic standpoint, Béjart was primarily interested in men. When Béjart's Ballet of the 20th Century went on tour to New York, City Ballet loyalists were shocked to see Balanchine's "alabaster princess" gyrating on a table as thirty-eight bare-chested men thumped and stomped around her. "Many of Balanchine's fans felt as

if Farrell had run off with a biker," the dance critic Joan Acocella wrote in a 2003 *New Yorker* profile.

Even as Suzanne cherished her adventure in Europe, she
never stopped missing Mr. B. When she tried to dance in a
classical style, she felt stifled: she wanted to move big and
fast, the way Balanchine had taught her. "Mr. B had infiltrated
my whole being—my ears, my heart, and my legs," she wrote.
She sent him letters, which he ignored, until—after five years
and one especially charming note—he didn't. "Dear George,"
she had written, after she bought a ticket to *Symphony in C*
and watched from the audience like any other fan. "As wonderful as it is to see your ballets, it is even more wonderful to
dance them. Is this impossible? Love, Suzi." Within months,
she was back at City Ballet. Balanchine's passion had cooled,
and, at last, their relationship could stabilize. The energy between them was different—less frenzied, more mature—but
the magic was still there.

Farrell was not just an instrument, passively following Balanchine's orders; she was an interpreter and even a cocreator.
Balanchine valued her ideas and encouraged her to follow
her instincts. In a rehearsal for his *Walpurgisnacht Ballet*, he
worked with his usual efficiency but struggled over how to end
the piece. He gave Suzanne vague instructions to leap onto her
partner's shoulder and then "do something else." Suzanne had
a sudden vision of "a figurehead on the mast of a ship" and
decided to embody it: "I released one leg into a wide circular
motion behind me and placed one arm over my head, palm at
a stiff right angle." The final tableau—the image that lingers in
the audience's mind—is of an imperious woman in a crooked,
airborne arabesque, held aloft like a statue or a goddess.

Balanchine's health was deteriorating, but energized, as ever, by Suzanne, he created some of his greatest work. In 1977, Suzanne danced the lead in *Vienna Waltzes*, an extravagant ode to beauty in which dozens of couples—men in tuxedos and women in ivory ball gowns and opera gloves—whirl across a stage lit by mirrors and chandeliers. In 1981, when his eyesight and hearing were almost gone, she opened in *Mozartiana*—a spectral, prayerlike "vision of heaven," set to a haunting score by Tchaikovsky. She danced for him until his 1983 death, which devastated her. "I was thirty-seven years old," she wrote, "but I felt like an orphan."

For the past forty years, Farrell has devoted herself to spreading Balanchine's work around the world, coaching young dancers in his technique and staging his ballets for foreign companies. She continued to talk to Balanchine long after his death, and her work helped her feel his presence more acutely. In 2000, she founded her own small troupe in Washington, DC. The Suzanne Farrell Ballet never commissioned new work; instead, each season, she chose a few Balanchine pieces to revive. Their last show, in 2017, was called *Forever Balanchine*.

After I finished Farrell's memoir, I opened my computer and browsed customer reviews online, postponing the moment when I would have to figure out how I felt. The first Goodreads reviewer, a reader named Sarah, had no qualms about picking a side. "Unbeknownst to Suzanne, George Balanchine is one of the great villains in literature," she wrote. Sophie shared Sarah's outrage: "In this era of #MeToo, I would hope that Balanchine's 'romantic' interest would be labeled as the disgusting pedophilia that it was." Another found the relationship "disturbing on many levels" and concluded that Balanchine was "a creepy old lecher." But not everyone agreed. "Despite a substantial age difference, this was a relationship built upon empathy, respect, and love," wrote one reader. Another felt sorry for Suzanne: "I found it sad that such a young girl had to struggle with the complexities of such a relationship with no support."

I read, too, the comments on Bettijane Sills's memoir from 2019. The theater critic Helen Shaw, who reviewed the book for the *New York Times*, found it "disturbing to see her protect a man who insulted and infantilized her," and characterized Sills's extreme dieting as "mental torture." Shaw points to one particularly cruel incident when Balanchine took Sills's hand and squeezed her fingers. "When I asked what he was doing, he reminded me of the story of Hansel and Gretel," wrote Sills. "Did I remember the old witch who in order to tell whether the children were plump enough for eating, would squeeze their fingers every day?" "*Get out*," thought Shaw. "But she danced for that witch for 10 more years."

Die-hard Balanchine loyalists, meanwhile—like an Amazon reviewer named Mary—praised Sills as "a keeper of the flame"; another commended Sills for owning "up that The Master had a right to dictate his ballet aesthetic . . . refreshing that the author doesn't make excuses for her own failings."

The blind passion of Balanchine's true believers—their refusal to hear a word against him—sometimes made me wonder if I had spent my adolescence in thrall to a deceased cult leader. I'm not the first to think in those terms. One prominent dance critic blames the powerful "Balanchine cult" for the neglect of other brilliant twentieth-century choreographers, like Antony Tudor and Roland Petit, in American ballet. Undeniably, there was an element of magical thinking in the memoirs I read. "He was going to live 'forever'—as he often told us," wrote Farrell, "and I believed him as I believed everything else he said." The language of faith and betrayal

infused the day-to-day workings of NYCB with all the gravity of a religious mission. "The presence of Balanchine always
hovered over us: icon, father, God," wrote Villella, clarifying
that Balanchine was too humble to present himself as a god—
merely as a kind of prophet: "he understood that his genius
had been conferred on him, he had been ordained by God."
Gelsey Kirkland, who broke ranks and publicly criticized Balanchine, was labeled an "apostate" in the *New York Times*.

I have a perhaps unsavory appetite for stories about modern-
day cults. I learned more than I ever needed to about Bikram
Choudhury, the yoga guru who made it trendy to work out in
studios heated to 104 degrees—a cruel enough legacy—and
was exposed in 2013 as a sexual harasser. I listened to multiple
podcasts about Keith Raniere, the soft-spoken founder of the
self-help group/sex cult NXIVM in upstate New York. I read
about how Raniere manipulated his inner circle into submit-
ting to sex whenever he wanted, demanded his followers have
his initials branded into their skin, and, according to a *Vanity Fair* exposé, leveraged "women's insecurities about their
weight . . . [and] severely monitored some acolytes' calorie
intake." He demanded one of his girlfriends maintain a body
weight of less than one hundred pounds and put another fol-
lower, India Oxenberg, on a diet of five hundred calories a day.

I understood that these details were meant to provoke
outrage—*Vanity Fair* called Raniere's fixation on women's
weight "one of the sickest aspects" of NXIVM—but it didn't
sound so foreign to me. After Balanchine complained that he
couldn't see her bones, Gelsey Kirkland whittled herself down
to a dangerous ninety pounds. She would have met Raniere's
requirements with flying colors. In *The Dancers' Body Book*,
a 1984 diet manual by Balanchine favorite Allegra Kent, a
110-pound dancer details how—to lose the ten pounds that

made her overweight by dance-world standards—she, just like Oxenberg, limited her food intake to five hundred calories a day.

One of the most effective aspects of Raniere's manipulation was how he wormed his way inside his victims' minds: by undermining and humiliating them, he wore down the women's confidence and turned them against themselves. He had such a strong psychological hold on his "slaves" that he didn't have to physically imprison them. One prosecutor told a jury: "The door was unlocked, but [one victim] felt she couldn't leave."

Even when Balanchine wasn't personally criticizing a dancer's body or pressuring her to lose weight, the women in his company knew what the "Balanchine ideal" was, and they devised extreme and creative measures to meet it. Before she entered NYCB at fifteen, Allegra Kent had a relatively relaxed attitude toward food. "After joining the company, however, I noticed everyone's fear of and obsession with food," she wrote. "So I began to worry about it, too." At one point, Kent installed a padlock on her refrigerator at home; only her son had the key, and "every time I wanted something to eat I had to go and get him to unlock it for me." When guests expressed concern, she swapped the padlock out for a hidden alarm inside the fridge. The door was unlocked, but Allegra felt she couldn't leave.

It's easy—for outsiders, at least—to recognize NXIVM as a cult, but it isn't always clear what counts; one person's cult is another's therapy or religion. In a *Guardian* article, the cult deprogramming expert Rick Alan Ross laid out ten signs that a group might qualify as a cult—a few of which describe Balanchine-era NYCB with almost eerie precision.

Warning sign number two: "No tolerance for questions or critical inquiry"—a good summary of the philosophy at SAB.

"We were expected to imitate and absorb, and above all to obey," Jennifer Homans, who studied at SAB in the 1970s, wrote in the prologue to *Apollo's Angels*. "'Please to do' was all the Russians could muster, and 'why' was met with bemusement or flatly ignored."

Red flag number seven: "Followers feel they can never be 'good enough.'" Balanchine exacerbated his dancers' natural tendency toward self-criticism by withholding praise, even for extraordinary performances. Maria Tallchief was one of Balanchine's most renowned stars—and, for six years, his wife—but she reminisced in *Dancing for Mr. B* about "the first time I've ever heard George say anything nice about my dancing"—decades after she had retired. "After a while, you think, *There's nothing I can do that will please this man*," one dancer said, in the documentary *In Balanchine's Classroom*.

Ross's ninth telltale sign: "The group/leader is always right." Consider Kistler: "You would do anything he said. If he told you to stand on your head, you would do it." Or Tallchief: "There was no doubt in my mind that everything Balanchine said was absolutely right."

Was Balanchine a predator hiding behind his art? Does he belong on the kind of list that was circulating in late 2017—the kind that cataloged the emotional and sometimes literal crimes of artists like Roman Polanski, Norman Mailer, and Harvey Weinstein? The kind that prompted one feminist critic to quote Walter Benjamin: "At the base of every major work of art is a pile of barbarism"?

It matters, I think, that Balanchine's dancers were willing and enthusiastic subjects. They may have been vulnerable, by dint of their youth or their low pay (Villella: "Some months the rent couldn't be paid, some days people went hungry . . ."), but they were also talented and ambitious in their own right.

How much should the feelings of the "victims"—their enduring anger, or their forgiveness—factor into our assessment of a perpetrator? Some of Raniere's acolytes defended him until the end; we are comfortable explaining this away as Stockholm syndrome. But to disregard the dancers' feelings about their own experiences with Balanchine would be to condescend; to deny that the women had agency and aspirations of their own.

And those feelings are, almost across the board, gratitude, pride, love. "Balanchine is my life—my destiny," Suzanne Farrell told the *New York Times* in 2017, when she was seventy-two. When I asked my old coach, erstwhile NYCB soloist Carol Sumner, what people misunderstand about Balanchine, she teared up. "When we say what he was like, nobody believes us. Nobody can believe that there was a man like Balanchine, like a saint."

Consider Bettijane Sills, the dancer who, no matter how hard she tried, could never bring her body into line with Balanchine's ideal. Part of her motive for writing a memoir, she explains, was to defend her late mentor from feminist attacks—"to dispel some misperceptions . . . concerning his attitude about women." Yes, he wanted his dancers to be very thin—but what people don't appreciate, according to Sills, is that he was right: ballet just "looks better on a trim body." And Sills disputed Helen Shaw's characterization of her relationship with Balanchine. In a letter to the editor, she insisted that the Hansel and Gretel incident was "amusing" at the time, "and it still is now." She believed it was Balanchine's right to dictate how his dancers looked, no matter what it cost them: "New York City Ballet was his company and he wanted his choreography and his dancers to shine."

Or Maria Tallchief. It's easy to read her romance with Balanchine as a protracted abuse of power. And maybe it was.

But it counts, too, that when she was in her sixties, Tallchief seemed to bear no bitterness toward Balanchine. She appreciates that he didn't let their split affect their working relationship: "I went back to the *Scotch Symphony* rehearsal, that he was choreographing for me, on the day our marriage was annulled," she said. She found a more suitable husband, and remained close with Balanchine until his death.

Or Darci Kistler, who was made principal in 1982—just one year before Balanchine died. "My very first class with the company, of course I was very nervous," Darci reminisces in *Dancing for Mr. B.* "And he came over and he slapped me really hard on the rear end, in front of the whole company." She smiles at the interviewer and giggles over the memory; as much as this sounds like textbook sexual harassment—if not assault—to her, apparently, it was charming.

Balanchine's practice of choosing a signature scent for his favorite dancers has become, for many, a notorious example of his desire for control. But not everyone understands it that way. Maria Tallchief wore Guerlain's L'Heure Bleue, which Balanchine picked out for her, for the rest of her life, after their separation and even after his death. And as a girl, Darci Kistler dreamed of receiving a special perfume from the great choreographer. "I only knew about the New York City Ballet from an article in *Vogue* magazine," she said. "I was really young and it talked about this man, and this man was George Balanchine. And he picked out perfume for all of his ballerinas. And it was just so wonderful that a man would do that, would pick out perfume for you." She smiles, swoons. "And he would say how he knew where each dancer was in the theater and who had been on the elevator and things." She knew then whom she wanted to work for.

Are these women merely "co-constituting their own oppression," as the critic Ann Daly argued in her 1987 paper "The Balanchine Woman"? It's possible. They seem, at the least, extremely comfortable with a power imbalance between the sexes.

What about the young dancers of today—the ones who learn Balanchine's technique, study with his disciples, and perform his ballets, but will never meet him? Even if they will never be personally harassed by him, they can still be shaped by his ideals—and his methods. The documentary *In Balanchine's Classroom* shows his dancers, now in their sixties, seventies, and eighties, coaching the current generation. I felt uncomfortable as I watched one of his disciples make a dancer—an accomplished principal at a major company—repeat a sequence so many times that she broke down in tears.

At the School of American Ballet, Balanchine is still worshiped as a hero. The school's Instagram account recently posted snapshots from what looked like a creepy birthday party, given that the honoree was long dead. The students wore party hats and wrote cards—"Happy Birthday, Mr. Balanchine!"—and red and yellow balloons were tied to the barres. Kids with perfect posture ate fruit off paper plates, and older girls in black leotards posed beside his portrait.

Balanchine's legacy is more than the legend of how he worked; it's the pieces he left behind, and what it feels like to watch and dance them. It's the ecstatic comments on the shaky YouTube footage of his choreography. "I feel so overstimulated I could pop . . . I could weep in gratitude for this pirated tape," one user wrote on a 1966 black-and-white clip of Suzanne Farrell. "Pure rapture . . . I'll be back tomorrow to watch it again. Another 10 times," wrote another.

It's the women who discover their strength through dancing

in these ballets. Balanchine died several years before dancer Eva Alt was born, and she first encountered his work when she began studying with one of his disciples at the age of thirteen. "That was absolutely what changed everything for me," she said in an interview with the *New Jock*. "Balanchine wanted you to bend more and move faster and be just more of everything. It was like letting me out of a box. I could be a wild woman when I danced. When I do Balanchine, I can rise above obedience. I don't have to just do perfect, you know, I can be more than that."

A Very Extreme Sense
of Escape and Control

When I look at the class picture, my eye jumps to Meiying. Not just because she's in the first row—the row where the shortest girls, the luckiest, were placed—but because she looks so at ease, as if she is genuinely enjoying herself. Her smile seems real, her pose effortless, as though gracefully crossing her hands above her outstretched leg were the most obvious thing to do with them. A wreath of delicate paper flowers peeks up from the top of her high, neat bun. I can almost imagine Meiying was born in first position. But her path to ballet was roundabout. An energetic child, her parents first enrolled her in gymnastics, at which Meiying—limber, tiny, and hardworking—excelled. Her coach suggested ballet as cross-training, but it wasn't until her parents took her to see *The Nutcracker* that she agreed. Her mom, who had been a modern dancer in her twenties, knew of the School of American Ballet's reputation, and figured Meiying might as well try. The day after her audition, she got a phone call: she would need a red leotard for her classes the next week. In her first year, Meiying was one of just two girls in her class chosen to play angels in *The Nutcracker*: the casting mistress already had an eye on her.

"I did not enter thinking ballet was gonna take over my life," Meiying said.

When Misty Copeland started ballet, she wanted only to appease the insistent grown-up coaxing her down from the bleachers where she sat, shyly hugging her knees. She couldn't have imagined that she would one day be a professional bal- lerina, let alone the most famous ballerina alive—a symbol of grace and resilience to people who have never heard of George Balanchine or Suzanne Farrell.

Misty, like Meiying, did cartwheels before she ever did a coupé. She taught herself to do splits and handstands as a seven-year-old, copying what she saw in a Lifetime movie about the Olympic gymnast Nadia Comăneci. "My legs just slid into position," she wrote in her 2014 memoir *Life in Motion*. "I didn't question why I could instantly do moves that it might take others months to achieve." Misty, too, hailed from a dancing family: her mom had been a professional cheerleader, and her older sister had been captain of the dance team. But Misty was five years older than Meiying when she entered a ballet studio for the first time at the urging of her middle school dance team coach.

"When I saw her in the gym, a tiny malnourished girl who stood with such poise and presence, I couldn't believe it," Eliz- abeth Cantine, the dance team coach, later told the *Guardian*. As Cantine began working with Misty in daily practice, she was stunned by how easily she picked up new steps and how naturally she moved. Misty had the ideal physique for ballet: long, thin legs; hyperextended knees; oversized feet. One day after practice, Cantine called Misty over and suggested she try a free ballet class at the local Boys and Girls Club. "I was caught off guard," Misty wrote. "Ballet? Why would I want to do that? I had never even seen one." But, ever the people pleaser, she did as her coach asked and walked over to the Boys and Girls Club after school. The ballet class would be held on the gym's basketball court.

Misty was too shy to introduce herself to the teacher, so she watched quietly from the bleachers as a dozen girls, most of them younger than her, engaged in an unfamiliar routine of "pointing, tapping, bending, and stretching." She was intrigued enough to come back the next day—and the day after that—but it was another two weeks before she worked up the courage to climb down from the stands and, in her too-big gym clothes and an old pair of socks, take up her place at the barre.

At thirteen, Misty was far behind her peers, most of whom had already been training for up to a decade. While they had been developing the obscure muscles needed for ballet—the hip rotators involved in turnout; the muscles around the ankle that stabilize the foot en pointe—she had been messing around at home and copying the moves she saw in music videos. They had favorite brands of pointe shoes and opinions on the relative merits of ABT and NYCB; Misty had never been to the ballet.

But, like Meiying, she was immediately singled out for her natural facility and charisma. The teacher, Cindy Bradley, had never seen such raw potential. Just two months after her first ballet class, Misty put on pointe shoes and stood on her toes—a milestone that most students spend years preparing for. "It was as if I'd been doing ballet all my life," Misty wrote, "and my limbs instinctively remembered what my conscious mind had somehow forgotten."

•   •   •

For much of Meiying's childhood, ballet was a refuge from the mayhem around her. She grew up just blocks from the World Trade Center. In the aftermath of the 9/11 attacks, her neighborhood was clouded in toxic dust, her family's apartment made unlivable by debris. Barred from entering their home, they bounced around between relatives' houses and temporary apartments. For months, nine-year-old Meiying slept on a bed that pulled out of the wall.

Our middle school was several miles north of the towers, but when we went outside at recess, to draw hopscotch courts on the sidewalk or play tag on a blocked-off side street, we could smell the fumes wafting up from the Financial District. I didn't really know what terrorism was, but I knew that everyone around me was on edge. Our teachers would stop teaching every time they heard the whir of a plane overhead, exhaling only when the sound had passed. Day after day, hoaxers called in phony bomb threats. At the sound of the alarm, we would throw down our pencils midproject, grab our jackets, and file outside, shivering and scared—and then, by the third or fourth time, shivering and bored—while a bomb squad spent hours searching the school.

That October, Meiying was cast as Marie in *The Nutcracker*. Now, after school, she didn't have to go straight home to the wrong apartment. Instead, she went to a rehearsal studio at Lincoln Center and pretended to be a German girl from the 1840s. She threw herself into the role, practicing late into the night, using her dog's crate and her stuffed animals as props. "I felt extremely connected to the character of Marie," Meiying says. "I lived and breathed her." Sometimes, she felt like she could disappear into the role—like she could merge with the character. "Ballet gave me a very extreme sense of escape and control." Putting on a beautiful costume, listening to live music, and going onstage, where everything played out in a way that she already knew, "was incredibly powerful," she says. "That saved my life."

Like most children, Meiying yearned to be taken seriously— and at ballet, she had real responsibilities. As Marie, she spent most of the two-hour ballet onstage. In Act I, her parents host a dreamy Christmas Eve party, where Marie dances with her friends, locks eyes with her godfather's handsome nephew, and opens presents, including an oddly seductive wooden nut-cracker doll. "I loved the professionalism of it," she says. In rehearsals, the ballet mistress would bend down and talk to her on her level, eye to eye, as if she were an adult who just happened to be small. "That was so empowering. She treated us with respect."

The most important moment, for Meiying, came in the midst of the tightly choreographed chaos of the battle scene. The Nutcracker and his army have picked off a few of the mice and distracted a few more with wedges of Styrofoam cheese, but the invaders haul off most of the soldiers and cor-ner the Nutcracker. He is lying on the floor beneath the seven-headed Mouse King when Marie has an idea: she pulls off one of her ballet slippers and hurls it at the monster. "She is so headstrong but also so brave," Meiying says. "When the man who's supposed to save her falls, she takes everything into her own hands." The wounded Mouse King turns, enraged, to look for the source of the tiny missile—giving the Nutcracker a chance to recover his bearings and stab his adversary. The Nutcracker then magically transforms into a prince, bows to Marie, and places a tiara on her head. The two children walk off, arm in arm, into a snowy enchanted forest. When the cur-tain rises on Act II, Marie and her prince have arrived in the Land of Sweets. The Sugarplum Fairy leads them to a throne, where they feast on cake and enjoy dances inspired by hot chocolate, marzipan, and candy canes.

For Meiying, *The Nutcracker* was only the beginning. Next came *Sleeping Beauty* and *Circus Polka* and *Harlequinade* and *A Midsummer Night's Dream*. She danced nearly every role in the children's repertoire, even traveling upstate with the company for the summer season in Saratoga. At home, she was still struggling with the aftermath of 9/11. But when the curtain rose, she was in a festive Candy Land in *The Nutcracker*. She was in a magical forest in *Midsummer*, a German village in *Coppélia*, a magnificent palace in *Swan Lake*. "I had the ability to escape into these fairy-tale stories and really live them."

Meiying felt sure of her future: she would graduate from SAB, join the company, and climb the ranks from corps to soloist to principal dancer. Her confidence wasn't unfounded. "I was very favored at SAB," she says. She was called "a delightful Marie, intelligent and dramatic" by the *New York Times* and was chosen to appear in a promotional documentary by the toymaker Mattel. *Living a Ballet Dream*—a companion film to *Barbie in* The Nutcracker—features six actual and aspiring ballet dancers, from twenty-five-year-old NYCB principal Maria Kowroski to eight-year-old Meiying.

Meiying wears a simple red practice leotard and blush on the apples of her cheeks; her hair has been scooped into two high buns on either side of her head, *Star Wars* style, and when she opens her mouth—to offer a shy smile or to explain what she loves about ballet—she reveals a gap between her two front teeth. It's not hard to imagine why the producers picked her out of all the girls in our class. Not only does she look like she might have escaped from a music box; she sounds entirely genuine when she says, "During the day, I look forward to the end of the day, so I can go to ballet." And when the camera zooms in on her face as she stands at the barre, performing a simple tendu or port de bras, her look is one of total concentration. She hasn't yet learned to keep her face neutral, to take every hint of effort and thought and force it down behind an expertly made-up mask.

"I like the movement and the music best about ballet," she says, as the camera cuts to her chasséing across the floor. "If I'm really into it, then I feel like I'm, like, flying and I'm a bird." She has the charming habit of veering between precocity and childishness; she sounds like a wise but tiny-voiced adult when she divulges her strategy for coping with stage fright ("I get nervous if I look at the audience so . . . I pretend it's not there and it's just a rehearsal and I just do my part") and her approach to her lessons ("I think the most important part of ballet class is when the teacher corrects me"), then reverts to an eight-year-old as she introduces us to her stuffed mouse, Willy, whom she totes around in her ballet bag (alongside her bobby pins, hairbrushes, and extra leotard and pair of tights). She lights up when she describes how, with "some lipstick, blush, and some eyeshadow," she can transform herself into a new character. For her peers at "regular school," as she calls it, playing dress-up is a rare treat—but for her, it's a part of her weekly routine. "It's really fun because usually girls my age don't usually—every day or every other day—get to put on makeup, except on Halloween."

Even as the trappings of ballet—the competition, the impossible physical standards, the punishing hours—can be a source of profound anxiety and distress, ballet itself—the movement, the music, the choreography—is simultaneously a salve for these emotions. I was a nervous, intense child. If my mom was late to pick me up, I was sure that she had been hit by a car. I loved how, at ballet, my anxiety-prone brain would shut down as I strove to make my fondue "look like melting ice cream," or my frappés "like popping a bottle of champagne." Ballet demanded absolute focus; it was impossible to worry about my performance on the next day's math test or my position in the middle school hierarchy while I listened to the music and thought about the placement of my hands and my arms and all ten of my toes. Onstage, we told stories that, like fables or religious myths, always ended the same way. *Reverence*—the post-class curtsy—was not just a step; it was a ritual.

I took comfort, too, in the familiar order of the barre—no matter who was teaching or how old I got, certain things remained the same. Pliés would always be followed by tendus, dégagés by grands battements. And never a day off. I bought a cassette tape called *Piano Music for Ballet Class* and diligently went through my exercises on family vacations and ballet-school breaks, steadying myself with a hand on a bookshelf instead of a barre.

The dancer's life is inherently ritualistic: the repetition of the barre; the preparation of pointe shoes; the application of makeup. Her day is ordered and predictable, from class in the morning to rehearsal in the afternoon and a performance at night. So is the larger arc of her career, at least as she imagines it—from student to corps dancer to soloist. (Lincoln Kirstein, a veteran of World War II, liked to call the School of American Ballet the "West Point of dance.") "People often ask if the discipline of my career is not irksome," the English dancer Margot Fonteyn wrote in her memoir. "On the contrary, I have found it an extraordinary advantage to have a rigid timetable prescribed for almost every day for the year." Dancers are notorious for inventing elaborate rituals of their own—adding yet another layer of order and regularity to their lives. Before going onstage, he told *Dance Informa* magazine, Christopher Charles McDaniel of Dance Theatre of Harlem listens to gospel music while chewing on Mentos and crackers. Kimberly Giannelli touches a lucky medallion and then stashes it in the right-hand corner of her makeup bag. Kleber Rebello, a former principal at Miami City Ballet, explained in *Dance Spirit* magazine that he lies down in the wings, knocks on the floor three times, and blesses the stage. When ABT principal Hee Seo crosses the street near the theater, she carefully avoids the unmarked pavement of the crosswalks, stepping only on the painted white strips.

"I think I was born worried," Misty Copeland writes in her memoir. However she was born, the chaos around her would have made anyone anxious. Her childhood was defined by a pattern of "packing, scrambling, leaving—often barely surviving," with the family's longest stint living in a violent neighborhood of Los Angeles. The fourth of her mother's six children, Misty didn't meet her birth father until she was twenty-two; her temporary stepfathers included a violent abuser and an alcoholic. "There wasn't a day that I didn't feel some kind of anxiety . . . I felt awkward, as if I didn't fit in anywhere, and I lived in constant fear of letting my mother down, or my teachers, or myself." She was so afraid of public speaking that she trembled when she was called on in class. (I wonder how common this is for bunheads.* Until high school—when my fear of getting a bad grade surpassed my fear of saying the wrong thing—I almost never spoke in class.)

---

* An obsessive ballerina—one who keeps her hair in a tight bun at all times.

Still, she exerted control however she could. She might not have been able to change the fact that she woke every morning in "a wall of sound, with children yelling, music blaring, and the television on full blast"—but she could get to school an hour early. She could work late into the night, studying by flashlight after her siblings had gone to bed. "I was very shy and definitely was the one in the family that blended in with the background," Misty said in the 2015 documentary *A Ballerina's Tale.*

Even before she discovered ballet, Misty took refuge in dancing. The only time she felt truly relaxed growing up was on Sunday afternoons, when—with the rest of her family focused on the football game on TV—she would hide in her mom's room, turn on Mariah Carey, and move. "Whenever I danced, whenever I created, my mind was clear," she wrote. "I didn't think about how I slept on the floor because I didn't have a bed, when my mother's new boyfriend might become my next stepfather, or if we would be able to dig up enough quarters to buy food."

Formal ballet training only amplified Misty's love for dance. She delighted in the challenges of ballet, and in her own success. In the studio, her shyness didn't matter; she didn't have to talk. "Each day I couldn't wait for the bell to ring after sixth period so I could rush out the door, jump into Cindy's car, and head to the studio."

As Misty was spending more time at the ballet studio, her home life was growing increasingly tumultuous. Her mother's fourth husband insisted the children stay silent at dinner and forced her brothers to have fistfights in the backyard. A few years into the relationship, Misty began noticing bruises underneath her mother's blouse—and her mom announced that the family was moving once more. Eventually, they ended up in a run-down motel beside the highway. But the studio was her oasis: there, as nowhere else, Misty was in control. The challenges were surmountable, and the path forward was clear. She quickly grasped the patterns and rituals of ballet class, and, unlike anything else in her life, they were predictable. "I was grateful to hide from the chaos for a little while at the dance studio, inside ballet, where there were rules and life was dignified," she wrote. "Beautiful."

Misty began spending weeks at a time at Cindy's house, where she was inducted, for the first time, into the rituals of an orderly family life: sitting down to dinner and talking about the day; lighting candles together on Friday nights. Ballet was part of the glue that bound the family together. Cindy's husband taught dance, and her three-year-old son took tap classes at her studio. Instead of watching football games on Sunday afternoons, the Bradleys put on archival tapes of Gelsey Kirkland dancing *Don Quixote* at ABT. Their poodle was named Misha, after Baryshnikov.

When Misty began performing in front of an audience, she discovered that the peace she felt in the studio was even more profound when she danced onstage. Just eight months after her first ballet class, she played the role of Clara in Cindy's version of *The Nutcracker*. Like Meiying, she disappeared into the role and—even though it was a local production— won attention from the press. The next year, she danced the lead in the higher-profile *Chocolate Nutcracker*—a retelling of the European Christmas classic in which Clare travels to Harlem and Jamaica instead of to Russia and Spain.

It's evident, from a video of a 1997 competition, that Misty's technique was still unpolished: she doesn't always close her feet in fifth position, and she stumbles when she lands a pirouette. Misty, at fifteen, had had only two years of training, but she chose a notoriously difficult solo—a big, bravura variation from *Don Quixote* in which the defiant Kitri twists and struts across the stage while fluttering a fan and flirting with the audience, finishing with a series of dizzying fouetté turns. But what shines through the old footage most of all is her obvious delight in dancing: her magnetic stage presence and her smile. The camera follows Misty as she brings the variation to a triumphant close and bounds off the stage, jumping up and down as though her tiny body can't contain her glee. "I got my fouettés in!" she yells, grinning. "I'm really happy!"

Four years later, she was a member of ABT's corps de ballet.

In 2013, the South African musicologist Clorinda Panebianco-Warrens interviewed seventeen professional ballet dancers about their experiences of being in "the zone." In combining physical activity with creative challenges, ballet can be a conduit to the elusive state of "flow"—a trancelike, even ecstatic feeling of total absorption. The person in flow is immune to distraction; the world melts away, leaving only the task at hand. The Hungarian psychologist Mihaly Csikszentmihalyi developed the concept through conversations with artists, including a composer who explained how, when his work was going well, he would stop thinking and let the music "just flow out." In flow or the zone, Csikszentmihalyi said in a 2004 TED Talk, "You know that what you need to do is possible to do, even though difficult, and sense of time disappears, you forget yourself, you feel part of something larger."

In what sounds like dictionary examples of flow, the dancers in Panebianco-Warrens's study recounted moments of elation ("your whole mind is in bliss of some sort, and your body, you don't feel tired, you don't feel sore"), a loss of self-consciousness ("I was just in my own space, I kind of became the character . . . you kind of forget who you are"), and a sense of ease ("your body just moves as it's supposed to"). Dancing with a live orchestra (as Meiying did in *The Nutcracker* and as Misty did nightly at ABT) was especially powerful. The countless variables affecting how a ninety-person ensemble sounds on a given night—from the musicians' energy to the conductor's mood to the timing of the audience's applause— mean that the dancers must focus even more intently on the moment. Almost all of the dancers described being "totally absorbed" while performing. "I wasn't thinking of what I was doing, it was just happening. I felt part of . . . an organism onstage; I wasn't separate," one said. Music was a key ingredient, playing "an important role" in fifteen of the dancers' experience of flow. One explained how "music takes the body where it wants to be." "You are in the music," said another.

Even though she won choice roles, Meiying, as a Vietnamese American, sometimes felt like an outsider. "The whiteness of that place is so palpable," she says. Every single one of our teachers was white; so were almost all of the NYCB dancers. "There was nobody in the company that looked like me. I had this ambition, but I knew there was a cap on what I could achieve." When she and a blue-eyed, blond-haired girl shared the role of Marie in *The Nutcracker*, it was the blonde who appeared on the promotional posters outside Lincoln Center.

Ballet makes no secret of valuing conformity; the corps, where every career begins, is meant to move as one. Historically, directors have been reluctant to cast dancers who stand out, whether in body type, height, or skin color. And some of Balanchine's beloved choreography traffics in racist stereotypes.

The Nutcracker's Act II dances aren't just playful homages to various types of candy; each one is also meant to pay tribute to a foreign culture—Russian candy canes, Danish marzipan, Spanish chocolate. In the "Arabian coffee" dance, which Balanchine intended as "something for the fathers," a sultry woman in a jeweled headdress and tassel-fringed bustier shimmies around the stage and writhes on the floor, setting off the bells on her ankles and wrists. The role was often performed by Aesha Ash, the only Black woman in the company. (In 1998, when Aesha was twenty, she had been singled out by the *New York Times* as one of the four most promising dancers in the corps; the critic praised her precocity and the sense of joy in her dancing. The other three dancers profiled all went on to enjoy illustrious careers, with two becoming star principal dancers and the third a celebrity choreographer. But within just five years, Aesha— still languishing in the corps—took Peter Martins's advice and left the company. Yet even as Martins was refusing to give her the featured roles she'd once been slated for, he used her image for marketing: one of the IMDb stills of *Living a Ballet Dream* features Aesha and Meiying doing tendus together.) In the "Chinese tea" dance, a (usually white) man in a straw hat and black wig, his face painted pale and his eyes made up to look slanted, would pop out of a lacquered box while pointing his fingers like chopsticks—all, in the story, to entertain Marie and her prince. "As a child, you feel racism, but you don't understand it," Meiying says. "How fucked is it that I sat onstage every night and I watched Chinese [Tea] ridicule being Asian while I sat on a throne pretending to be German?" (In a rare concession to modern critics, NYCB modified the original costumes and choreography in 2017.)

If ballet had at first been the salve for Misty's anxiety, it was also, at times, the source. As a new member of ABT's corps, she had to learn entire ballets in a matter of days while proving herself to her new boss and navigating thorny dynamics with her new colleagues. When the other dancers talked about summers in Europe and weekend homes, she had nothing to say. Misty was the only Black woman in a company of eighty. "I was a little brown-skinned girl in a sea of whiteness," she wrote. "Certain people, they'd come in and cast ballets and wouldn't even give me the time of day or the chance to see if I was talented enough to portray certain roles," she told *New York* magazine in 2014. "It's a visual art form, so they're judging me on my physical appearance, and some of them just don't want to see brown skin on the stage." When she was cast in the "white ballets"—classic narrative ballets featuring airy spirits and ghosts and flocks of swans—she had to paint her face and arms white to blend in. (Not to mention her shoes: until a few years ago, pointe shoes only came in peach-colored satin. Darker-skinned dancers had to hand-dye or paint each pair to match their skin tone—adding yet another step to the arduous process of breaking them in.) Misty felt so out of place that, when the historically Black Dance Theatre of Harlem made her an offer, she almost accepted. But ABT had been her dream ever since she had watched those videos of Gelsey Kirkland and Baryshnikov at Cindy's house. "I couldn't give up . . . If I had to work ten times harder than everyone else, then I would."

But some things were beyond her control. Misty was rehearsing late one evening when she felt a sudden pain in her lower back. For a couple of weeks, she tried to ignore it, but the pain didn't go away. When she finally went to the hospital, she learned that she had a serious stress fracture and would have to take several months off. At one of her follow-up appointments, a doctor asked her about her period.

As a malnourished teenager, Misty had had all the muscle definition of a rubber band. In footage of her dancing at Cindy's studio, her fouetté turns and jumps look almost implausible on her skeletal frame. I know, intellectually, that these steps require tremendous strength and stamina—but Misty appears to be made of elbows and bones. This was the body she had when she was anointed a prodigy and when she won her first contract with ABT. At nineteen—six or seven years past the age when most girls start menstruating—she was still waiting.

The doctor put her on birth control, and over the next few weeks, Misty went through an accelerated puberty. She sprouted breasts, gained ten pounds, and finally got her period. When she got back to ABT, directors and wardrobe staff were startled by her transformation. Before, Misty had barely needed a bra; now she couldn't find one that fit under her costumes. Not long after her return, she was called in for a meeting with ABT and told that she needed to "lengthen"—one of the ballet world's euphemisms for "lose weight."

As Meiying entered her teens, the magic of performing was tempered, somewhat, by the increasingly harsh realities of the studio. As a child, her stage presence and charisma had been enough to stand out, but as we got older, the scales tipped toward technique. As she asked more of her body—higher extensions, stronger insteps, cleaner lines—she was dismayed to find that it didn't always comply. After years of forcing her turnout, her hips ached all the time. Her body was still growing, but it was also starting to wear out. She felt shooting pains every time she lowered her leg from a grand battement—and we might do a hundred grands battements in an average class. Going on pointe when we were twelve was not the rite of passage she had hoped for; the structure of her ankle and toes, she discovered, made pointe work almost unbearably painful. But she didn't want to give up. She didn't want to admit that the activity that had brought her so much joy, that had even saved her life, was now causing her so much pain. She was determined to find a solution. In between classes and rehearsals and school, Meiying squeezed in MRI scans and physical therapy sessions. Desperate to regain her teachers' favor, she turned against herself. "I started swallowing this pain and then blaming myself for it."

Meiying devised a private, ritualistic grading system, giving herself points and demerits based on how many corrections she received in class and how well she implemented them. At night—no matter how tired she was—she would go to her room and, as if to atone, stretch for a number of minutes determined by the day's score. But hard work could only get her so far. At her end-of-year evaluation, she was told that her feet were too flat and her neck was too short.

As Meiying's future began to look less certain—pointe work wasn't getting any easier, and her neck wasn't getting any longer—she wondered how much more she could take. The summer she was fourteen, she and Emily were accepted into the same summer intensive at the Miami City Ballet School. She flew down to Florida, trying to get excited about the prospect of eight-hour days in the studio and a new set of teachers to impress. But her heart wasn't in it. One night, at the end of a long, hot day of classes, Emily's mom took the girls out to dinner. It was a rare treat—a break from their nonstop training. Away from the campus, Meiying relaxed. Her feet hurt. She thought about her peers in high school, who were spending the summer at sleepaway camps, hiking or fishing or learning to canoe. She wondered what it was like to be normal—not to worry about what role she was up for next or which toe pads might blunt the pain of pointe shoes, but about who was going to the next house party or what books had been assigned for English class.

Meiying and Emily had been inseparable since they'd met as eight-year-olds. They shared everything, including the dream of becoming professional dancers. Now, six years later, Meiying, exhausted and sore, turned to Emily and gave voice to the blasphemous thought that had been brewing for months. "It hurts too much," she said. "I don't think I can do this for the rest of my life."

Not long after, Meiying stopped going to ballet. Instead of sprinting for the door as soon as the school bell rang, she lingered in the hallways, chatting with friends, and then took the subway home. It didn't occur to her that she might try a different, less punishing style of dance, like modern or jazz; she believed she had failed at the only kind of dance that mattered.

She applied herself instead to becoming "normal." She read all seven Harry Potter books, one after the other. As if preparing for a new role, she made a list of what regular teenagers seemed to do, and then diligently checked them off. She went to basketball games with a posse of girls, got drunk at homecoming parties, and even joined the cheerleading team.

But as Meiying tried to adjust to her new life, she realized how much she had relied on ballet—the structure it gave her days, the purpose it gave her years. She tried to care about school. But it all felt so banal. For as long as she could remember, her life had been organized into cycles of auditioning, rehearsing, performing, and recovering. Now she was just a regular high schooler. She joined student clubs and got invited to all the right parties, but she still felt lonely. She had lost her community, her sense of purpose, her sense of moving toward something.

In ninth grade, Meiying had danced for hours a day; by eleventh grade, she was so depressed that she could barely move. She often felt as if she were watching her own life through frosted glass, and her memories from high school are still hazy. She sleepwalked through her senior year and enrolled in a small college in rural New England. She can't remember much about starting college—only that it was cold. On weekend nights, she stayed in the library until it closed, then wandered around campus alone. After less than a semester, she dropped out and moved back home.

Misty left the "fat talk" meeting and cried. "I had no idea how to handle that," she said in *A Ballerina's Tale*. "I had no idea how to take care of my body." Fueled, for once, by anger, she refused to diet; instead, she called Krispy Kreme and placed a corporate order for two dozen donuts. It was the beginning of a cycle of self-sabotage: she would binge at night, in the privacy of her own apartment, and wake up dreading the prospect of looking in the mirror in class. "Thinking that I was fat became a paralyzing mental loop," she wrote, "and I was paranoid that everyone could see it."

Over the years, Misty and ABT reached a truce: she stopped bingeing, eventually adopting a balanced, pescatarian diet, and—in a testament to her star power—they accepted her more muscular frame. As she has risen through the ranks of ABT and booked modeling and commercial gigs, she has been celebrated for breaking the waiflike mold. (Of course, what passes for mold-breakingly muscular in the ballet world is still so desirably thin by the rest of the world's standards that she is often asked for diet tips in interviews; her image appears on the cover of a bestselling book of nutrition advice.) "My curves became an integral part of who I am as a dancer," she wrote, "not something I needed to lose to become one." In 2015—just a year after writing those words—Misty was promoted to principal, becoming the first ever Black woman to reach the highest rank at ABT. She had also, by then, become so renowned that she was publicly congratulated by the likes of Hillary Clinton and Prince.

Does ballet have something to offer those who are not prodigies—even those who have no special facility for ballet? In 2006, the Birmingham Royal Ballet in England invited a group of disadvantaged teenagers to spend a year and a half training with their coaches. The goal of the program was not to transform the children into masters of ballet technique, but to introduce them to the structure and discipline of ballet. (A documentary crew followed the project, producing a series that eventually aired on British public television.) The teenagers were struggling with nearly every horror imaginable; watching them describe the traumas they had suffered—sexual abuse, rape, abandonment, bullying, domestic violence, dead mothers, absent fathers—was like peering into a kaleidoscope of human suffering. Richard—so shy he could not make eye contact with the cameraman—had been living alone at the YMCA ever since his parents told him he was too expensive to feed. When eighteen-year-old Duane started the program, he had just been released from prison. Fourteen-year-old Shireenah explained matter-of-factly, her face clear of emotion or self-pity, that her father had murdered her mother. ("So, um, I don't see my dad that often.")

Before the teenagers started the program, their only exposure to ballet had come through stereotypes. Christina, who dropped out of school at eleven, thought ballet was about "little tutus and men in tights"; Alex thought that "ballet men" were "poofs." There was culture shock on both sides. The ballet teachers were accustomed to unquestioning obedience in their charges—not unexplained absences and the occasional fistfight. They had never had students who juggled classes with court dates or came to rehearsal in dollar-sign necklaces and sweatpants. Outside the studio, the children's lives were chaotic, their futures uncertain. But every afternoon, they entered a realm of order and dignity. The beauty and romanticism of ballet—and the devotion of their teachers—were as foreign as the French names for the steps. Many of them welcomed the structure they found in their classes. "This is giving us something to focus on and stops us worrying about other stuff in our lives," said a self-aware sixteen-year-old named Cesia. "I ain't good at talking to people, but I can dance in front of them," said the painfully timid Richard. They became acquainted, too, with the emotional release of exhaustion. "I didn't think it'd be that intense," said Linden, sweating but grinning.

"Do you feel cleansed?" asked one of the teachers, at the end of a long rehearsal. Shireenah didn't hesitate to answer: "Yeah!"

When Shireenah Ingram started the ballet program, she was grappling with a painful reversal that most don't confront until middle age: the person who raised her—her grandfather— was now relying on her for care. He had lost his eyesight and could no longer make a cup of tea or go to the bathroom on his own. When a social worker encouraged Shireenah to apply, she was surprised. "I thought it was not for someone like me, being quite tall and broad," she told me over Zoom. But she loved her classes at the Birmingham Hippodrome; she was awed by the "professional presence and discipline" of the teachers and dancers.

Shireenah knew it was too late for her to become a ballet dancer, but—buoyed by her teachers' praise—she decided to pursue acting. After finishing high school, she signed up for websites like Casting Call Pro and StarNow and took whatever jobs trickled in—as an extra in movies or an actor in community theater. After a few years, she signed with an agent and worked her way up to commercials and TV. "The ballet project really changed my life," she says. "The discipline I was taught of picking up the choreography, coming prepared, how we should be in rehearsals—that gave me such a strong foundation of how I wanted to lead my life going forward. It built the foundations of my acting practice." When I spoke to Shireenah, I couldn't detect a trace of the sullen teen who told her counselor, on camera, that she had no one to talk to. She was bubbly and outgoing and excited about her life. In the middle of our conversation, her phone rang, and she excused herself—it was her agent, calling to see if she could squeeze in a gig in Prague the following week.

Peter Lovatt, who founded the Dance Psychology Lab at the University of Hertfordshire, once asked a thousand people why they dance. One of the most common responses was that dancing lifted their mood, even alleviated feelings of depression. Dancing is the only time "I feel happy and I can't stop smiling," said a middle-aged man. "In troubled times dance has always been my 'salvation,'" said a fifty-nine-year-old woman. Even a single dance session can have a significant impact: in a German study from 2007, psychologists invited a group of patients who had been hospitalized for depression to dance to the Jewish folk song Hava Nagila for half an hour. After just thirty minutes, they scored higher on measures of vitality and lower on symptoms of depression. (This effect can't be attributed to the joyful music alone: patients who spent the same half-hour period listening to the song without dancing actually wound up feeling more depressed.)

To dance is a universal impulse. Before infants walk or talk or even crawl, they move rhythmically in response to song. (Search "babies dancing" on YouTube, but only if you're prepared to lose at least half an hour.) In a 2010 study by a pair of European psychologists, infants sat on their mothers' laps while either music or a speech played over a set of loudspeakers. Afterward, the researchers analyzed videos of the babies and found that they made more "rhythmic movements"— gestures repeated at least three times in quick succession— when they heard the music. They also smiled more.

All over the world—from the Na Nach mystics who jump on top of vans in Israeli cities, to the clubgoers who rave in sweaty basements—dance is an ecstatic release, a ritual celebration, a spontaneous expression of joy. Like hypnosis or dreams, it's a conduit to an altered state and a sense of oneness with the world.

But not everyone is comfortable improvising. The clear rules and structure of ballet allow those of us who feel self-conscious grabbing a stranger's hand or randomly jumping up and down to access the freedom and joy of dance. Babies may happily move to the beat, but as we grow up, the urge to avoid embarrassing ourselves starts to compete with the urge to shake our hips. I dread the moment, at weddings, when the DJ invites all the guests to the dance floor; unless I've had several drinks, I hover on the sidelines, scanning for a conversation to join. I can only let loose to music under the cover of darkness, or in the privacy of my own room.

The ballerina who is formidable in the studio but awkward and stiff on the dance floor is a subset of the uptight-bunhead stereotype, parodied and immortalized in the ballet canon. In the 2003 rom-com *Uptown Girls*, an eight-year-old hypochondriac named Ray (played by Dakota Fanning) loves her weekly ballet class (populated, in the film, by several of my SAB classmates, including Emily and Flora) but freezes up when, toward the end of class, the teacher announces that there are five minutes left: Time to freestyle! While the other girls cheer the news—Emily pumps her fists and does a cartwheel—Ray packs her bag, storms out of the studio, and starts buttoning up her crisp, white blouse.

The nineteen-year-old narrator of Sophie Flack's novel *Bunheads*, Hannah, a professional dancer with a thinly veiled New York City Ballet, is confident dancing before an audience of two thousand discerning New Yorkers. But when a new "real-world" friend invites her to a party and she finds herself in a throng of college students gyrating to Beyoncé, she doesn't know what to do with her body. "The funny thing is that I'm embarrassed to dance in a situation like this; I don't know how to do it like a normal person," Hannah says. "I'm used to having everything choreographed for me, not all improvisational and loose."

At summer programs, we were sometimes required—in a token gesture at rounding out our education—to take classes in hip-hop and jazz. I was terrible at them, but I secretly took pride in the teachers' admonitions to let go: I was an incorrigible bunhead. I recently dug up an old VHS recording of an end-of-summer recital from a program I attended in 2005.

After a twee ballet piece, in which we tiptoed in and out of dainty diagonals while holding pastel scarves above our heads, the piano faded out, and the music changed. The volume rose, and Paula Abdul giggled and moaned: "Work it, baby!" I watched the tape with my mom, and we laughed so hard we cried—but even as I experienced a full-body cringe, I wanted to defend the thirteen-year-old half-heartedly undulating on the screen. Watching her, I remembered the precise strategy I had deployed for getting through the piece, doing just enough that I wouldn't stand out—carefully going through the motions of the choreography, making sure I was in the right place at the right time—but without actually committing to the dance. Instead of shimmying my shoulders or shaking my hips, I pointed my feet and squared my back as if I was in ballet class—clinging to the rules that made me feel safe.

The regimented discipline of ballet can be a lifeline for those suffering from trauma or going through uncertain times. I wasn't surprised when millions of lapsed dancers flocked to virtual ballet classes at the start of Covid. Confined to my one-bedroom Brooklyn apartment in March 2020, there were days I doubted my own existence. Without really thinking about it, I rested a hand on the kitchen counter and started doing tendus—front, side, back, and side; right leg, left leg . . .

But it works in more quotidian times, too. We all—to some degree—long for boundaries. We all reckon with a tension between our desire for freedom and our desire for order; between the risk of chaos and the risk of repression. "Anxiety is the dizziness of freedom," wrote the philosopher Søren Kierkegaard—the consequence of looking too long into the "yawning abyss" of possibilities. So—in order to survive—we close our eyes to some of them; we give ourselves borders and box ourselves in. We build cocoons, metaphorical or not. The writer Jessica Gross takes comfort in small spaces and calls herself a "claustrophile"; in an essay for Longreads, she writes ecstatically of "the pure relief of containment" afforded by a small study carrel, a cramped train cabin, a corner seat.

There is a scene in the popular TV show *Fleabag* in which the rudderless protagonist, who has for ten episodes been struggling to find some kind of anchor—to a relationship or an ambition or a community—breaks down and confesses her true desire. "I want someone to tell me what to wear every morning," she says. She is sitting in a confessional booth, crying in front of a priest who is also the object of her latest sexual fixation. "I want someone to tell me what to eat. What to like, what to hate, what to rage about, what to listen to, what band to like, what to buy tickets for, what to joke about, what not to joke about. I want someone to tell me what to believe in, who to vote for, who to love and how to tell them." This scene was endlessly memed, and praised for its relatability. The speech "resonated for reasons totally outside the show," wrote a reviewer for Vice: "We are surrounded by so much *stuff* . . . that often it can be hard to root out what you really want or think or even know." *Fleabag* captures the fantasy of surrender—of throwing up your hands and letting a ready-made ideology, or even a single person, fill in for the whole hard work of becoming.

When I watched this scene, I thought about ballet, and how it fulfilled so many of these desires. I thought about how dancers don't have to decide what to wear in the morning. I thought of Balanchine, who told his dancers who to vote for (conservatives), who to love (him), and what to eat (not much). Of how Toni Bentley had captured the dancer's mentality— the perverse pleasure of abdicating responsibility—in her first memoir. At twenty-two, she already understood: "We have no choice; we choose to have no choice."

The cost of having choices is high: you might make the wrong one. Those who thrive in ballet find ways to express themselves, to maintain their individuality while staying within the bounds of traditional etiquette and technique. It's the tension between the system and the individual that creates an electric charge for the viewer. Misty's stardom stems from her pristine classical technique, and from the many ways in which she conforms, as much as from her difference.

Little Rats

Growing up, my dad often took me to the Met on Saturday afternoons. We would stroll through Central Park, past the tourists tossing coins into Bethesda Fountain and lazing on rowboats in the lake, past the pretzel carts and peanut stands, until we reached the magnificent art palace on Fifth Avenue. We collected our "M" buttons and clipped them to our shirts and then walked through the Great Hall, gazing up at the grand columns and archways all around us. We could have seen treasures from ancient Greece or mummies from Egypt or masterpieces from the Dutch Golden Age, but I knew exactly where I wanted to go. Up the staircase and to the left, ignoring the sculpture court on the right and the Spanish relics on the left, through the photo exhibit, into European Paintings, and there they were: my beloved Degas.

I would hurry past his figurines—there was something eerie about those dark naked shapes, with their blurry faces and sloppy bronze skin—and arrive, at last, at the paintings: luscious dreamscapes, lovely dancers in turquoise tutus and lace bodices with red ribbons in their hair; dancers practicing at the barre, stretching and preening backstage. I looked at them so long I felt like I could crawl into the frames, could leave behind the crowded neon chaos of 1990s New York and live in this world of quiet beauty, of violins and lamplight and watering cans in the corner. When I was done staring at these scenes—or, more likely, when my dad had tired of watching me—it was time to visit my favorite piece of all: *Little Dancer Aged Fourteen.*

Degas's sculpture of a poor Paris Opera student stands in the middle of the room, elevated and alone, her feet apart and her hands clasped behind her back. I circled her on her pedestal, examining her half-closed eyes and her strange, flat face, admiring the real silk ribbon in her metal braid and the cotton tutu around her waist. From one angle, she looked proud, as if she were peering down her nose at me; from another, I thought she seemed tired but at peace, lost in some private fantasy. Or perhaps she looked resigned, like the best she could do was to shut her eyes to the world. (In my favorite picture book, she waited until the last visitor had left the museum and then came to life, jumping down from her pedestal to haunt the empty galleries.)

My dad would try to interest me in the Rembrandts and the Vermeers—but these excursions, for me, were always about Degas. One afternoon, we visited the museum's gift shop, and I was allowed to pick out one poster for my bedroom wall at home. I could have chosen a print of *L'Étoile*, Degas's rendition of a beautiful, blushing ballerina, dancing in the spotlight with a look of ecstasy on her face, or of *Deux danseuses sur scène*, in which two delicate women pose prettily en pointe. But I knew which one I wanted; it wasn't even close. *La classe de danse* (1874) captivated me.

At first, it was beauty that drew me in: the dolled-up dancers, the flurry of puffy tutus and flowers in dark hair. But the more I looked, the more layers of complexity revealed themselves: the ambiguous profile of the portly ballet master. The anxious look on the dancing girl's face, her expression hidden by lipstick and rouge.

I step back, take in the whole busy scene. A girl in a pink sash performs an arabesque while a dozen other pupils wait their turn, warming up or gossiping in the back. One girl massages her neck; another fixes her costume in the mirror. The competition is tangible: the dancing girl is under close observation. One of her classmates watches with both hands on her hips, as though reluctantly impressed; another bites her fingernails, as though unsure if she can measure up. But there's no doubt as to whose opinion matters, or who is at the center of the girls' orbit. Students and their mothers are packed into the corners of the room, but a wide swath of empty space surrounds the ballet master: no one dares infringe. He has gray hair and a matching gray suit, a ruddy and unreadable face. He leans on a heavy wooden cane. Power, and the possibility of violence, cling to him: Does he use his walking stick to keep time, or to strike his students' turned-in legs?

It wasn't until I returned to the Met as an adult that I realized *La classe de danse* was not the only Degas painting that featured a man. As a child, I had been fixated on the women, their frilly tutus and their glamour. So I was surprised to see—lurking around the edges of many of the paintings I had loved—dozens of dark, unmistakably masculine figures. Men in top hats—some without faces, like figures from a bad dream—hovered in the shadows or in the wings, slovenly and menacing. As soon as I noticed them, they were all I could see; I wondered how I had ever looked at these scenes and seen anything else. I was an adult, too, when I learned about the life of Marie van Goethem, the muse for the *Little Dancer* sculpture I'd always loved. I read Camille Laurens's *Little Dancer Aged Fourteen* and learned how, as a Parisian ballet student, Marie earned extra money for her family by posing for artists; how she was expelled from the Opera when these sittings interfered with her rehearsals. (The dancers were known as *petits rats de l'opéra*, or "little rats," according to the nineteenth-century poet Théopile Gautier, because of their small size and their "gnawing and destructive tendencies.") I read about how Degas gave her features associated with immorality and the lower class (high cheekbones, thick hair) and how she was ridiculed when the sculpture was first exhibited in a Paris salon. About how she was called ugly and sickly and depraved; how she was likened to a criminal and an ape. One revolted critic wrote that she had "a face marked with the hateful promise of every vice." I had always thought she was pretty.

I learned, too, about how those men on the sidelines of Degas's paintings had real-life counterparts in the rich men who scouted for lovers and prostitutes among the fresh-faced young girls at the Opera. And how the girls' mothers would often act as pimps, arranging the sale of their own daughters. (When Marie van Goethem was born, the age of consent in France was thirteen; it had recently been raised from eleven.) But I already knew that, although women in ballet may be center stage, dangerous men are loitering just behind the scenes.

Girls and women made up the vast majority of students and dancers, but at every level, men had the upper hand. In the classroom, boys were scarce and therefore favored. The School of American Ballet awarded them automatic scholarships, while girls owed several thousand dollars in annual tuition. Male dancers were three times as likely to find a full-time job in a company, according to *Advice for Dancers*, by the psychologist and former New York City Ballet member Linda Hamilton. Men were the all-powerful directors, the vaunted choreographers. From 2018 to 2020, according to the Dance

Data Project, men choreographed eighty percent of the work performed by America's fifty largest companies. And as recently as 2016, all fifty-eight of the pieces on New York City Ballet's program were made by men. Our bodies were instruments and they belonged to other people: to choreographers and partners and directors—to men.

Girls are trained not to create new work but to join the corps de ballet, the ensemble where all professionals get their start, and where the majority spend their whole careers. The corps is the backbone of the ballet: the low-ranking women who play the anonymous snowflakes, flowers, peasants, and swans. (Though men, too, pass through the corps, most of the iconic corps roles—the shades of *La Bayadère*, the swans of *Swan Lake*—are for groups of women. Men are more readily promoted; they stand out without trying.) "The rule is if we don't notice you, you're doing a good job," says the ballet mistress of England's Royal Ballet. Before a dancer can be considered for solo roles, she must first succeed at blending in—a humbling rite of passage. (The American Ballet Theatre dancer Devon Teuscher told *Pointe* about the whiplash she experienced after being promoted to principal; about how alien it felt to be asked for her opinion. "I remember starting to work on *Swan Lake*, and my coach, Irina Kolpakova, asked, What do you want to do at this moment? And I was like, What do you mean? You tell me what to do!") To succeed in the corps takes tremendous discipline and reserve. There is no room for argument or interpretation. The dancer must forgo her own artistic flourishes—her individuality, her ego—for the sake of moving as one. A single foot out of line, a tendu a breath too soon, can ruin the effect. She must put her trust in the choreographer and his vision. But the result, when it works, is breathtaking. Some of the most memorable scenes in the ballet canon are not solos or pas de deux but the extravagant beauty of dozens of women dancing—the haunted Willis orbiting Giselle's fresh grave; the fuchsia flowers waltzing through *The Nutcracker*'s Land of Sweets. It's hardly surprising that women raised in this world shy away from choreographing—from telling others what to do. That they find it more natural to take direction.

*   *   *

I was twelve years old and had never so much as held hands with a boy. At middle school dances, I huddled with my girlfriends, studiously avoiding eye contact—let alone actual contact—with the opposite sex.

And now I was standing on the side of the studio, my time running out in four-beat increments. The middle-aged pianist in the corner, who had no doubt seen this ritual a hundred times, tapped out the bars of some generic tune. I looked at my partner, assigned based on our heights—a reedy, dark-haired boy in the standard uniform of black tights and a white T-shirt. I had never spoken to him before. His hand was wrapped around another girl's waist as she held an arabesque en pointe.

The girls outnumbered the boys five to one, so we shared them, rotating in and out while they kept dancing. When the exercise ended, my rival ran off gracefully and I ran in, taking her place. I wondered who was sweatier, who was prettier, who he preferred. I was too shy to look directly at my partner, and, mercifully, the choreography did not require it. I arranged my feet in fifth position with my back to him, relevé'd onto pointe, and felt a pair of strong hands on my waist. For the first time in my life, I could turn not just two but three, four, five pirouettes. All I had to do was balance, secure in the knowledge that he would lend me momentum and catch me if I fell. When I reached the highest point of a jump, he lifted me another three feet; it was the closest I had ever come to flying. Then the music ended, I ran off to the side, and another girl stepped in. I had never felt so ecstatic, or so replaceable.

The first time I danced with a boy in real life—a couple years later, in my middle school gym—was fumbling and chaotic. Whose hands went where? What was I supposed to say? Who was meant to initiate, to lead?

The dynamics of classical pas de deux, meanwhile, were clear. "The women were fillies and the men were jockeys," Edward Villella wrote in his memoir, *Prodigal Son*. "During the pas de deux I felt I was holding the reins, leading the ballerina through her paces, directing her movements around a track." The woman is the ornament; the man is in control. He lifts her up and sets her down, spins her around while she silently poses. The very act of rising onto pointe renders the woman precarious: perched on her toes, she is "far easier and lighter to manipulate . . . as well as being appropriately vulnerable and dependent upon our male support," as Toni Bentley put it in a 1983 article for *Rolling Stone*. I sensed, on some level, that it was too easy—that I was giving up on something—but still, I took comfort in the choreography, in the prescribed nature of our roles.

I have sometimes wondered, in my post-ballet life, if I have replicated that dynamic—if I internalized the doctrine of passivity, and if it affected my relationships. For more than a year in my early twenties, I was involved with a man I never called first. No matter what I wanted to say—no matter if I was bored or upset or just wanted to chat—I waited. Meanwhile, after months of interning—running errands, sorting mail, and

writing late at night—I landed my first real job at a magazine. My articles were picked up; my bosses praised me, as did
strangers online. But the confidence I was developing at work
had no bearing on my behavior in private.

When I began reading about Margot Fonteyn, I squirmed
with recognition. On one level—the level on which she was an
ultraglamorous superstar—she was entirely unrelatable. But
on another, her story felt strangely familiar.

In the 1940s and '50s, Margot Fonteyn helped to elevate
English ballet from a minor diversion, on par with the circus,
to a mainstay of British culture, with fans in the Palace and a
permanent home in Covent Garden. Her foreign tours did so
much to restore England's postwar reputation that, in 1956,
Queen Elizabeth anointed her a dame. When Margot danced
in New York, her admirers camped out overnight, sleeping in
the subway station to be closer to the box office at Lincoln
Center. Most ballet dancers are lucky to extend their careers
into their midthirties; Margot celebrated her sixtieth birthday
by starring in a new ballet. Her strength and tenacity as a
dancer are legend.

Offstage, meanwhile, she was pathologically unable to
stand up for herself. One colleague described her, in a documentary, as "the most passive person I have ever known." As
a young dancer, she accepted a meager salary without complaining. She had imbibed the company ethos of what her
biographer, Meredith Daneman, calls "vocational frugality,
which preaches that one must be grateful to scrape a living
for the privilege of doing what one loves."

When it came to romance, Margot's passivity made her
easy prey. With striking dark hair and a magnetic presence,
she attracted legions of admirers—accomplished and famous
men from the worlds of theater, politics, and the arts. She was

always fashionably dressed, often by the likes of Christian Dior and Yves Saint Laurent.

But in the theater where she spent her formative years—she enrolled in de Valois's ballet school at fourteen and became a full company member at fifteen—she had developed a sense of herself as expendable. The gender ratio was stacked against her. Of the three dozen members of the company, Daneman estimates that "only a handful" of the men would have been interested in women. "And in some ways these unambivalent 'he-men' would have been the least romantically acceptable of all," she writes: swaggering womanizers, "cutting a swathe through the ranks of the more foolishly susceptible girls in the corps de ballet." Still, competition was fierce. As one ballerina put it, "If there was a man around, you grabbed him." (That line has been haunting me ever since I read it; it perfectly captures my own mentality during my ballet years—a mentality that followed me through my late teens and early twenties. It wasn't until I downloaded Tinder in New York that the illusion of scarcity was finally shattered.)

Margot spent much of her young adulthood in thrall to the composer and conductor Constant Lambert, who had a violent temper, a drinking problem, and—when he started pursuing her—a pregnant wife. Constant was a worldly twenty-nine-year-old, the son of a prominent painter and a confidant of socialites and celebrities. He was a prolific reader and a famous wit; the economist John Maynard Keynes considered him one of the most brilliant men he had ever met. When Margot first caught Constant's eye, she was a sheltered fifteen-year-old, self-conscious about her ignorance of the world, even as she was also starring in a ballet he had scored. "Why on earth wasn't I educated properly?" she used to ask her mother, who pulled her out of school at fourteen. When the art historian

Kenneth Clark, enthralled by Margot's dancing, invited her to join a group of critics and choreographers for dinner, she was too embarrassed to speak.

Still, Margot resisted Constant's advances for months. Margot was glamorous and immaculately groomed; Constant was jowly and overweight. But he gave her records to listen to and books to read—James Joyce, D. H. Lawrence, Baudelaire—and eventually wore her down. "In a funny sort of way, he educated her," one of her fellow dancers told Daneman.

"I used to look at him and think, 'How could she?'" Julia Farron, one of Margot's contemporaries, said. "I don't understand how she managed, because she was so beautiful and he was so ugly," said another.

Nevertheless, it was Constant who held the upper hand and Margot who ran after him. She looked the other way when he ogled—and slept with—various girls in the corps. She took care of him when he drank too much and tracked him down when he wandered off into the night. "Constant would find somewhere to drink after the show," one of their friends told Daneman. "She'd pick him up from the gutter." He didn't always limit his drinking to after the show, either; he was once so inebriated while conducting *Hamlet* that he fell off the podium and into the pit.

For the first few years of their affair, Constant was still living—and fighting—with his first wife, Florence Kaye. Florence once told the police she was screaming because of a toothache, when in fact she was screaming because her husband had attacked her. (Margot would later admit to a friend that he had been violent with her, too.) Eventually, they divorced—but instead of committing to Margot, Constant eloped with a new woman. He didn't bother to let Margot know; rather, Daneman wrote, "she was merely left to find out by what means she might—like a dancer reading on a public notice board that she had lost a leading role."

The relationship was over, but a pattern was in place. Margot spent much of her remaining twenties and early thirties—when she wasn't dancing for Queen Elizabeth or posing for the cover of *Newsweek* or *Time*—pining after men who were hard to pin down. It didn't matter if they were married, mean, drunk. And, in spite of his appalling treatment, she never stopped missing Constant. Years and many men later, she still kept a framed photo of him beside her bed.

She despaired of ever finding lasting love. "The man I could marry did not apparently exist, and without such a love I would descend into the abyss when my career ended, or so it seemed," she thought, according to her memoir, as she approached her thirtieth birthday. Still single five years later, she started to panic.

She was thirty-four when a Panamanian diplomat named Roberto "Tito" Arias—an acquaintance from a long-ago tour to Cambridge, and now Panama's delegate to the United Nations—bought a ticket to see Margot in *The Sleeping Beauty* in New York. Margot guarded her pre-show privacy fiercely; she had been known to drop her rigorously polite demeanor when interrupted before a performance, once hissing at a ballet manager to "Get out!" of her dressing room. But when Tito arrived at her door at intermission—she was fixing her headdress for Act II—she did not send him away. Aurora was one of Margot's favorite roles, a showcase for her acting as well as her ballet technique, but he did not compliment her performance—only announced his desire to see her outside of the theater. The next morning, he called her hotel. "Darling, I have to leave for Panama at noon, so I want to have breakfast with you," he said. It was too early, she protested: she was barely awake. "It doesn't matter," he replied. "Order me some coffee and I will be right over." Half an hour later, he was sitting cross-legged on her floor and asking her to marry him— never mind the fact that he was already married, with three children. "My wife will divorce me," he said, in what Fonteyn remembered as "a lazy voice." The next day, he phoned her from Panama to tell her that his wife had agreed to separate. "Don't be crazy," Margot cried. "I hardly know you. I don't love you." Within months, they were engaged.

Tito was a master of grand romantic gestures—dropping off one hundred red roses in a limo; meeting Margot's train with offerings of diamond jewelry. But it is unclear how well the couple got to know each other, or how much Margot understood about her suitor's politics. Tito hailed from a powerful and conniving right-wing Panamanian family; his father had been president twice, his uncle three times. He socialized with Aristotle Onassis and Winston Churchill and the local dictator Manuel Noriega. Fomenting revolutions was a hobby of Tito's—he claimed to have plotted seven—though his enthusiasm surpassed his skill. A few years after they wed, Tito recruited Margot to help smuggle weapons into Panama on a fishing boat—a clumsy scheme that was quickly intercepted, landing her in jail and him in the trunk of a friend's car, being ferried to safe haven in the Brazilian embassy. (At least, the ever grateful Margot notes in her memoir, she was given "the VIP suite," with such luxuries as a bedside table and sheets that "looked clean.")

Even when he wasn't getting his wife arrested, Tito was a terrible husband. He was unreliable and inattentive, dismissive of Margot's intellect and indifferent to her career. (Even so, Margot took pains not to make him jealous; after her wedding, she canceled the press clipping service that she had retained

for years, and stopped scrapbooking her reviews.) Margot—
who taught herself French by reading Proust, and was pen
pals with Graham Greene—confided to a friend that "he held
her cognitive powers in such poor regard that he barely spoke
to her except to introduce her at parties." Tito's "philandering
spirit" has its own entry in the index of Daneman's biography;
his "elusiveness" gets four pages. Rumor had it that his infidelities began even before their honeymoon in the Bahamas
had ended. He humiliated Margot by flaunting his affairs—a
long-term relationship with his secretary, one-night stands
with women in Panama—and, like Constant before him, flirting with her colleagues in front of her. "He would grab the
youngest, prettiest little corps de ballet dancer at a party and
sit her on his knee, with Margot standing there, pretending
to laugh it off," one company member recalled. Margot com-
forted herself with the tales of her beloved ballets: after all, she
reminded herself, the mythological shepherd Daphnis hadn't
stayed faithful to Chloe—a role Frederick Ashton created for
her—but there was no doubt that Daphnis loved Chloe, or
that the ballet was a romance, and a masterpiece.

In the early 1960s, Margot was approaching the age at
which most dancers—even primas—retire. But she didn't
feel ready to step aside, and the Royal's director, Ninette de
Valois, suggested that dancing with a younger man might prolong her career. De Valois didn't know, when she arranged for
forty-two-year-old Margot to partner with the twenty-three-
year-old Russian defector Rudolf Nureyev, that their chemis-
try would electrify the ballet world. Margot's grace coupled
with Rudolf's charisma, her experience with his energy, her
British reserve with his wild exuberance, were dynamite. The
Guardian's dance critic called them a match "made in heaven."
The *New York Times* said that to see "Fonteyn and Nureyev

together . . . was almost indescribably special." It strikes me as ironic that this partnership—the pinnacle of long-suffering Margot's career—was built on a balance of power that was, at last, almost egalitarian. When she reflected on the relationship in a BBC documentary, she was able to acknowledge, for once, her own accomplishments (even if they were couched in her usual self-deprecation). "I would go out on the stage thinking, *Who is going to look at me, with this young lion leaping ten feet high in the air and doing all these fantastic things?* And then Rudolf had really a deep respect because I was this older, very famous, established ballerina. And he felt a bit—'Well, when I'm on the stage beside her, who's going to look at me?'"

Offstage, Margot and Rudi delighted in each other's company, flirting and partying and debating the finer points of ballet technique. Margot's friends noticed a new levity in the ever-dutiful ballerina. But Rudi—like so many of the men in Margot's life—had a nasty streak. A dancer told Daneman about one *Giselle* rehearsal where "suddenly Rudi let fly at Margot. He swore at her. He was evil. And she just stood there and took it, and then quietly left the studio." Margot's colleagues—who expected their lead ballerina to be treated with reverence, or at least a modicum of respect—were horrified.

When Margot and Rudi were cast as the leads in *Giselle*, thirty thousand people applied for tickets. Tito, presumably, could have bypassed the application, but he didn't bother. He rarely watched Margot dance, though his schedule was undemanding; he devoted more time to his dalliances than to any kind of work. "Whenever we were traveling, and Tito used to promise to come and join the tours with us and everything—and he never did, you know—once he did," Margot's assistant, Joan Thring, said in Tony Palmer's 2005 documentary *Margot*.

"She was on the phone with him all the time, and pleading with him. He had no reason not to join the tour, three-quarters of the time." Even after reading a litany of Tito's infidelities and offenses, I was especially outraged when I learned about his attitude toward his wife's career. I expect my boyfriends to promptly read everything I publish, including my tweets.

When Tito did show up, he refused to congratulate Margot, instead complaining afterward: "You know I not like ballet." Still, he encouraged her to keep dancing; he enjoyed spending her money. "It's difficult to retire a good racehorse," he said. (Both horses and dancers, he explained, need careful exercise and a lot of food.)

Through it all, Margot worshiped him. His cruelty only fanned the flames of her devotion. Her blind loyalty frustrated her friends. "If he'd said, 'Run down naked into the Thames and swim to the other side and bring me out that stone,' she'd have done it," one told Daneman.

In 1965—when he and Margot had been together for about a decade—one of Tito's rivals shot him five times, leaving him paralyzed from the waist down and barely able to speak. (Margot, in her account, portrayed Tito's adversary as motivated by politics, though some say that he was having an affair with his assailant's wife.)

Margot's career was at an all-time high, but she didn't hesitate to cut back and care for her husband. "Had Tito died," she wrote, "I would be totally unable to continue living, let alone dancing." When he was taken to Stoke Mandeville Hospital in Aylesbury, about an hour outside of London, Margot booked herself a room nearby and learned to drive so she could eat breakfast with him before commuting to morning class. She became a fluent interpreter of his slurred, barely audible speech, translating his whispered words for his family and friends. To lift his spirits and reinflate his ego, she asked him to dictate notes about his life and his business ideas, transcribing them for his "autobiography."

In photos from this time, Margot—who was in her mid-forties—looks as vulnerable as ever: her eyes are still searching, her smile tentative, as if she's begging you to like her. She makes me think of a porcelain doll with a few cracks, or a child with Halloween wrinkles. Her face is beautiful but eerily blank. When the *Guardian* interviewed her in 1970 about one of her signature roles, she demurred, self-effacing as ever: "Anybody who's knowledgeable about *Giselle* wouldn't consider I do it well either, because you could find many, many dancers who could do the ballet much better."

When Tito regained some mobility, he decided he wanted to move back to Panama. He bought a ranch in a remote part of the country, and Margot cheerfully agreed to join him there. She left the Royal Ballet and lost contact with most of her friends; they could reach her only by sending letters to a post office an hour's drive from the ranch. The farm had no phone line or electricity. "No amenities at all," Tito's son recalled in Palmer's documentary. "No amenities to the point there wasn't even a hygienic facility."

"From Dior suits and seams up the back of her legs and Elizabeth Arden–dyed hair—from that she went to this farmhand," one of her horrified colleagues told Palmer. Sheep wandered freely in and out of her bedroom. One visitor remembered watching her "cutting up Tito's food while her own got cold." Another recalled that she would go to bed "fully clothed so she could wake up every three hours and turn him . . . he was a big dead weight." Margot saw it as her duty not only to nurse and feed him, but to keep him entertained. She diligently listened to the radio, tuning in to stations around the world so she could talk to him about international affairs. "Life was a constant struggle to keep him from being bored," she told *Vanity Fair* writer Maureen Orth.

Even as Margot martyred herself for her husband, he refused to change. Being confined to a wheelchair didn't stop him from carrying on an emotional affair with Anabella Vallarino, a socialite he had been sleeping with before he was shot. When Margot occasionally left Panama for dancing engagements, Anabella would move in and take her place. Back in the UK, Margot reprised her usual roles, playing teenagers well into her fifties. "She was having a lot of difficulties with her feet and everything, but when she came onstage, I couldn't believe it was her," the dancer and director Peter Wright, who saw her in *Romeo and Juliet* in 1975, told Palmer. "She looked about sixteen. She looked like a young, young girl."

Tito, meanwhile, drained Margot's savings, renovating the ranch and buying fancy cows even as she wasted away. "Tito only liked the best, and cattle are very, very expensive," said a friend of Margot's. He followed his whims, however extravagant: if he decided he wanted to go for a swim, then a driver would be commissioned to take him to a pool and a servant would be hired to help lower him into the water. In a single afternoon, according to a friend of Margot's, Tito might run up a tab of six or seven hundred dollars (more than five thousand dollars in today's money).

Margot "was literally starving," said one of her friends. "She had no money at all. When I say no money, I mean, nothing, living off cornflakes." The year Tito died, in 1989, Margot auctioned off most of her jewelry at Christie's.

In 1990, Maureen Orth visited Margot in Panama, where she lived in a ramshackle house with a corrugated iron roof and—although Orth estimated the temperature to be over one hundred degrees in the shade—no air-conditioning. Prizes won by Tito's cattle were on display in the living room, Orth noted, but every memento of Margot's forty-five-year ballet career had been hidden away. When Orth tried to turn the conversation toward dance, Margot seemed uncomfortable. "All I was ever trying to do was what was expected of me," she said. "And I always felt inadequate."

Margot lived for only a year after Tito's funeral. She died at the age of seventy-one, isolated from her many fans and friends, and asked for her ashes to be buried at Tito's feet. "When Tito died she just gave up," Tito's sister told Palmer. "It was her choice." When a friend of Margot's visited the cemetery, the custodian "didn't seem to know anything about Arias and Fonteyn." He searched his records while Margot's friend waited. When he finally located Margot Fonteyn, her name was misspelled.

Was Margot happy on the farm? As much as she insisted that she was, her friends in London didn't believe her. "I guess it was part of what she had to do to endure it," said one Royal Ballet dancer who spoke to Palmer. Margot's old colleague shakes her head. Fashionably gaunt and carefully groomed, she wears subtle gold earrings and coral lipstick. "Here she was saying just how wonderful it was to have the cow in the kitchen when they're having breakfast." Her voice drips with sarcasm; a chandelier glitters above her head. It is impossible to imagine that this woman has ever come within fifty feet of a cow. "Oh my God. She talked about that all the time."

"She's happy with her cows," said Rudi, in archival footage that appears in the same documentary. He reclines in front of a mirror, looking completely at home in a baroque burgundy getup that might have been either a costume or a bathrobe. "Maybe it was empty, this glamorous world, and I think life with cows probably was more meaningful." His lips tremble; he bursts out laughing. It is beyond his imagination.

But when I watched footage of Margot on the ranch, I wasn't so sure she was faking her contentment. I watched her sit beside Tito's wheelchair and look at him adoringly, her silver hair pinned up in a bun, her posture immaculate as ever. I watched her lay her manicured hand on his paralyzed one and lift a forkful of food to his mouth. I watched her choke up as she recalled the moment, twenty-five years earlier, when she learned that Tito had been shot. And I believed Tito's son when he said: "After he died, life lost all sparkle for her."

Margot's ability to swing between opposite poles of triumph and abjection—to bask in forty-three curtain calls, then go home and babysit her self-centered husband—is a testament to the lesson she absorbed in the studio: that women, however celebrated, are still at the mercy of men; that her most important role was not as Princess Aurora or Giselle or the Swan Queen, but as her husband's helpmeet.

But if Margot found some kind of satisfaction in romantic suffering—if she even relished her own powerlessness—she was hardly the first woman to do so. "Is there a particular kind of abjection that some of us are drawn to, participate in, possibly romanticize, even though nothing about our external lives necessarily suggests it?" Katie Roiphe asks in *The Power Notebooks*, her meditation on women who are "strong in public, weak in private." Roiphe considers luminaries such as Sylvia Plath, who wrote that her husband, Ted Hughes, was "the only man I had ever met who I could never boss," and Edith Wharton, who wrote to her ambivalent boyfriend: "I don't want to win—I want to lose everything to you." I can believe that Margot Fonteyn, like Wharton and Plath, took a perverse pleasure in suppressing her own desires; in agreeing to become an ornament.

When I think about Margot's choices—about how she minimized her accomplishments and prioritized her husband—I think of how normal it seemed to me, growing up, for men to be in control—to wield a dictatorial level of power over the lives of company dancers and students. Margot and I were seventy-three years apart—but the ballet world, in that time, was largely impervious to the progress wrought in the world outside. When Peter Martins occasionally dropped in on our SAB classes, lowering himself into a plastic chair as though it were a throne and wordlessly staring at us from the front of the room, the atmosphere would shift, darken. We could feel the teachers tensing; we suddenly felt like we were on their team. They didn't have to tell us to straighten our knees, point our toes extra hard. I cringe when I remember how we tried to impress Martins. The proudest moment of my ballet career was on one of these occasions, when the teacher chose me to demonstrate a combination—or maybe it was only a step—at the barre.

Not so long before, Martins had been arrested on charges of beating his wife, Darci Kistler, a dancer nearly twenty years his junior. She called the police in the middle of the night and told them her husband had pushed her, slapped her, and thrown her from room to room. In an affidavit quoted in the *New York Times*, she said she had cuts on her ankle and bruises up and down her arms and legs. Martins spent the night in the Saratoga Springs jail—but Kistler refused to testify, and the charges were dropped three days later.

Ballet insiders, meanwhile, rushed to Martins's defense. It was "a personal matter," a member of SAB's board told the *New York Times* days after the arrest, in July 1992. In December of that year, a fawning profile of Martins appeared in the *Los Angeles Times*. The writer, Scot J. Paltrow, paints him as a beleaguered hero, and lingers with almost erotic attention on the handsomeness of the "former heartthrob danseur noble"—on his "imposing" six-foot, two-inch figure and his "long index finger." He quotes a childhood friend from the Royal Danish Ballet School, who compares the young Martins's looks to those of a Greek god—as if that might excuse his behavior. Martins's attack on his wife is framed as an unfortunate hurdle in an otherwise impressive career; he is depicted as the victim of scandal-hungry headline writers and stubborn Balanchine loyalists rooting for him to fail. Insiders—including his wife—rallied around him. "I feel so upset for Peter and for us that anything like this happened," Kistler told Paltrow. "It's awful that everybody found out about this. I'm behind Peter in everything he's doing."

"We have the highest regard for Peter and the deepest admiration for the work he has done, as we do for Darci," said the chairman of NYCB's board.

Martins was untouchable. In her roman à clef, *Bunheads*, former corps dancer Sophie Flack describes a tyrannical director (she calls him Otto Klein) whose "word pretty much determines the course" of the dancers' lives. "And we can never question him—I hardly know anyone who's even talked to him."

Perhaps he preferred nonverbal communication. "The word 'looming' is what I use," Meiying says. "There was never a moment where I was not scared of him." Once, in a rehearsal for *Midsummer Night's Dream*, she was waiting in the wings when she felt a big, clammy hand on the back of her neck. "I remember him coming up and putting his hand on the back of my neck and just standing there like that." He continued to grip her neck, unnecessarily, as he steered her to her mark onstage.

When Lily was sixteen, a teacher—an older woman she trusted, who had known her since she was a child—took her aside. "When Peter Martins looks you in the eyes," the teacher said, "you need to stare back." Lily was grateful for the tip. She started spending extra time in front of the mirror before her classes with Peter, carefully applying dark liner around her eyes. One Saturday morning at the barre, not long before hiring decisions would be made, Peter and Lily locked eyes, and for ten interminable seconds, she held his gaze, "giving him the best mix of fierce and smoldering I could muster." Afterward, she felt like she had passed some kind of test.

Her intuition was confirmed the following year, when Martins hired her as an apprentice with NYCB. That same year, Lily—then eighteen—began dating a twenty-nine-year-old principal dancer from Denmark. Lily is twenty-nine herself now, and the idea of dating an eighteen-year-old strikes her as absurd. But at City Ballet, age-gap relationships were just part of the culture; to be deemed worthy of an older man's attention was a badge of honor, an anointment. In an environment where women were commodities, it was only natural that men would pluck their teenaged girlfriends from among the freshest ranks of barely legal recruits. Lily often woke to see she had missed four a.m. calls from another principal; she delicately deflected, careful not to cause offense.

When, in 2017, a handful of dancers spoke out about how Peter Martins would grab women by the neck, favor women who slept with him, and berate dancers who gained weight, he resigned (although he denied the allegations). But even then—his autocratic reign over—most dancers didn't dare criticize him; many still went out of their way to defend him. Their loyalty was too ingrained. For years, they had starved for him and slept with him; now they would stay silent for him.

In a 1987 paper bluntly titled "The Dancer as Masochist," the Canadian psychologist Jock Abra compares the relationship between a dancer and her director to that of masochist and sadist. "To an almost unmatched degree," he wrote, dancers in a ballet company are "regulated by other people, by teachers, directors, choreographers, etc., and their arbitrary, capricious judgments . . . They do as they are told without complaining . . . and virtually forgo personal responsibility or independence."

From a young age, Abra writes, ballet dancers are taught "to accept . . . external authority and discipline unquestioningly." They conform to strict codes of dress, hairstyle, and makeup—no matter their preferences or natural proportions. As adults, their bodies become the passive site of the choreographer's creative control—like "canvas for the painter" or "stone for the sculptor." Dancers readily compare themselves to objects or tools. One young Canadian dancer, interviewed for a 2011 sociology paper called "Ballet and Pain: Reflections on a Risk-Dance Culture," hid an injury during an audition because, she said, hiring an injured dancer would be like "buying a shirt that has a hole in it." In her memoir *Winter Season*, Toni Bentley wishes she could erase her own needs and desires, the better to channel Balanchine's vision. "It's a pity he needs a hundred individuals as his tools rather than paintbrushes," she writes, when her colleagues are negotiating their contracts. "What would have happened if van Gogh's brushes one day had refused to be manipulated because they wanted better living conditions?"

The dancer's submission may be extreme—but, according to the psychoanalyst Natalie Shainess's *Sweet Suffering: Woman as Victim*, "no woman in our culture can be completely free of masochism." *Sweet Suffering* was published in 1984, and it is no longer in print; its author is no longer alive. Some of Shainess's ideas are laughably outdated. References to penis envy and the Oedipus complex abound. A hysterectomy—the surgical removal of the uterus—is, in her telling, not a treatment for fibroids or prolapse, but rather a "somatic self-rejection" and a "symbolic castration."

And yet the themes Shainess explores—and the self-defeating feminine behaviors she describes—are uncannily resonant. I couldn't stop highlighting as I read, and sending photos of underlined passages to female friends—which elicited responses like: "Yes to everything [crying emoji]"; "oh my goodness i should really read this"; "Pls save this book for me."

While a masochistic woman will surely "suffer," in Shainess's words, from a desire to be hurt sexually, it's in her everyday interactions that her guilt and self-doubt are most destructive. She writes of a female patient who dreads her appointments with her (male) gynecologist—his exams are "rough and painful," his bedside manner condescending—but who is so unwilling to offend him that she hires him to deliver all three of her children. And of a single woman in New York who drops all of her commitments when a new romantic prospect invites her on a road trip to the Midwest, inadvertently sending him "the message of absolute submission."

I took Shainess's forty-five-item "Are you masochistic?" quiz, and answered yes to several questions. (Number eleven: "Are you afraid to send back a dish that has something wrong with it or is cold?" Number forty-one: "If you were on a dark, deserted street, would you feel obliged to stop and answer a man who asked for directions?") I cringed when she used—as examples of masochistic behavior—exact things I had done, like letting a bad date up to my apartment because he said he needed the bathroom.

But, according to Shainess, I can hardly blame myself. Growing up in a culture that views them as helpless and weak, girls are practically destined to develop low self-esteem. Even in a progressive society with ample opportunities for women, we can't escape ancient, misogynistic ideas about our worth: our first and most powerful lessons about the sexes still come from our mothers—who were in turn shaped by their own mothers. We need to go back only a generation or two before we reach women who barely questioned their second-class status.

It makes sense to me that dancers can't always shed this obedient mindset when they exit the studio. That it can infect, even shape, their relationships with men in everyday life, and that even stars like Margot Fonteyn—invincible onstage—are susceptible to a childlike mentality, to acting the ingénue all the time.

Brought Up to Turn Off

Rachel was fourteen—the same age at which Marie van Goethem was immortalized in wax and bronze—when she was chosen to spend a day posing with the Degas at the Met. She walked through the galleries with a curator from the museum and a New York City Ballet dancer, a man in his thirties. What did Rachel think about when she looked at the *Little Dancer*? the curator asked. Perhaps Rachel was projecting when she imagined how Marie was feeling: "Probably she was just hoping not to mess up." And what would Rachel want to wear, if an artist made a sculpture of her? She would prefer a longer tutu. That day, she was wearing a knee-length skirt, a prim cardigan, and a pair of ballet flats. She and the NYCB dancer posed for a photo in front of the statue: Rachel struck an arabesque and he stood just behind her, one hand holding her hand in front of her body, the other cupping her chin.

Rachel already had plenty of experience being touched. She first went through the motions of a courtship when she was just nine years old. In a high-ceilinged rehearsal room at Lincoln Center, under the exacting instructions of the children's ballet mistress, she learned the steps choreographed in 1954 and memorized by dozens of little Maries before her. (A natural onstage, with dark hair and dark eyes, Rachel had been a shoo-in for *The Nutcracker*'s young lead.) She lay down on two pushed-together chairs—onstage, they would be replaced by a bed with a ruffled skirt and a princess-worthy pillow—and closed her eyes, pretending to be asleep. The little boy cast as her prince tendued toward her, pretending to carry a golden tiara in his hand, and roused her with a tap on the shoulder; she opened her eyes and gasped in delight. He brushed his lips against her hand, laid the imaginary crown gently on her head, and knelt in front of her. She slid down from the chairs and the tiny couple walked off, arm in arm, gazing into each other's eyes. They practiced the scene so many times, they never had to worry about slipping on the specks of paper "snow" that fell, sometimes in clumps, from the ceiling; so many times that their courtship became second nature. Three or four nights a week, from just before Thanksgiving until a few days past New Year's, Rachel fell in love onstage.

But Rachel would reach her early twenties before she let herself experience desire—unruly, chaotic, private. Unscripted, and for herself. Meanwhile, in middle and high school—when most adolescents begin exploring their sexuality—Rachel was monomaniacally focused on ballet. "You're brought up not to think about sex," one School of American Ballet student told the journalist Suzanne Gordon. "You're brought up to turn off, not on." There was no room in Rachel's head for sex. "That part of my brain was not awake," she said. Her environment made it easy to avoid dating: her SAB friends were gay guys and girls, and she barely knew who was in her class at the Professional Performing Arts School.

Rachel and the other bunheads would show up at school bleary-eyed for their eight a.m. class, already wearing leotards under their clothes, and stare at the clock until nine thirty, when a bus would take them uptown for their morning ballet class, and their real day would begin: technique, pointe, and mandatory pas de deux classes, in which Rachel's male classmates—under the matter-of-fact direction of a teacher (often male)—would hoist her into the air by her stomach, armpits, or thighs, or hold her by the hips as she silently struck a pose. Boys' "hands were practically in my vagina" when she was fifteen, she says. There was no room to argue or opt out. "It was like, 'This is how it works. You don't have a say in it.'" When sixtysomething Peter Martins—who stalked the halls as if he were surveilling his empire, and occasionally taught class—wrapped his hands around her waist as she demonstrated a pirouette, she considered it a privilege.

*   *   *

Rachel is tall and dark-haired, with a Julia Roberts smile; the *New York Times* once compared her to a doll. As far as Rachel was concerned, though, her body was a machine—a ballet machine that sometimes malfunctioned. Rachel's weight has never risen above the low end of healthy; in photos from her ballet years, she looks, to the normal eye, slim and fit. If she was not as emaciated as was in fashion in the early 2000s, she had no extraneous flesh, either.

But Rachel felt acceptable only for a brief period in her teenage years when a wisdom tooth extraction left her unable to chew solid food. As she entered adolescence, her teachers began telling her to "lengthen," or to work on her "condition." At sixteen, she was sent to the nutritionist, who recommended she fill up on peanut butter. By this point, Rachel was already well versed in the fad food plans of the mid-2000s: she knew about all three phases of the South Beach Diet, and which types of protein were permitted on the Zone. She could never bring herself to commit, though, to the simple diet that was so popular with her classmates: eat as little as possible. They competed to see who could eat the least without passing out, and silently egged each other on: "It was like, 'You're eating five bites of yogurt? Oh, I'll eat four.'"

Malnourishment is a mood-killer. Anorexia, according to the psychiatrist Hilde Bruch's classic 1978 primer *The Golden Cage*, is "characterized by the avoidance of any sexual encounter, a shrinking from any bodily contact." Research from Innsbruck Medical University in Austria shows that women with eating disorders have pivotal sexual experiences, from their first kiss to their first orgasm, years later than their peers, and are less likely to describe their first sexual encounter in positive terms.

In 1944, the University of Minnesota physiologist Ancel Keys, hoping to better understand the effects of the famines that were ravaging much of Europe, recruited thirty-six healthy young men for a risky study of starvation. For the first three months, the men—who lived in corridors and rooms in the university's football stadium but otherwise led a normal life of work, school, and exercise—ate a healthy diet of about 3,200 calories a day. In the next phase of the study, which lasted for six months, their diet was slashed to two meals a day (the menu featured wartime European staples like cabbage and boiled potatoes) and amounted to about 1,570 calories. It's probably a sign of my still-skewed standards that this number struck me as relatively normal; I was surprised to learn, in Todd Tucker's 2006 book *The Great Starvation Experiment*, that the men began wasting away within weeks of adopting it. But one of the first and most dramatic changes was the men's loss of interest in dating and sex. The men were in their twenties and thirties, but most gave up on trying to date. Erotic fantasies disappeared from their diaries. One man tried to persevere despite his hunger pangs, and invited a female lab technician to see *To Have and Have Not*. But as soon as he entered the cinema, he was distracted by the smell of popcorn in the lobby. The romance between the dashing Humphrey Bogart and the sultry Lauren Bacall couldn't hold his attention, either: he was too focused on a scene of Bogart eating dinner.

Most of Rachel's teachers used innuendo to criticize her weight—but Peter Martins was blunt. "Your body is a problem," he told her, just before she graduated. He would not be offering Rachel a place with the New York City Ballet. She swallowed the insult and auditioned for just about every other company in America.

Rachel was eighteen when she moved to the West Coast to join the corps of a small but well-regarded local ballet company. In some ways, she was mature beyond her years: a sophisticated performer, cool under pressure. But in others, she was entirely unprepared for adult life. She had only nominally attended high school. She had no friends outside of ballet and had never been on a date. Her new boss was another moody middle-aged man. He could joke around, or he could snap, flying into a rage if a dancer was half a count offbeat. The women—or "girls," as they were called, and as they thought of themselves—knew not to talk back. "We just would scramble to fix it or make sense of what had gone wrong."

In her first year there, Rachel shared a one-bedroom apartment with another dancer and biked back and forth to the theater, too broke to buy a car. Alone in a new city, she attracted a roster of suitors. But she couldn't see that the men in her life wanted more than friendship. "Flirting—I don't recognize that as anything other than people talking to me," she says. One man in particular, a fellow dancer, seemed to always want to hang out; once, he invited himself over to her apartment and lay down in her bed. Rachel thought this was a funny thing to do; it was only after being confronted by his angry girlfriend that she realized he had been hitting on her. Throughout her life, physical contact had been so constant that touch and romantic gestures had been desexualized. If a man gripping her thighs in a partnering class was just being professional, then how was she supposed to know that a man gently brushing her arm, or letting his hand linger on hers, meant something else? Rachel's body was a serious thing, an instrument for her art—she couldn't conceive of it as a site of pleasure or play. Besides, after hearing over and over that her body was "a problem," she couldn't imagine that anyone would want her.

It had been a few years since I'd quit ballet when I met M, and it would be a few more before I would start to shed the beliefs I had developed about myself in the studio. It was a sweaty Friday night, and I found myself huddled up with him in the corner of a house party—the kind you attend when you're twenty-two, where the guest list includes everyone the hosts have ever met and the music is so loud you have to lean in close to be heard. Whenever the conversation petered out, M would revive it. I couldn't figure out why he kept talking to me, or why he texted me later, inviting me for a drink the following week. We ran in similar circles; I assumed he wanted a new friend. I said yes.

When I entered the bar he had chosen and noticed that it was more like a lounge—that the lights were dim and the walls were red—I thought it was an awkward choice. He must not have been here before, I thought. It didn't occur to me that the romantic setting might be intentional. When, somewhere around cocktail number three, he took my hand, which was resting on the table, and cradled it in his, I figured he must be drunk. *I'll pretend not to notice,* I thought. I don't want to embarrass him. It was only after we left the bar, and his mouth was on mine, that I realized I was on a date.

It was all so much easier at ballet, where I never had to worry about how to navigate ambiguous romantic situations; where there were no such situations to navigate. Growing up, I felt—at least at ballet—blissfully exempt from that sort of thing.

❄   ❄   ❄

In September, my classmates would come back to school with suntanned shoulders and tattered friendship bracelets and stories of their first, fumbling kisses. For my ballet friends and me, though, summer was not a time to explore, but to double down. When school let out in June, I decamped to unglamorous locations like Carlisle, Pennsylvania, and Tuscaloosa, Alabama, for full-time training programs with strict curfews and frequent assessments, dreaming of how high my extensions would be, how pointed my feet, by fall. "I've been waiting so long to get to ballet camp, that I can hardly believe I'm here!" I wrote in my diary.

In one dreary college town, I started my days with technique class at nine and, if I was slacking, finished with repertoire at five—but I usually attended the optional after-dinner class, which ran until eight and gave us ninety minutes before curfew. Just enough time, if we were feeling rebellious, to walk to the ice cream shop in town, conspicuous bunheads in our rolled-up tights and slicked-back hair. The dress code mandated that we wear black leotards in "traditional, conservative styles only—no embellishments" and buns with "all bangs neatly pinned or sprayed back." If we were late to class, we might be banned from recreational activities on Sunday, our day off. But the strictest rules governed our interactions with the few boys who attended. Not only were we "absolutely not permitted in rooms of the opposite sex at any time"; according to the handbook, "displays of affection are almost always inappropriate and should be avoided."

On a rare night off, our counselors treated us to a screening of *Center Stage*. Most of us had already seen—if not memorized—the cheesy 2000 teen movie set at the fictional American Ballet Academy. Still, we tensed when Maureen, the star of her year, was asked out by a handsome pre-med student. "The thing is, I've got priorities," Maureen sputters, panicking. "You only get to be a dancer for ten years, maybe fifteen if you don't get injured, so for the next decade at least—"

"Hey," her suitor interrupts, apparently wondering why she's acting like he demanded she set her toe shoes on fire. "All I'm asking for is a date." But the joke was on him. He didn't understand. Romantic entanglement represented a threat of the highest order, and in our black-and-white world, ballet and sex were not compatible. One prestigious summer program in New York housed female students in a literal nunnery in Greenwich Village. Even for the older girls—even for professionals—the taboo held strong. "To have a boyfriend jeopardized the possibility of dancing for Balanchine," Gelsey Kirkland observed. "Marriage was thought to be the kiss of death." We could have only one true allegiance, and it must be to ballet.

One of the most popular ballet movies of all time is 1948's *The Red Shoes*, about a dancer who—torn between her husband and her career, and believing her director's message that "You cannot have it both ways"—throws herself in front of a train instead. "Considering the tragic ending," writes Melissa

Klapper in *Ballet Class: An American History*, "there is a certain irony to the fact that, as British film critic Ian Christie commented, *The Red Shoes* 'launched a thousand dance careers.'"

I don't think it was so ironic. I complained about the lack of men as loudly as everyone else, but secretly it was a relief. In fact, even if the program had had an equal balance of boys and girls and mandated coed sleepovers every night, I'm sure I still would have found a way to avoid interacting with the opposite sex. I was too shy to flirt; I handled my crushes by pretending they didn't exist. At ballet, this made me feel virtuous instead of deficient.

The idea that women must choose between work and love did not originate in the ballet world. As women began making inroads in the workforce in the mid-twentieth century, the age-old debate over whether ambition compromises femininity, undermines the ability to be a good mother and wife, intensified. We invented a bogeyman image of the career girl: a crusty woman with sensible shoes and a hole at the center of her heart. "However large the brain may grow / the lashes and the earrings must keep pace," the poet Rachel Wetzsteon wrote in her 2006 poem "Love and Work"—in which an intellectual narrator anticipates a lonely future featuring "a crowded bookcase and an empty bed." The phrase "having it all" was coined in the 1980s—giving us a convenient shorthand with which to argue about whether it's possible for women to succeed in both the professional and domestic spheres. The debate was reignited in 2012 by a popular *Atlantic* essay, according to which—despite all the progress wrought by feminism—it was not.

Even today, women and girls who speak up are sanctioned,

slapped with labels like "pushy" or "bossy." As recently as 2014, according to a paper in *Sociological Science*, American high school seniors ranked breadwinner-husband plus homemaker-wife as the best of several possible domestic arrangements; only five percent considered it "desirable" for a mother to work full-time. "The phrases sometimes used for men who partner with successful women—taking it in his stride, not put out by, OK with, dealing with, cool with—are reminders that female success can be regarded as some kind of intrusion or inappropriate behavior," the critic Rebecca Solnit observed in the *Guardian*.

The hurdles are even higher for women who want to make art, which requires unusual dedication and a stereotypically masculine indulgence of ego. "Can a woman who is an artist ever just be an artist?" Rachel Cusk asks in a 2019 *New York Times Magazine* essay. "The male artist, in our image of him, does everything we are told not to do: He is violent and selfish. He neglects or betrays his friends and family." She profiles two accomplished female painters whose careers have been limited by child-rearing and overshadowed by men—powerful critics and careless lovers and famous fathers. Can a woman who is an artist ever just be an artist? The question haunts the piece. The implicit answer is no.

Female dancers occupy a unique position, as liberating in some ways as it is restrictive in others. They can devote themselves fully to their art and their ambitions without sacrificing their femininity. When I read *Bunheads*, I was struck by the line "the drive to succeed is as natural to us as breathing." I can't imagine that sentiment—that declaration of naked ambition, no apologies or qualifications—being expressed by a girl in my English class or orchestra practice in 2003.

Dancers are exempt, too, from one of the most rigid expectations of women: having children. Even if they are physically capable—and many are too thin to menstruate—pregnancy would compromise their instrument and keep them off the stage in their prime. "Childbearing does not pose a choice for the ballerina," Toni Bentley wrote in *Rolling Stone*. "The decision is self-evident. There is no pregnant dancer." Dancers can forgo the responsibilities of marriage and children while maintaining their femininity—while even becoming the most hyperbolically feminine versions of themselves.

✳   ✳   ✳

Carol Sumner was seven when she announced to her parents that she would never marry or have children. It was 1947, and this was an unusual sentiment for a little girl in Brooklyn to express. But Carol had other plans; she wanted to become a movie star and live in Hollywood. She eventually made it to California, not as an actress but as a dancer on tour with the New York City Ballet.

Carol danced for Balanchine from 1958 to 1978, and she was still, I sometimes thought, dancing for Balanchine when I met her in 2004. She looked so serious when she demonstrated a step—her chin lifted, her eyes elsewhere—I used to wonder if she was communing with the late ballet master. When she corrected me, she seemed to channel Mr. B: "You know, dear," she would often begin, an echo of his Russian accent in her husky smoker's voice.

I don't remember exactly how I found Carol. I must have heard a rumor that some of the more successful girls—like Rachel—had been going to her for private lessons. This wouldn't have been talked about openly, since we weren't supposed to take classes outside of SAB; we couldn't risk someone interfering with our curriculum, which, as we were often told, had been designed by Balanchine himself.

Somehow, though, I found myself at the barre at City Center, where in the 1950s Carol had performed with the nascent New York City Ballet and where in the mid-2000s she taught fifteen-dollar open classes for "adult beginners." Most of Carol's regulars were twentysomethings just looking to work up a sweat before happy hour, so when I—a hard worker with a few years of good training—turned up, she lavished attention on me. Soon, I was supplementing my SAB classes with biweekly lessons with Carol.

I was twelve or so, and I felt invisible at SAB. After two years as a member of *The Nutcracker*'s battle scene ensemble, I had been hoping for a promotion to the more demanding role of candy cane—the most desirable part that girls my height were eligible for. In the weeks leading up to the audition, I studied archival footage of the dance and practiced all the time, staying late in the empty studio after class and waking up early to run through it before school. When the big day arrived, I stood in the corner with the other aspiring candy canes—a few dozen of us were competing for sixteen spots—and watched as, one by one, my rivals demonstrated the steps that I had been working on. When my turn came, I leapt across the floor, trying to cover as much space as I could and resisting the temptation to check myself out in the mirror. It was only an eight-count phrase but, with so many judgmental eyes on me—the ballet mistress at the front of the room, my classmates on both sides—it felt like hours. As I neared the corner of the studio and the next girl began to dance, I stole a glance in the mirror. *I look good*, I thought, for once, watching my feet carve half-moons in the air. I held my head high as I ran off to the side and joined the other girls waiting to learn our fate.

When everyone had taken her turn, the ballet mistress consulted her clipboard and began calling out names.

Laura, she said.

Ellie. Christina. Shana.

The lucky girls ran forward to the center of the room, suppressing their smiles, too well-mannered to visibly gloat. I stared at them with envy. Twelve places left. I held my breath, willing the next name to be mine.

Emily. Pauline. Olivia.

Nine places.

And then I heard it.

Alice.

I ran up to join them. My hard work had paid off. How could I ever have doubted myself? I would have a future in ballet after all. I would graduate from SAB, I would join the company, I would be the greatest dancer who ever lived—

"Oh," said the ballet mistress. She looked at me as though surprised to remember I existed. "Other Alice."

There wasn't just another girl waiting to take my place; there was even another Alice.

The task I had set Carol was largely impossible. I wasn't just looking for a coach to help me fine-tune my feet or my turn-out; I was looking for someone to turn me into a different dancer, with more talent. But Carol—whether because she had a delusional belief in my potential or in her own teaching— was determined to try.

Carol was in her sixties and hadn't performed in thirty years, but she made herself up each morning as though she might wind up onstage at any time: thick eyeliner, penciled-in brows, a bright red lip that would have been visible from the fourth ring. She wore baggy shirts and tight black leggings, and if her body was no longer the perfectly honed tool it had once been, then you couldn't tell once she started moving: her legs were nimble, darting out from her body as if they were living things; her feet were arched and strong, launching her into the still-buoyant jumps for which she'd once been famous. (Balanchine had often compared her to a bird.) Carol would look, then, like some kind of ageless hybrid, with the face of a middle-aged woman and the body of a young girl.

Carol was born in 1940, in the working-class Brooklyn neighborhood of Bay Ridge. Her father worked on the stock exchange—doing what, exactly, she was never sure—and her mother, as a young woman, had been a restaurant hostess. Growing up, Carol danced around the house to boogie records and took a weekly tap class at the local Moose Lodge, but she didn't start serious training until, at thirteen—thanks to a tip from a neighbor and an ad in *Dance* magazine—she found a ballet teacher on West Fifty-Sixth Street. Soon, she was taking the subway to Manhattan four days a week and buying dollar-fifty balcony tickets to Balanchine's New York City Ballet. She saw *Agon* and *Allegro Brillante* and she felt something stirring inside her: she wanted to know the man who had made these spectacular works, and she wanted to look like the women who danced them. She went to the ballet as often as she could, and afterward, she would stand outside the stage door and wait for the dancers to come out. The first time she met Balanchine was when she asked him for an autograph.

Just one year after discovering the New York City Ballet, she auditioned for SAB. When Carol learned that she had been accepted, her mom went back to work, this time in a department store, to pay the tuition. Carol didn't care that she was placed in the beginner's class; she didn't think she deserved much. She just liked dancing and seeing the company members up close. Now, instead of waiting for them outside the stage door, she could peer in on their classes, even flirt with the men on their way out.

Carol worked hard and soon made up for her late start. She catapulted through the ranks of the school and, at eighteen, landed an apprenticeship with the company. Some dancers struggle with the decision to cut short their education, but not Carol. "Did I miss not having gone to college? Heavens, no!" she said in a 1983 interview for the book *Balanchine's Ballerinas*. "I hated school."

For months, Carol was too intimidated to even say hello to her new boss, the great George Balanchine. "I'm this little kid from Brooklyn," she thought. "What am I gonna talk about to him? How I get here on the subway?"

But Balanchine noticed her; it would have been impossible not to. With her high cheekbones and blond hair, the young Carol Sumner could look icily unattainable, even haughty; or she could crack a wide, dimpled smile and look adorable. (A critic for the *Asbury Park Press* once complained that she was "too cute.")

Right away, he singled her out for solo roles—Sacred Love in *Illuminations*, Marzipan in *The Nutcracker*. She was still relatively new to ballet, but what she lacked in technique, she made up for in sheer power of will. And besides, if Mr. B thought she was ready for these roles, then who was she to argue? One day, the wardrobe supervisor, whom the dancers knew as Ducky, pulled her aside. "You know where you're going?" Ducky asked. He pointed to the ceiling. "You're going straight up."

As Carol grew more secure in her dancing, she worked up the courage to share some of her opinions with Mr. B. He started taking her out for dinner, and a friendship blossomed.

The dinners migrated from restaurants near the theater to his condo on the Upper West Side. He would make them a salad, pour a glass of wine, and tell her stories about his life back in Russia. Mostly, though, they talked about ballet.

Carol came to SAB with her natural talent and her good looks—but she gives Balanchine all the credit for what she became. "He literally made beautiful women," she said, and she loved him for it. Even Balanchine's staunchest defenders tend to see his obsession with Suzanne Farrell—and his refusal to let her husband dance—as an embarrassment. But not Carol. "I was really on Mr. B's side," she said. "After making Suzanne look like that, and giving her those beautiful ballets, how could Paul Mejia steal her out from under Mr. B?"

"I was a Balanchine girl," she said. To be a Balanchine girl meant not to be anyone else's. Carol was often asked out on dates, which she sometimes accepted, and which sometimes turned into affairs. But her boyfriends had to understand: ballet, and Balanchine, would always come first. She bowed out of the balancing act that ensnares so many women; she had a playbook on how to engage with the opposite sex.

There is a photo of Carol and Mr. B—she looks like she's in her late twenties—standing together on the sidewalk outside the stage entrance. Balanchine is dressed conservatively, in a dark jacket and tailored pants, while Carol's pale arms and upper legs are bare; she wears hot pants that end at the top of her thighs and go-go boots that don't quite reach her knees. Her hair hangs down her back in a long, tight ponytail with the distinctive swoop that suggests it's just been released from a bun. Half of her face is hidden by big, movie-star sunglasses. Her back is to the camera, and she smiles coyly over her shoulder, while Mr. B stands beside her, squarely on both feet, facing us. It's a striking image—for the beauty of the two figures, and for the play of the light: the pale stems of her legs and the dark lines of his, like the keys of a piano, or the costumes in *Agon*. But the most striking aspect of the picture is the link between its two subjects. One of Mr. B's hands rests on Carol's cheek; the other is tucked casually in his pocket. He isn't looking at her, but at someone, or something, outside the frame; she, too, is following his gaze. His fingers are hidden behind her face, but they seem to be tilting her head just so: the gesture makes me think of a breeder presenting his favorite steed. But Carol is grinning, posing, colluding: she is undeniably delighted. She is relishing her role as coquette.

"You're a really good girl," Rachel's director said. She was twenty, and she was about to learn whether her contract would be renewed. Just a few days earlier, she had been thrown into *Swan Lake* at the last minute, learning an injured colleague's part just half an hour before the curtain rose. Rachel had a reputation for picking up new steps right away, and she had danced three different parts that night—the kind of heroic feat often rewarded with a promotion or at least a chance at solo roles or, at the very least, not being fired. But her boss continued: "We really like you, but you're in a terrible condition." He told her to work on her body over the summer and come back for another assessment in the fall. He couldn't understand why she wouldn't lose weight; perhaps, he offered generously, it was outside her control. He told her to go to the doctor and have her thyroid checked.

Rachel was too stunned to reply. Ever the "good girl," she mumbled her thank-yous and held in her tears until she had left the room. She thought about what the summer would hold: about how she would weigh herself every day, log all of her food, and punish herself with extra sessions at the gym. She had worked toward this job all her life; she was supposed to be living her dream. But when she thought back on her first year of company life, she remembered how she had been passed over for the roles she wanted and knew she could do. She remembered how she had called her mom, frightened, after she'd caught herself standing at the top of a flight of stairs and wondering how hard she would have to jump to get time off. And in the days after her meeting, she felt a new emotion bubbling up: rage. She looked at herself in the mirror, and she saw her body as it was: a fit, healthy size two. For what may have been the first time in her life, she went back to her director and said: No thank you.

It was only after she had flown home to New York, after she had moved in with her parents and woken up in her childhood bedroom, that it hit her: she had no job and no plan.

A few years ago, in the course of promoting my first book, I found myself in a small studio at the back of the *Guardian*'s London office, posing for a photo to run alongside a Q&A I'd given a month or two earlier. I tried to remember what I'd said in the interview and started sweating through my freshly applied makeup; I knew I had stumbled over my words, picturing how they would look in print before they had even left my mouth. The day of the photoshoot was so much easier. The photographer, a man, told me to look this way and that, to touch my hips, cross my arms, clasp my hands behind my back, and I happily did as I was told. (I thought back to the middle school afternoons I'd spent watching the contestants on *America's Next Top Model* learn how to "smize" and told myself they were finally paying off.) At one point, the photographer told me to lie on the floor with my head on a pillow, and then did something that surprised me: He asked if it would be okay for him to come closer, and for him to adjust my arm. I wondered if I'd heard correctly; I might have asked him to repeat himself. I didn't hesitate to say yes.

At twenty-seven, of course, I could hardly attribute all of my ideas about men and women and boundaries to ballet. In her book *Girlhood*, the writer Melissa Febos coined the term "empty consent" to describe the unwanted touches that women—who have "spent their entire lives being socialized not to upset or disappoint people"—endure. It's easier just to give in than to protest "the impulsive fondling of pregnant women's bellies, hugs from mere acquaintances, sex that we simply aren't in the mood for." Unwelcome touches have haunted Febos throughout her life—from age eleven, when an aggressive neighbor pulled her into a bathroom and fingered her, to last year, when a stranger at a party rested his hand in the small of her back.

Febos worked in a BDSM dungeon in her twenties, and she wonders whether the experience of constantly tolerating touches that didn't turn her on could have eroded her sense of autonomy. Sex workers are experts at feigning pleasure—at arousing others while suppressing their own desires. For centuries, ballet dancers were seen as naturals for the sex trade: in nineteenth-century France, wealthy men were invited into the foyer where the dancers rehearsed so they could check out the goods up close. The underage trainees in Paris were so frequently sold to upper-class men—often by their own desperate mothers—that the spread of syphilis was blamed on ballet.

In the early 2000s, the sex predator Jeffrey Epstein scouted for victims at New York ballet schools, including an Upper West Side studio where I took open classes. Young, precarious, naïve about the world, and accustomed to following orders: ballerinas-in-training were the perfect victims. Epstein's lackeys would lure young dancers to his mansion under the pretense that he was looking for a personal trainer or a private dance instructor. A woman named Lisa told the *New York Times* how, as a seventeen-year-old aspiring dancer, she had gone to Epstein's town house, expecting to teach a dance class; how, instead, Epstein had offered to buy her pointe shoes and then assaulted her. Epstein abused Lisa for years, stopping only when she no longer resembled a teenager—at which point, according to court documents, he told the twenty-five-year-old "to go to her dance studio and find other dancers."

✳   ✳   ✳

Carol loved Balanchine, but he could be possessive. "He was very grabby," she said. "He was always wanting the girls. He'd be arrested now, he'd be in jail now." She laughed heartily. "It was good for us innocent ballerinas." But Balanchine didn't like it if Carol showed interest in another man. At one point, she developed a crush on a fellow company member. "Let me experience something," she thought. "Let me be in love, or attracted." But Mr. B scolded her: "You know, dear, why do you cast pearls before swine?" He didn't need to worry, though. Carol was satisfied with her life. She already had a man who loved and understood her: who appreciated not only her beauty as a woman but as a dancer. "And you're never gonna get anything like that again," Carol said, sounding wistful. "There'll be some hitch to it, some catch."

Carol saw the relationship as pure, but Balanchine was also her boss. In 1964, six years after joining the company, he promoted her from corps dancer to soloist. But Ducky's prophecy never quite came true. "I would love to be a principal," Carol told John Gruen in 1970. "Naturally, it's what every ballet dancer works for." Carol was a stalwart, not quite a star. *Newsweek* described her as "the backbone of the company," and she was often mentioned in reviews, but rarely in more than a few words. A typical write-up noted "Violette Verdy and Carol Sumner also dancing well," or "Carol Sumner and Sara Leland were good." When Carol retired in 1976, she was still listed as a soloist. She makes a cameo in Suzanne Farrell's memoir, and appears as a footnote in Jacques d'Amboise's five-hundred-page *I Was a Dancer*: "Carol Sumner, a very attractive ballerina with NYCB, danced in the company for years, and later became a teacher."

As her stage career wound down, Carol discovered that she still had a purpose: she could further Balanchine's legacy by teaching the next generation. She set up her own academy in Connecticut, modeling it after SAB, and trained her students in the Balanchine technique. Over the course of a decade, she built the school into a local powerhouse and SAB feeder, though she eventually wearied of the interpersonal drama involved in managing and fund-raising—she believes she was persecuted for her loyalty to Balanchine—and shut it down.

"We dancers all knew that we should leave our boyfriends three blocks away and then walk to the theater," an anonymous Balanchine dancer told Linda Hamilton, a clinical psychologist who, before going to grad school, spent nineteen years with the New York City Ballet. "And no kissing on the streets!" In spite of her best efforts to hide her relationship, she was found out. "He was furious," she said, and Mr. B retaliated by taking her out of ballets.

Hamilton specializes in treating dancers and has for decades been a leader in issues like body image, sexism, and competition in ballet. Since 1992, she has written a popular advice column for *Dance* magazine, fielding questions from young readers wondering how to get a more pronounced arch, how to avoid being typecast, how to deal with teachers who yell at them and bosses who try to seduce them. Many of her advice seekers fear that dating would interfere with their work. In her 1998 guidebook, *Advice for Dancers*, she quotes a young dancer who is desperate to crush her feelings for a castmate. Hamilton consoles her with a somewhat clinical recommendation: so long as it's only an infatuation, "you could be back to normal in as little as six weeks." In the meantime, Hamilton suggests she channel her feelings into her dancing.

Hamilton devoted a chapter of her book to the challenges dancers face in forming relationships. "When I was a dancer, I remember being told that marriage was taboo and that even having a cat would detract from my work," she wrote. But she insisted that times had changed and it was, in fact, possible to have both. As evidence, she cited two dancers who might serve as "role models." Mikhail Baryshnikov—who is a once-in-a-generation celebrity, and also a man—found time to have four children by two women. And NYCB principal Darci Kistler is "now happily married to the artistic director of the company, Peter Martins, and has a lovely baby girl." *Advice for Dancers* was published six years after Martins was arrested for beating Kistler.

A few years ago, I wrote a profile of Alexandra Ansanelli—a celebrated dancer whose star was still on the rise when she suddenly decided to retire from the Royal Ballet, baffling her colleagues and fans. When I met her seven years later, she was living with her parents and working as a medical assistant on Long Island; I wanted to understand why she had given up the life she had worked so hard for. When she quit ballet at twenty-eight, she told me, she had only ever kissed a man onstage. Her commitment to her art had been total. From a young age, "I really just gave up life to pursue ballet," she said. At twelve, she left her cozy world on Long Island—her Quaker school, her soccer teammates, and her science classes—to live in Manhattan and train full-time at SAB. Four years later, she was dancing with the New York City Ballet. She could have coasted on her natural talent and striking beauty—with her dark hair and pale skin, she looked like a porcelain doll—but she never stopped pushing herself. If she ever had a free hour, she would go across the street to the performing arts library and watch videos of her idol, Gelsey Kirkland. After curtain call, she would stay up all night, reliving the show, and go to class delirious the next morning. After eight years at NYCB, she moved to London to join the Royal Ballet. Although Alexandra spent four years in England, she rarely strayed outside the three-block radius of the Royal Opera House and her apartment. She had few friends, let alone a romantic partner; her first kiss was in a pas de deux. Her colleagues tried to include her, but she kept her distance, wary of other people's demands. "I don't think I ever had a very deep connection to one person, because I was very involved with myself," she told me. "My marriage was to my work, and it was impossible for me to give emotionally to anyone else. The balance that I wanted, I didn't want to wait to have."

Carol is in her eighties now, and she suffers from no such regrets. When I messaged her recently and asked her how she had been, she said she had kept busy during the pandemic, "analyzing comments on FB, mostly about Mr. B and the old NYCB." In her black-and-white profile picture, she is glamorous and young, dancing in Balanchine's *Divertimento No. 15*. Her profile is like a museum of Balanchine and the glory days of New York City Ballet: archival photos from the 1960s and '70s—Carol in the studio with Mr. B; Carol in an arabesque onstage—which inspire lengthy reminiscences, technical debates ("This moment is a sissonne, not a glissade, no?" elicits eighteen replies), and tributes to Carol's beauty. ("Now there is a Balanchine ballerina," one woman commented, on a photo of Carol balancing on one leg; "This is just adorable. It makes me feel young again!" wrote another, on a photo of Carol—looking, with her bangs, like Audrey Hepburn— sitting cross-legged on the floor and gazing up at Edward Villella, who hangs in the air in a split leap.) One discussion of Balanchine's musical genius ends when Carol writes: "Off to teach a Mr. B style class!"

Last summer, Carol and I met for lunch near her apartment in Hell's Kitchen. I hadn't seen her in years, but she looked just as I remembered: hair still blond, eyes still lined, lips still painted red. At one point—we were discussing Balanchine's *Serenade*—she demonstrated, there at the café, a port de bras: lifting her arm gracefully above her head and tilting her upper body back behind the table. The old look came over her face, the one I remembered: the illusion of youth. She was performing still.

When Carol looks back on her career, her only regret is that she didn't give herself more completely to Balanchine. "You know, he liked me as a woman," she said. "A lot." But she resisted. She had wanted to protect a sliver of time, of space, that was hers alone; she wanted her freedom. She knew that if she succumbed, she would have to give up everything—flirting with men and going on dates, caring for her many cats and dogs. Now she sometimes wishes she had given in; she wonders if she could have been Mrs. Balanchine Number Six. But she tries not to dwell on what might have been. "I was so happy being in the Company and I'm still a happy person because I got what I wanted," she wrote on Facebook.

After catching up for a couple of hours, Carol and I made our way from the restaurant to her apartment around the corner. It was a short distance, but it took a while; she seemed to know everyone on the block. She stopped to say hello to a group of young men—her neighbors—gathered around a boom box on the sidewalk, and seemed delighted to find herself in the midst of an impromptu dance party. We walked into her lobby, and Carol introduced me to the woman who worked behind the front desk. "Doesn't she look great?" the woman said to me, nodding at Carol. "I tell her she needs a man in her life."

Just Try to Look Nice, Dear

Perfect," she croaks. "It was perfect." Nina Sayers's voice is barely audible as she collapses onto a mattress behind the just-lowered curtain. A few feet away, the audience roars. Nina is in her late twenties, and her entire life has been building toward this: her triumphant debut as the Swan Queen. Now she is bleeding from the gut, soaking the gauzy layers of her ivory-colored tutu, but she doesn't look like she's in pain; she looks elated. Mortal injury is a small price to pay for her perfect body, her perfect technique, her perfect performance in *Swan Lake*. Like a robot that has achieved its programmed purpose and has no more reason to exist, she dies.

The final scene of Darren Aronofsky's ballet horror movie *Black Swan* may be over-the-top—but just as ridiculous as the idea that Nina could have danced the finale with a self-inflicted stab wound in her stomach is the idea that she could have delivered a perfect performance in a two-hour ballet. It is impossible for the human body to perfectly execute even one step, let alone a whole sequence of them—not that that stops dancers from trying, or from berating themselves for falling short. "In my experience, no species of performing artist is as self-critical as a dancer," Susan Sontag, who often attended the New York City Ballet, wrote in the *London Review of Books* in 1987. "Each time I've congratulated a friend or acquaintance who is a dancer on a superb performance—and I include Baryshnikov—I've heard first a disconsolate litany of mistakes that were made: a beat was missed, a foot not pointed in the right way, there was a near-slippage in some intricate partnering manoeuvre."

Ballet attracts children who are already prone to perfectionism—who would rather repeat the same small movements over and over than play in the sandbox or run after a ball—then trains them to "self-correct": to look in the mirror and scan for flaws. And there were always flaws, not only in our dancing—the feet could be more pointed, the hips more turned out, the movement more fluid—but in our bodies: the beauty standards of ballet are rigid. A woman is expected not only to be rail-thin, but to have a specific set of features no diet can change, including narrow (or nonexistent) hips, a small head, and a short torso atop long legs. There are an almost infinite number of ways to deviate from the ideal. Meiying was told that her neck was too short; another classmate was informed that her arms were too long.

It was hard to pick which of my classmates to focus on in this chapter. None of them, really—none of us—escaped the scrutiny of our bodies unscathed; we are all prone to seeing the world through what Emily calls "the ballet lens." Lily, my tall friend and battle scene comrade, had a bout of anorexia so severe, she passed out on the subway; Rachel, the dark-eyed Marie, endured "fat talks" from the age of thirteen until her retirement at twenty-one. But it was Emily's story that I couldn't stop thinking about. Others may have been more extreme, but they were also more contained: episodes that had been processed and consigned, more or less, to the past.

Emily's story, though, is messy, and ongoing. Emily is thirty, and if you came across her Instagram, where she posts pictures of herself in swimsuits and crop tops, you might mistake her for a fitness model. For years, she worked at an upscale health club and has the kind of thin-but-toned body used to sell memberships—the kind of body that makes you feel like it's a good idea, urgent even, to join a gym with eucalyptus-scented towels and a saltwater pool, and to throw in a package of personal-training sessions, too.

But body dysmorphia, Emily told me, is a daily presence in her life. Some mornings, she changes her outfit five or six times; she gets stuck in front of the mirror and doesn't feel comfortable leaving the house. She understands, on some level, that she is a "normal skinny person," and she can speak eloquently about the messed-up standards that have shaped her self-perception—but she also can't stop fixating on her imagined flaws. She is living proof of the paradox that self-awareness doesn't always translate into change. When Meiying tells her that her body is perfect, that most women would envy her, Emily knows, on some level, that this is true; she knows, at least, not to argue. But it has no effect on the way she feels, and she is pretty sure it never will.

I remember Emily as a tiny powerhouse of a dancer, precocious and strong. Ballet is in Emily's blood: it has been at the center of her life for as long as she can remember, even before she started formal training at the age of five. Emily's mother, Linda, was a principal dancer with the Metropolitan Opera Ballet, and her father was a dancer and—alongside Rachel's dad—a stagehand at Lincoln Center. (I remember taking open classes with Linda; she looked like a diva, with her enormous, made-up eyes and sharp black hair, but when she spoke, she had the gentle manner of a kindergarten teacher. We adored her.) Emily's older brother, Ryan, was a golden child of the

School of American Ballet: the suave Nutcracker Prince at age twelve ("I don't really get nervous," he told a reporter) and a member of Pacific Northwest Ballet by nineteen.

Emily, meanwhile, felt safest when she didn't have to talk. A born performer with the same dark hair and doleful eyes as her mother, she loved how she could express herself without opening her mouth. Emily was accepted into SAB when she was eight years old, and she stood out right away—for her precocious technique, her intense focus, and her tininess. The smallest in the class, she was assigned to stand in the first place at the barre. While everyone else had to crane their necks to see the tips of their toes or the top of their head in the mirror, Emily had an unobstructed view of her body—which, at eight, she could still enjoy. Naturally petite, she felt sorry for her classmates who were already preoccupied with dieting. Once, she walked into the dressing room and saw two girls crouched over a single M&M, cutting it in half. She knew there was something not right about this; she couldn't have guessed that, soon enough, her own behavior would be just as disturbing.

But that first year was a dream. Emily and Meiying—who stood next to each other at the short end of the barre—were the only ones in their class chosen for *The Nutcracker*. They were the youngest guests at the Stahlbaums' Christmas party and the most diminutive angels in the Land of Sweets, criss-crossing the stage with miniature Christmas trees in their hands and golden halos on their heads.

⁎   ⁎   ⁎

In 1962, Gelsey Kirkland made her stage debut in the same role. By the time Gelsey, a ten-year-old student at SAB, was cast as a *Nutcracker* angel, she was already racked by insecurity.

Born on a spacious farm in Pennsylvania to a playwright father and an actress mother, Gelsey recalls her early years—catching fireflies in a jar, splashing around in a lake, doting on her pet horse—as a time of Edenic bliss. But this period came to an abrupt end when she was not yet four. With her father's work drying up and his fortune dwindling, the family—Gelsey, her parents, and her vivacious older sister, Johnna—relocated to a cramped apartment on the Upper West Side. In New York, Gelsey and Johnna shared a bedroom, and with only a curtain between them, their rivalry flourished. Johnna was a social butterfly; Gelsey was so shy that, like Emily, people sometimes assumed she couldn't talk.

Gelsey's father had once hoped to publish an autobiography. Instead, a few passages from his notes wound up posthumously in his daughter's. He called the sale of the family farm "the end of me," and, after the move, acted as if he had no future. Always a heavy drinker, he descended into alcoholism, starting each day by throwing up in the bathroom. The family reorganized itself around his mood swings, but the children couldn't always escape his rage. Once, after Gelsey tried to stand up for her mother, he chased her out of the house with a kitchen knife. Gelsey's mom was now the breadwinner, and money was so tight that Gelsey was put to work as a reluctant child model. Still, Gelsey's mother made sure her girls had activities like camp and Sunday School and, fatefully, ballet lessons.

Gelsey took no pleasure, as a child, in the news that she had been accepted to SAB: after all, her lifelong rival—her older sister—had gotten in first. But she soon discovered that ballet offered a refuge from her father's anger and a way to communicate without speaking: it "gave me a creative arena in which to vent my rage," she wrote in her memoir. But it was also a breeding ground for her insecurities. She never relied on her natural talent but worked with fanatical intensity, inventing new and destructive ways to push her body beyond its limits. She spent so many hours hopping around in her sister's pointe shoes, before her teachers had deemed her feet strong enough for pointe work, that she had developed disfiguring bunions by the time she was eleven.

She didn't rely on her natural beauty, either. As a teenager, she visited a series of plastic surgeons, falling into a cycle of procedures and disappointments. "I would become hooked on the pain, addicted to the voluptuous misery that bound my sexual identity to ballet, to an ever-increasing threshold of anguish," she wrote. She had silicone lip injections and breast implants before she had ever had sex.

Gelsey was thrilled to catch Balanchine's eye, but his attention could also be a curse. One day, when she was a teenager, he halted class and approached her at the barre. "With his knuckles he thumped on my sternum and down my rib cage, clucking his tongue and remarking, 'Must see the bones.'" She weighed less than a hundred pounds, but she took it to heart when he said, "Eat nothing."

Forty years later, the instructions were less explicit. But the euphemisms Emily started hearing as she entered her teens—to "lengthen" and "tone up"—amounted to the same thing. Our classmates were going through growth spurts, their legs stretching into string beans that catapulted them into bigger jumps and higher penchés, but the only changes Emily noticed were the faint curves showing up around her hips and chest. She counted calories and portioned out her meals, but the fat talks stopped only when she developed an intestinal problem that left her unable to eat solid food.

When Emily was twelve or thirteen, she began to suffer from mysterious headaches and stomach pains. She spent nights in the hospital, doubled over in pain, and endured invasive tests for Crohn's disease, allergies, and irritable bowel syndrome. Meanwhile, her appetite disappeared. She lost fifteen pounds in a couple of weeks. Her mom would try to cajole her into swallowing a few bites of salad, but Emily couldn't keep it down. Part of her longed for a diagnosis, but sometimes, she thought the pain was a fair price to pay for her new physique. She liked the way her emaciated body looked—and so, it seemed, did everyone else. Emily was so weak that she struggled to get through short variations in class, but her teachers said she looked good. And they weren't the only ones who were watching. Emily sometimes felt as if her body were being monitored by everyone in her life. Her classmates envied her transformation and asked her what her secret was. Even her mom—who was careful never to criticize her daughter's body—complimented her.

But Emily's illness, which was eventually traced to a thyroid problem, was cyclical; sooner or later, her symptoms would subside. Her appetite would come back, and with it, her normal body. The fat talks would resume. "The only way I'm gonna be accepted is if I'm ill," she realized. At her end-of-year evaluation when she was fifteen, Emily's teachers suggested she try modern dance. Emily understood this as the insult it was: in their world, to dance anything other than ballet, to do it anywhere but at the New York City Ballet, was to fail. The school had felt like her second home for six years, but the verdict was final: she was not tall enough or thin enough, and she was no longer welcome at the School of American Ballet.

Gelsey Kirkland starved, and her career soared. She was fifteen when she was handpicked for the New York City Ballet and introduced to the public as one of Balanchine's "baby ballerinas." The *New York Times* quickly recognized her as "a special talent," with "grace, heat, and spirit." She danced the most demanding roles in the classical repertoire—*Swan Lake, Coppélia, Don Quixote*—and partnered with an exciting Soviet defector, the up-and-coming star Mikhail Baryshnikov.

It wasn't just Gelsey's technical prowess—her superhuman balance; her precise petit allegro, for which Balanchine nicknamed her "speedy-feet Gelso"—that made her a star. It wasn't just her theatricality, her determination to imbue even plotless, abstract dances with drama and emotion. She was becoming known for her vulnerability—for the feeling you got, watching her, that you were looking at a super-talented girl-woman, a damsel in distress. Decades before the fashion world embraced the waifish aesthetic of Kate Moss and heroin chic, Gelsey was the poster child for anorexic glamour.

When I watched videos of Gelsey from around this time, I was mesmerized, but also disturbed. She seems to anticipate the music, as if she's coming from inside it, or it's coming from inside her. As the obstinate Kitri in *Don Quixote*, she performs feats that require incredible strength—fouetté turns and stag leaps and hops on pointe—but she has all the muscle definition of a pencil. Her thinness is shocking. Her feet look too big for her legs, her head too heavy for her neck. There is a built-in drama to her movements, even on film—I knew

YouTube would have warned me if Gelsey collapsed in this clip, but I still couldn't help wondering if her body was going to give out. Her glittering black bodice calls attention to the bones jutting out of her chest. The juxtaposition of beauty and bony pallor is breathtaking.

Gelsey Kirkland described her eating disorder as an inevitable side effect of the "concentration camp aesthetic" that dominated the New York City Ballet: it was, she argued, a reasonable response to the pressures of her environment. She certainly wasn't the only dancer who relied on diet pills or starvation. In 1997, the New York doctor Michelle Warren estimated ballet dancers' rates of eating disorders as twenty times higher than the general population.

One early study of young dancers and their diets came out in 1979, when a pair of Columbia doctors interviewed sixty female students at New York's elite Joffrey Ballet School. The girls exercised for six hours a day, six days a week, but consumed, on average, only one thousand calories a day. "Food faddism approaching the bizarre was not uncommon," they write in the journal *General Hospital Psychiatry*. "Some were on 'lettuce diets,' some on 'yogurt diets,' and one girl ate only carrots and developed clinical evidence of carotenemia"—her skin was turning orange.

Robust research into dancers' eating habits, though, is surprisingly sparse. One aborted study gives a hint of why. In the 1990s, Warren and a colleague designed a longitudinal study of girls beginning their training at SAB. They intended to follow the students and monitor their eating habits for three years but had to abandon the project after just one: between sixty and seventy percent of the girls stopped cooperating. "Basically when the girls started getting into trouble, they didn't want to answer questions," Warren told the *New York Times*.

Emily left SAB with her confidence shattered. Still, she couldn't imagine a future other than as a dancer. Nor was she preparing for one; she had already transferred to the academically lenient Professional Performing Arts School. She kept up her dance training at the studio where her mother taught and, at eighteen, defied SAB's predictions by landing an apprenticeship with the Orlando Ballet. It wasn't New York City Ballet, but after years of rejection, she was thrilled to have a job in her chosen field. Her first season passed in a haze of hard work. She continued to watch her diet carefully, maintaining a very low body weight as she danced corps roles in *Peter and the Wolf* and *Giselle* and learned solo parts in *The Nutcracker*.

But she soon realized that her problems had followed her to Florida. She went into meetings with her director, eager to learn how she could improve, only to be told that her legs were not long enough. The faces at the fat talks were different, but the message was the same. "That was all I ever heard," Emily said. "'You're a strong dancer, you're good onstage, but you're not skinny enough.'" At twenty-two, she was let go.

In 1970s New York, ballerinas like Gelsey Kirkland were as beloved as movie stars. But Gelsey wasn't enjoying her fame. She was filling her stomach with celery juice and emptying it with enemas and laxatives. From time to time, she binged on junk food, then swallowed syrup of ipecac or shoved her fingers down her throat. Sometimes, she felt her heart skipping beats and wondered if she would die. Relief came only at night, when she dreamed that she was someone else. Meanwhile, her career reached new heights. The *Chicago Sun-Times* swooned over her body, "slim as a reed and light as a feather." "At 5 feet, 4 inches tall and weighing only 97 pounds, Kirkland suggests a fragility beyond this world," the *New York Times* wrote in 1975.

Gelsey's success did little to bolster her self-esteem. If anything, public praise had the opposite effect, heightening her imposter syndrome. "I could not bring the opinions of others into accord with my heart, which seemed always on the verge of breaking," she wrote. Dancing coveted parts in Balanchine's *Harlequinade* and *Jewels*, she "collapsed into tears after almost every performance." When her mother went backstage to congratulate her, she would inevitably find her doubled over, inconsolable.

When a foot injury forced Gelsey offstage, her anorexia intensified. Banned from dancing, she had no idea how to fill her time. She spent her days lying in bed, waiting for her foot to heal, and poured all of her energy into maintaining her weight. "I hobbled to the bathroom scale and balanced on one foot to check my weight several times a day," she wrote. "I went on a ration plan to stay at ninety pounds." She slashed her food intake to a single green apple—sliced, ritualistically, into quarters—and four tablespoons of cottage cheese per day. "I was proud of myself for keeping my physical instrument tuned to perfection. I actually assumed the ascetic routine was part of the commitment that Balanchine had been advocating all along."

Hunger goes hand in hand with paranoia. As Gelsey's eating disorder spiraled out of control in her early twenties, so did her mental state. On a New York City Ballet tour to Moscow, she became convinced that the radio in her hotel room was a spying device and went on the offense: she attacked it with the hammer she used to break in her pointe shoes, tried to smother it with a pillow, and finally destroyed it with coffee-soaked tampons. The old-world glamour and explosive dancing of the Russian ballerinas fueled her sense of inferiority. Feeling even more insecure than usual, she decided to limit her diet to coffee and candy bars. "Since I was flying into the unknown, my primary goal was to maintain control," she wrote. "Purification and punishment seemed to go hand in hand."

By the end of the five-week tour, her skin had taken on a greenish tinge. Her friends warned Balanchine that she was unwell, but he insisted that Gelsey go ahead and perform. "Just try to look nice, dear," he said, as he handed her "vitamins"—which she later came to believe were amphetamines. When she got back to New York, she was so weak that she could hardly walk. But, at less than ninety pounds, she was finally satisfied with her physique. "In my eyes, emaciation gave my upper body . . . swan-like definition," she wrote.

Kirkland's memoir, *Dancing on My Grave*, can be melodramatic. (The tone is clear by page one: the book is dedicated to her colleague Joseph Duell, a rising star who leapt from his window the day after dancing in *Symphony in C*.) When it was published in 1986, Gelsey—thirty-four years old and newly retired—was bitter, angry, aggrieved. She was out to settle scores. Her thesis is that ballet is cruel, and the supporting evidence is her life. *Dancing on My Grave* made her a pariah in the ballet world—the only world she had ever known. (She eventually apologized, in a 2007 interview with *Dance* magazine, to the people she offended in the book, "such as Baryshnikov and Peter Martins.")

One of her most notorious confessions is the volume of cocaine she consumed during her career. When one of her dance partners, Patrick Bissell—who would die of an overdose a few years later—introduced her to the drug, she took to it with suicidal enthusiasm. Cocaine served a dual purpose: it helped her suppress her appetite and forget the pressures that drove her to fast in the first place.

The first time she got high, she felt "no worries, fears, anxieties, nerves, nothing: only bliss, a fantastic sense of well-being." For once, she was happy with her physical form. "My body glowed," she wrote. "I felt light as a feather." Within weeks, she was using all the time. The first time she danced on coke, in a rehearsal for *Le Corsaire*, was a revelation. "The drug made the work bearable," she wrote. "It was painless for the first time." She danced with abandon, no longer needing to analyze every step.

Gelsey's lifelong paranoia and self-loathing were like kindling, and cocaine the fuel that set the whole thing on fire. Her behavior became so erratic that fans took bets on whether she would turn up for performances. On one occasion, she kept the audience waiting for an hour, then ran away in a taxi. On a tour to Boston, she crossed another threshold and went onstage high. She thought she might be dying and was sure the audience would catch on. But they were oblivious, blinded by the talent she couldn't destroy. One Boston paper compared her to "some lyrical phenomenon of nature." Another, disturbingly, fawned over her figure, calling her "a small wistful waif . . . no bigger than a child."

A few years before Gelsey, emaciated and fearing for her life, finally quit ballet, PBS filmed her dancing "The Dying Swan." The melancholy solo suited her diminished technique; it's more gesture and emotion than bravura jumps or showy turns. Her wispy arms flutter and her fragile back arches as her feet skim the floor, beating as if they have a life of their own. She has stripped the short piece of its few frills; all that remains is raw feeling, the frightened look on her pale face. Her white costume brings to mind a shroud as much as a swan's feathers. Her death throes are faint as she kneels on the floor and collapses. With the PBS broadcast, she reached a bigger audience than ever before: the public embraced her at her weakest, her most fragile.

Who would Gelsey have become if her mother had not enrolled her in ballet lessons in 1960? Was she destined—by some combination of biology, bad luck, family history—to struggle with addiction and eating disorders no matter what? Or did something in the physically grueling, body-obsessed world of ballet trigger her perfectionism, her self-loathing, her drive to disappear? It is, of course, impossible to say. (Balanchine's defenders argue for the former, dismissing her as a basket case or a bitter opportunist blaming her own demons on ballet.) What we do know is that she learned young, in the studio, that thinness and beauty meant attention and success; and that, as an adult, that lesson was reinforced by critics, fans, and lovers in the real world.

Of course, it isn't only in ballet that women's fragility is fetishized. Many women notice depressing social rewards for losing weight.

*   *   *

"I can feel your ribs," my date says, wrapping his hand around my torso, pulling me closer on the couch. The bar is dark and my shirt is thin. His fingers move methodically across my chest, searching out each rib and pressing into it as though he can't believe his luck.

Like Emily, I spent my childhood scrutinizing my body in the floor-to-ceiling mirrors of the studio on Sixty-Fifth Street. I looked on in horror as my hips widened, each millimeter making my dream of becoming a dancer more far-fetched. I fantasized about slicing off my thighs, trimming the muscles on my calves. I remember being told that the mirror was a tool, that we should use it to correct our technique. Of course, we used it to compare ourselves to each other. Our skintight leotards left no room to hide. I could recognize my classmates by the slant of their hips, the arches of their feet. I envied Ellie's spindly legs, Emma's delicate hands, Lily's jutting collarbone. "Don't look down, Alice," my teachers scolded. "What's so interesting on the floor?" But I couldn't raise my eyes and risk catching sight of myself in the mirror. (Eventually, I mastered the art of looking without seeing: of lifting my eyes without focusing my gaze, letting my field of vision blur.)

When we became dancers, our teachers warned, we could be photographed from any angle, at any moment: we must never let our guard down. I imagined critical eyes surrounding me all the time. I internalized the mirror, and constructed more mirrors in my head. I absorbed the punitive beauty standards of classical ballet and counted the ways I didn't measure up.

I hated the ways my body changed, hated that I couldn't control it. One year, I was in the running; the next, I was mostly ignored. I was kicked out of SAB, but I couldn't accept that my ballet career was over. I enrolled in a second-rate program and spent the next few years drifting around, dreaming of re-auditioning for SAB, making a dramatic and increasingly implausible comeback.

Still, it wasn't until my early twenties, years after I quit ballet, that I developed an overwhelming fear of gaining weight; that I discovered the giddy pleasure of going six, seven, eight hours on water and green tea. I chewed strip after strip of strawberry-flavored gum and, on nights I was alone, ate rice cakes drizzled with soy sauce or, when I lived in England, Marmite. (Even though their food intake was strictly limited, the men in the Minnesota starvation experiment had access to as much water and gum as they wanted, and I understood why they enthusiastically availed themselves of their gum privileges. One man, who chewed as many as forty packs a day, spat out so much gum that he measured his daily output in a beer mug.)

I felt very productive, feeling my body shrink, and as my BMI dropped from the "normal" range to "underweight," I was rewarded for it. I was told that my body was tiny, perfect; I was approvingly called a waif. The man who liked my ribs took me to his beach house and bought me thirty-dollar plates of pasta I didn't eat.

By this time, I had spent years as a resident of the "pedestrian" world—which afforded its female citizens the luxury of wearing pants but still, undoubtedly, valued thinness. I wondered if I could trace my unnatural standards back to ballet; I wondered if I was trying—now that it was too late—to look like the dancer I'd never become, as if trying to prove my fidelity to an ex-lover who had moved on. I thought of a friend of mine, who joined AA after breaking up with her sober boyfriend. She wasn't an alcoholic, really; she just wanted to feel close to her ex.

※   ※   ※

It may seem inevitable that students of a physical art form will develop an intense relationship with their bodies. But it's the environment, too—the leotards and mirrors—that make girls feel so exposed, like specimens beneath a microscope. In the

studio, so-called junk—leg warmers, warm-ups, and sweats—
was forbidden. I remember what a treat it was to be allowed,
occasionally, to wear a "ballet skirt"—a short strip of gauzy
fabric—in class. I wrapped the skirt—a privilege reserved for
pointe class or variations—around my waist and instantly felt
less naked and more confident. Psychologists have confirmed
that the standard class uniform contributes to dancers' poor
body image: in one study, written up for the journal *Social
Behavior and Personality*, young dancers took class either
in a leotard and tights or in loose warm-up gear. Afterward,
the ones who were allowed "junk" were more likely to agree
with statements like "I like my body" and "I enjoy looking
at myself in the mirror during class"; they were more able to
recognize that, compared to "normal society," they were "on
the thin side." Another study, this one in *Perceptual and Motor Skills*, showed the harmful impact of the mirror: college
students who took a semester-long dance class in a standard,
mirror-lined ballet studio felt less satisfied with their bodies,
at the end of the term, than a group of women who took the
same class in a mirror-free space.

Excessive "mirror gazing" and "mirror checking" are both
occupational necessities for dancers and clinical features of
body dysmorphic disorder. A woman named Louise, who was
interviewed as part of a British *Journal of Health Psychology* study on body dysmorphia, admitted to having once gotten "stuck" in front of the mirror, unable to move—even to
eat or drink—for eleven hours straight. Even as Louise knew
that the longer she stared, "the more distorted everything becomes," she couldn't look away. The dysmorphic women were
both tortured by mirrors and dependent on them. "I do feel
kind of bereft if there are no mirrors," said another woman. "I
feel really like kind of an addict without their drug."

In 2001, a team of German psychologists had dozens of elite teenaged dancers fill out detailed surveys about what they thought of their bodies, rating several aspects of their physique on a scale of one to seven. The aspiring ballet dancers assessed their bodies more harshly than students at a local high school: even though they more closely resembled society's "ideal," the dancers were likelier to say that their bodies were ugly and poorly proportioned. Whether or not they had full-blown eating disorders, they had a mindset analogous to people with anorexia, who, when asked to sketch their emaciated bodies, draw curves that don't exist. The culture of ballet is so powerful, the ideals so seductive, that even not-so-serious students are at risk for body dysmorphia: one study, published in the journal *Psychopathology*, showed an elevated rate of eating disorders among girls who took as few as two or three classes a week and had no intention of pursuing a career in ballet.

Whenever I entered a room, I used to note the location of the mirrors, the way a nervous flier might scan a plane for emergency exits. I orbited them: sometimes I wanted to be near them, to check if my hair had gotten frizzy or a pimple had bloomed; sometimes I wanted, self-protectively, to avoid them. But I never wanted to be confronted with a mirror, or even a reflective surface, without being ready.

I remember the first time I was in a house free of mirrors: at my grandfather's shiva, when I was ten. The mirrors in the house had been covered in accordance with Jewish custom, and I remember how jarring it was to look for my reflection and not find it. It took a while to lose the habit of looking in those mirrors. I would go to the bathroom and be surprised, and then relieved, to see a dark cloth instead of my own im-

perfect face. I felt that I'd been somehow absolved of responsibility for my appearance. For a few, precious hours, I almost
forgot about how I looked.

Ballet's obsession with thinness is often traced to Balanchine,
who had a personal preference for willowy women; all of the
ones he married were leggy and lithe. Yet, ever since the birth
of ballet in seventeenth-century France, "the idea was to create some kind of Apollonian image—an ideal sort of body,"
the scholar Jennifer Homans said in an NPR interview. Our
image of perfection has changed over the centuries, following fashion, politics, and arbitrary fads. Degas's dancers had
soft curves and even cleavage. In 1800s Italy, Marie Taglioni's
skinny legs were considered a liability; a hundred years later,
in Russia, the lanky Anna Pavlova drank cod liver oil in an
effort to bulk up.

But by the mid-twentieth century, it wasn't just in Balanchine's company that dancers were starving themselves. In
1963, a promising young dancer named Heidrun Müller, who
was just out of one of Dresden's top ballet schools, was offered a spot in the corps of the Berlin State Opera—on condition that she lose weight. The nineteen-year-old Müller, who
had gained a few pounds while immobilized by an injury, took
drastic measures to meet the Opera's demands. She told the
writer Maja Langsdorff how she narrowed her diet to one
food at a time—eating only oranges one day, only sauerkraut
the next. After hearing that she could burn extra calories by
shivering, she arranged to be pulled across a lake by a boat
while lying on an air-filled mattress in its wake.

And while Balanchine doled out insane dieting advice

("Eat nothing") to some of his dancers, he also made exceptions: Melissa Hayden, one of his favorites, had bulging muscles in her thighs; Suzanne Farrell was five eight and Gloria Govrin, another muse, was a voluptuous five ten. (In giving Govrin a chance, Balanchine was defying the 1950s expectations of what a dancer should look like; as a teenager, she had been advised to move to Las Vegas and become a showgirl. "He once told me that he never saw anybody my size move the way I moved, and he was intrigued," Govrin told NPR in 2017.) Archival photos from the early days of City Ballet show women who, by the aughts, would not have made it past the front door.

Maybe it was after seeing these pictures that, in my diary, I fantasized about Balanchine's resurrection. It was 2004, and I wasn't doing well at SAB. My teachers were mostly ignoring me in class, and I had been cast—for the third year in a row—in the same small role in *The Nutcracker*. When I was feeling confident, I imagined that my teachers were underestimating me, and I blamed the casting director's indifference on my above-average height. "I'm tall, so I bearly [*sic*] got to be in anything," I complained to my diary. I dreamed about the ultimate validation, from an authority higher than the casting mistress. "Sometimes at Ballet, I hope Balanchine will walk in and say he never really died. He liked tall dancers." (In reality, I was not even so tall, and I grew up to be only five-foot-five.) But in Balanchine's absence, his "ideal" had hardened into law. By the time I arrived at SAB, the standard was so specific and severe that even actresses and gymnasts seemed to have it easy by comparison.

Michelle was the rare child who did not intend to become a dancer when she auditioned for SAB. By the age of eight, she had already discovered her talent for gymnastics; dance classes were only supposed to help with the line of her body on the beam. But she soon found that she excelled at ballet, too: the grace and rhythm that she had honed at the gym translated easily to the studio, and then the stage. She played a party girl in *The Nutcracker* and a butterfly in *Midsummer Night's Dream*, and at twelve she gave up gymnastics to focus on ballet.

I don't remember interacting with Michelle so much as I remember staring at her. At nine, she looked different in a way I didn't understand. She reminded me of the girls I saw on the Disney Channel or in the Gap catalogs that showed up in the mailbox at home: shinier, somehow, than the rest of us. (It was only later, looking at old photos, that I realized this might have had something to do with a precocious ability to contour and a sophisticated set of caramel highlights.) In the class picture, she looks less like a child than a scaled-down news anchor: her hair sleek, her eyeshadow the same shade of pink as her leotard.

Not long after Michelle committed to ballet, her experience at SAB began to change. Performance opportunities tapered off, replaced by extra pointe classes. "The fun and games were over," she told me. The competition with her classmates intensified. "There was a lot of favoritism."

Michelle was used to being one of the favorites. She heard about her classmates being called in for "weight warnings," but Michelle—naturally petite, with long legs and narrow hips—had so far escaped criticism of her body.

But when she was fifteen, Michelle was told, at her end-of-year meeting, that her dainty frame had a defect after all. The shape of her calves, according to her teachers, was all wrong. Strong and slightly bowed from the years she had used them to grip the balance beam, her calves, she learned, were ruining the smooth silhouette of her legs and putting her dreams at stake. She was sent home for the summer with a warning: her advancement to the next level was not guaranteed; she would be reassessed in the fall. "If my legs came along, they would take it from there," Michelle remembered. She had three months to deal with the problem of her calves.

Michelle was not in the habit of questioning her teachers. She set about working to reshape her lower legs: at the prestigious summer intensive at the Pacific Northwest Ballet School, and in the many private lessons she squeezed in on the side. At home, in her spare time, she did thousands of tendus and visualized her calf muscles wrapping themselves more tightly around her shin bone.

But as she was toiling away at the barre, trying to rid her body of the evidence that she had ever been a gymnast, a seed of doubt took hold. She began to wonder if she was trying to force her body into a mold that it didn't fit.

When Michelle got back to SAB in the fall, her teachers were pleased with her progress. Her regimen of relentless tendus had worked, and she was promoted to the advanced division, from which New York City Ballet's apprentices are culled. Michelle settled back into her old routine—gritting her teeth as she rose onto pointe, smiling through the pain, and striving for her teachers' approval. But something inside her had shifted. She couldn't drum up her old enthusiasm. She missed gymnastics—the thrill of hurling herself through space without worrying about the size of her calves. Just a month into the school year, she confided in her mom, who had spent years shuttling her to dance classes and rehearsals and summer programs. "Honestly, I'm just not happy here anymore," she said. "I don't really want to be doing this anymore."

It had been over three years since Michelle had set foot in

the gym. But in just a few weeks, it all came back. Twisting in the air and landing on a razor-thin beam was, for her, like riding a bike. Her calves got rounder, but her coaches didn't care, and neither did she. She felt gloriously free to focus on her artistry and form, and not on her body. "Gymnastics thin is not ballet thin," she said. In gymnastics, a fit body was a byproduct of intense training—not an end unto itself. "You need to have power. You need to have brute force. I didn't feel as physically scrutinized as I did in ballet."

In 2010, when she was eighteen, Michelle moved to Michigan to train full-time. With the same determination she had once applied to the project of reshaping her calves, she now prepared for the Olympic trials. Once again, her hard work paid off, and in 2012, she flew to London to compete.

A mash-up of instrumental punk music boomed out around the O2 Arena as twenty-one-year-old Michelle, in a glittering leotard the color of a ripe tomato, turned her body into a rocket, flipping through the air with her legs in a pike and tossing off graceful pirouettes in between tricks. No matter how risky the stunt, how dizzying the turns, her smile—a more genuine smile than the one she wore in her ballet class picture—never faltered.

*   *   *

Even as the discourse around bodies has become more polite, dancers are still seen as fair game. In a 2010 review of *The Nutcracker*, the *New York Times* critic Alastair Macaulay wrote that Sugar Plum Fairy Jenifer Ringer—who had once struggled with anorexia, and had recently given birth— "looked as if she'd eaten one sugarplum too many." He defended himself against the ensuing online backlash: "If you want to make your appearance irrelevant to criticism, do not choose ballet as a career."

But of course, no woman can make her appearance irrelevant to criticism. I like Olivia Laing's description of femininity, in her book *The Lonely City*, as a "perpetual, harrowing, non-consensual beauty pageant." The dancer's preoccupation with her body is only an exaggerated version of what all women contend with. In a recent Gallup poll, twice as many women as men—one in five—said that they worry about their weight *all the time*; only eighteen percent of women—and thirty-two percent of men—said that they never did. It's estimated that anorexia is three to four times more common among young women than young men. And women are not only expected to stay thin, but, more than ever, to hide the effort it takes. The body positivity movement has changed the way we talk about weight—has made it taboo to admit to being on a diet, and has compelled Weight Watchers to rebrand as WellnessWins—without much changing the standards women are expected to meet.

When the writer Alana Massey shrank to a size zero in her early twenties, she was at first delighted by the flood of male attention that rushed in. But she soon realized that, as much as men appreciated her new body, they were turned off by her refusal to deviate from the routine that kept it small. "As relationships advance, romantic partners become visibly disappointed and even annoyed that maintaining thinness is not a matter of a quick jog and 100 crunches," she wrote in a 2014 essay in the *New Inquiry*. "For a thin woman to betray the reality of her diet and regimen for staying that way would spoil the fantasy of a woman who is preternaturally inclined to her size rather than personally preoccupied by it."

Helen Gurley Brown—who, as the longtime editor of *Cosmopolitan*, helped define the modern feminine ideal—would agree. In her bestseller *Sex and the Single Girl*, she advises women to master elaborate recipes for chocolate soufflé, breakfast steak, and lobster en brochette—then warns that they should be cooked or consumed only in the presence of men. "What you feed him and them bears no resemblance to what you should be feeding *you* when they aren't around," she wrote. When women are alone, they should subsist on tuna fish, yogurt, and cottage cheese—saving up calories for those hearty romantic dinners. "Keep your lips zipped" about your own diet, she advised: let him think your figure is an accident. I hear myself tell my boyfriend I'm eating ice cream when I'm really eating a frozen dessert made of fava beans, artificial sweeteners, and air, whose only resemblance to ice cream is that it is cold.

But dancers are exempt from this double bind. They don't have to hide the colossal effort they make. For them, dietary sacrifices don't signal vanity or an adherence to old-fashioned ideals, but commitment to high art. During the press tour for *Black Swan*, Natalie Portman gave journalists the kind of quotes that guaranteed their pieces would go viral. While preparing to play Nina, she lived on carrots and almonds and lost twenty pounds. "There were some nights," she said, "that I thought I literally was going to die." Her costar, Mila Kunis, exercised thirty-five hours a week and chain-smoked to manage her hunger pangs. These actresses—who undoubtedly watch their diets no matter what they're shooting—do not usually share the graphic details so freely.

Every Friday morning, I log on to nymag.com and click over to the Grub Street Diet: a weekly feature in which a stylish, accomplished, or otherwise enviable New Yorker logs all of her meals for a week. This is not a habit I am proud of, but it makes me feel better to check Twitter and see that I'm not the only one. And I've noticed a pattern on social media: if the author is a thin woman, and if her diet seems carefree and carb heavy, then she will be celebrated. The writer Jia Tolentino describes herself in her entry as "extremely enthusiastic about food." She eats lunch at eleven in the morning, so she can eat lunch again at two. "I must eat every three hours or shut down emotionally," she claims. Her tri-hourly meals consist of things like ramen, rigatoni, carrot cake, cinnamon-raisin bread, pasta with lamb sausage, deviled eggs, and steak tartare. The diet reinforced Tolentino's status as the consummate cool girl. "Perfect perfect perfect," one woman tweeted. A journalist joked about having the column tattooed on her body.

The author Alissa Nutting's entry was even more extreme— and garnered even more praise. Nutting pounds hot dogs (two per bun), nachos, Doritos, and pepperoni pizza topped with Oreos ("I love hotel rooms with two beds: one for me and one for my delivered pizzas"). One Grub Street editor declared Nutting's diet her all-time favorite. Others called it "a masterpiece," "true genius," "my favorite thing in the history of ever."

Misty Copeland's Grub Street Diet is not like the others. She does not conceal how little she eats, or how carefully. "Really starving" after ballet class, she picks up a smoothie—which is "like a meal for me." From Saturday evening until Sunday night, she abstains from food entirely. ("This was a fasting day, which is something I do if I feel like I need to cleanse . . . I'll just drink a ton of water all day. You go 24 hours without eating.") Her indulgence is cheddar biscuits at Red Lobster— once every two years.

✳   ✳   ✳

In 1984, Gelsey withdrew from a gala in which she was set
to star. She had recently fallen in love with fellow addict Greg
Lawrence, whom she met outside her dealer's door, and who
helped her see that ballet and drugs were killing her. The couple then fled to a farmhouse upstate to listen to Beethoven,
read Plato, and get clean. Two years later, sober and ostensibly
stronger than ever, Gelsey flew with Greg—now her husband,
and the cowriter of *Dancing on My Grave*—to London for
a comeback, a final performance of *Romeo and Juliet*. (She
recounted their sojourn in London in a second memoir, *The
Shape of Love*.) After a long day of rehearsals with the Royal
Ballet, Gelsey met Greg for dinner at an Italian restaurant near
their flat. The waiter, "a silver-haired man with the natural gift
of talking with his hands, had raised them in despair" when
Gelsey gave him her order, "refusing sauce or pasta." Later,
when she declined dessert, he began "gesticulating almost
tragically"—until Greg stepped in to explain, in a single word:
"Ballerina." Right away, the waiter forgave her. "Ah ballerina!"
he said. "I see. She not eat . . . she dance!"

As Emily boarded the plane home to New York, unemployed
and in pain, she thought about her skinny colleagues who
had kept their jobs, and she wondered if she would still be
in Florida if she were taller or thinner. But she resolved to
push on. She would use the time off to get her hips fixed—
they had been hurting for years—and then embark on another
round of auditions. At the doctor's, though, she learned that
the damage was worse than she had thought: years of overuse

had worn down her cartilage, and her hips would have to be surgically reinserted in the sockets. But Emily was hopeful. As a nurse wheeled her into the operating room, she thought, *I'm gonna feel so good! I'm gonna get another job!*

But when Emily left the hospital, she couldn't walk. Accustomed to having almost total control over her body, it hit her that she would have to relearn the most basic movements. She lay in bed, watching TV, and fell into a depression. She felt like she had nothing to work toward: no show to get in shape for, no company director checking in. *Why am I even trying?* she wondered. In between Netflix binges, she replayed the cruelest comments she had heard about her body. It was six months before Emily could get through a class again.

As Emily slowly regained her strength, she realized it was performing, not ballet, that she missed the most. She signed up for acting lessons and hired a voice coach, and started going to auditions for anything she could find—from musicals to movies to burlesque shows.

"Cattle calls" are notoriously dehumanizing: aspiring actors complain of feeling objectified and replaceable as they try to stand out among hordes of similarly talented, similarly striving peers. But Emily found them empowering. If she was rejected for a certain role, she didn't assume it was because of her body; maybe, she understood, the director wanted a tap dancer instead of a ballerina, or a blonde instead of a brunette. Unlike in a ballet studio, everyone looks different; some girls even looked "like her." (Emily said this as though her physical defects are so obvious they don't need to be described, and so dreadful that they can't be named.) But these girls who "look like her"—girls with those unspeakable breasts and hips—wore as little clothing as they could: they came to auditions in sports bras, thigh-skimming shorts, and high heels that emphasized their curves: they seemed proud of their bodies.

I was younger than Emily, still a teenager, when it dawned on me that my standards might be extreme. It was Tyra Banks, the nineties supermodel who reinvented herself as the ruthless host of a reality TV show, who led me to this realization. I can't remember how I stumbled on *America's Next Top Model*— only that I was instantly hooked and slightly ashamed: I was supposed to care about Latin grammar and classical dance, not a vapid modeling competition. Still, there was something uniquely soothing about watching a mean supermodel tell a parade of beautiful young women what was wrong with them: the beautiful women's eyebrows were too thin or their teeth were too far apart or their hair was too brown (except when it was too blond). I was all too comfortable ogling and assessing the contestants and, like Tyra, breaking them down into parts.

I must have spent dozens of Wednesday nights watching that show. I watched the women pose with live tarantulas and hunks of raw meat; I watched them pour olive oil on their legs and "smize" inside a giant salad bowl. But the dramatic photoshoots and makeovers mostly blurred together, washing over me like some kind of sedative. It was a relatively tame scene that had me glued to the screen, and that I can still recall in vivid detail.

The contestants had been sent to an amateur dance class, ostensibly to improve their posing, and they filed into a studio in leotards and lined up at the barre. I remember looking at these young women, who met the physical requirements of a fashion model in the mid-2000s, and, without thinking, scanning their bodies for flaws. I remember thinking that few of them would pass muster in a real ballet studio. One girl's thighs were too wide; another's torso was too long. Yet even as I scrutinized these models the way I always looked at bodies in leotards, I also had a dim awareness that what I was doing was off somehow. The women I knew outside ballet—my classmates and teachers at school, and the girl-boss writers for *Seventeen* and *Teen Vogue*—criticized the fashion industry for glorifying women who were too thin. *America's Next Top Model* had even been singled out for promoting an unattainable ideal.

Even though I know that no book reviewer or editor would ever critique my body—and even though I understand, intellectually, that the ballet standards are outrageous—I can't fully break out of the ballet mindset. In the morning, I look at my face as if it's a first draft: What should I emphasize with makeup? What should I edit out? I was so afraid of "bulking up" that I didn't touch free weights until I was twenty-eight; the same fear has compelled me to cut short bike rides and long runs. Like Gelsey, I have perched one-legged on a scale, balancing on the ball of my foot and postponing the moment of truth. I can't stop comparing myself, absurdly, with dancers. When the NYCB principal Lauren Lovette told the *New York Times* in 2021 that she'd gotten healthier and wouldn't be "dancing at 94 pounds anymore," I should have been happy for her. But that wasn't my first response. My first thought was that I was excited to know Lovette's weight; I opened a new browser and googled her height.

When, in her late twenties, Emily missed ballet enough to brave an open class, she hid her body under baggy leg warmers and sweats. In times of stress, fasting remained a comfort-

able coping mechanism. After a breakup a few years ago, she stopped eating completely; the resulting weight loss felt like the silver lining of her heartbreak. She wondered how long she could survive without food—maybe she could finally take class without layers of "junk."

Crown of Thorns

When I was nineteen or twenty, I had a boyfriend, one of my first. One night, as we lay entangled in my too-small single bed, I shifted my body in some small way—I repositioned a cramping leg or I let my head fall on his shoulder—I don't remember how, exactly. What I remember is what he said next: "Ow." It rolled off his tongue like he wasn't thinking, wasn't censoring himself. "That hurts."

I couldn't believe what I had heard. He had registered his own pain and deemed it worth expressing. I apologized and withdrew my leg or my head, and his moment of discomfort was over.

I thought of all the small pains I had experienced in my time with him—an uncomfortable thrust, an arm too heavy on my arm. I would have let my limbs go numb before I would have said, "Ow. That hurts." Pain seemed so inevitable that I had taught myself to ignore it. It was more important to spare his feelings and preserve the mood than to feel better.

Throughout our lives, women suffer from all kinds of extra pain. We have more nerve receptors than men and, literally, thinner skin. In the lab, women exposed to the same electric shocks and hot and cold stimuli register more acute pain. From the time girls learn where babies come from, they anticipate the pain of giving birth (and know they will be stigmatized if they try to minimize it with painkillers). From puberty through middle age, women risk cramps, migraines, nausea, and muscle aches every month. Pain is often a facet of girls' sexual initiation, and many just accept it. "The sex was always painful but I thought that perhaps that was the price of being loved," the sex worker Liara Roux writes of her first romance. In a survey (described in the *Journal of Sexual Medicine*) of over seventeen hundred men and women in the United States, thirty percent of women say they experienced pain the last time they had sex, compared with just five percent of men. And for some, the pain is excruciating: as many as one in six women suffer at some point from vaginismus, a condition in which their vaginas contract in painful spasms when touched.

The most common response to all of this is to grit our teeth. We even teach ourselves to tolerate pain beyond that which is biologically necessary: "Beauty is pain," we tell ourselves as we trip down the street in high heels or pay to have hot wax smeared on our bare skin. (Between 2002 and 2010, according to a study in the journal *Urology*, emergency room visits for pubic grooming injuries increased by a factor of five; the most at-risk group was young women.) We shove ourselves into Spanx or Skims, cutely named shape-wear so constrictive that, like old-fashioned corsets, they can cause blood clots and fainting spells. It isn't only the results of these procedures—the hairless crotches and the slick waistlines—that make us feel like women; it's the process of enduring them. In her memoir *Sick*, the writer Porochista Khakpour reflects on a lifetime of physical and mental anguish—and on how her identity as a person in pain has been intertwined with her identity as a woman. Growing up, she looked forward to getting her period—"the affliction that it seemed everyone I knew got to complain about." When she fainted after emerging from a too-hot shower, at the age of thirteen, it felt, on some secret level, like a longed-for rite of passage, a fast-track ticket to fulfilling her gender identity. It was also, she wrote, "the first time I got to feel like a woman"—and the dawning of her realization "that perhaps ailment was a feature central to that experience." Dainty and fragile, she felt like an ideal woman—"like a crystal ballerina."

Women are incentivized to downplay and conceal their discomfort; if we admit we are in pain, we risk being cast as hypochondriacs or hysterics. The word "hysteria" comes from the Greek for "uterus": ancient medics, according to Maya Dusenbery's book *Doing Harm: The Truth About How Bad Medicine and Lazy Science Leave Women Dismissed, Misdiagnosed, and Sick*, thought that the uterus was an independent organ, roaming around the woman's body and causing aches and pains if it strayed off course. Even after doctors discarded that idea, they still believed that hysteria was an epidemic. "As a general rule, all women are hysterical and . . . every woman carries with her the seeds of hysteria," a prominent French physician wrote in the late nineteenth century. Even today, doctors doubt women's reports of their own pain. In a 2008 study of patients in a Philadelphia emergency room, men with abdominal pain received medication after forty-nine minutes, while women had to wait sixty-five.

※   ※   ※

Some followers of Freud believed that women were born with a taste for suffering and submission: influential psychoanalysts understood masochism and passivity as inherently feminine traits, a direct result of women's anatomy. (In this paradigm, sadism and virility are fundamentally masculine.) A woman lacks a penis, and so she feels defective; she wants to sleep with her father, and so she feels guilty; she bears children, and so she feels pain. A few years after Freud's death, one of his disciples, the psychoanalyst Helene Deutsch, argued that masochism is not inborn, but develops as an adaptive response to women's life cycles and circumstances. "The psychological task of puberty and menstruation . . . consists in the establishment of a new passivity drive that prepares the woman for masochistically suffering man's sadistic onslaught," she wrote in *The Psychoanalysis of Sexual Functions of Women*. It is self-protective for women to give in to the inevitable, even to embrace it. A few years ago, a data scientist analyzed millions of Pornhub searches and found that the primary consumers of videos featuring violence against women were women.

Even as we punish women for complaining, we relish stories, real and made up, of their suffering: Miss Havisham in her burning dress, Anna Karenina underneath a train, Sylvia Plath with her head in the oven. In *The Empathy Exams*, the essayist Leslie Jamison meditates on the impossibility of communicating female pain. She wants to write about her heartbreak and self-harm, but she is afraid of conforming to melodramatic clichés. "I knew better . . . than to become one of *those* women who plays victim, lurks around the sickbed, hands her pain out like a business card," she wrote. Hip, contemporary women, whom Jamison dubs "post-wounded," are acutely aware of—allergic to—tropes of female vulnerability. "We're attracted to it and revolted by it; proud and ashamed of it. So we've developed a post-wounded voice, a stance of numbness or crutch of sarcasm . . . that seems to stave off certain accusations it can see on the horizon: melodrama, triviality, wallowing . . . The post-wounded woman conducts herself as if preempting certain accusations: don't cry too loud, don't play victim, don't act the old role all over again." But that doesn't mean she doesn't hurt, or want her pain acknowledged. Jamison admitted "the possibility that being a woman *requires* being in pain; that pain is the unending glue and prerequisite of female consciousness." Which is to say: it's complicated.

For dancers, it's less complicated. No one embraces pain more fully: the pain of contorting their bodies into impossible shapes—twisting the legs to turn outward from the hips; forcing the weight of the entire body onto the tip of one toe, then hopping up and down on that toe. The pain inherent in whittling their bodies into the toothpick figure Balanchine preferred.

But they suffer in silence. One of the first lessons dancers learn is to keep their expression pleasant no matter what: never to complain, even with their eyes. We learned to dissociate the look on our face from the ache in our feet, to always keep our expression regal, serene.

(These ingrained habits can carry through into dancers' adult communication styles. Popular hashtags on the relentlessly positive ballet-themed corner of Instagram include #happy ballerina, #iloveballet, #ilovemyballerinalife, #somuchfun. One professional dancer I corresponded with used flower emojis where most people would put commas; another ended every sentence with at least one exclamation point.)

We looked up to women who danced through unbearable pain, who ignored life-threatening injuries. We learned about the Russian ballerina Anna Pavlova, who, in 1931, died of pneumonia in a Dutch hotel, refusing to undergo an operation that might have left her with a less-than-perfect body. Her stamina was Herculean. She assembled her own troupe in 1910, trekking all over Latin America, Asia, Australia, and Africa on crowded trains and dirty boats. She and her band of dancers, stagehands, and musicians got ready in dressing rooms flooded with sewage and performed on makeshift stages in churches and schools. "Our work became a concentrated form of punishment," one company member wrote. They sailed to Ecuador on a cattle boat and danced in 102-degree heat. Pavlova was almost fifty when she died, and she was still traveling and performing at a relentless pace; she was only on the first leg of a planned transatlantic tour when she ran a fever so high she was finally forced to lie down. We learned her apocryphal last words—"Get my Swan costume ready."

Almost no one who saw Pavlova dance is still alive, and the footage that survives is scratchy and faint. I grew up hearing her name mentioned in reverent tones, but when I watched the clips recently, I was underwhelmed. Frilly costumes obscure half of her body. Her extensions are low; her feet are virtually flat. Her technique could be bested by any twelve-year-old at Youth America Grand Prix. It's not for the memory of her dancing but her willingness to suffer that her legend endures.

We learned about the Spanish ballerina Tamara Rojo, who was starring in *The Nutcracker* when she felt a sharp pain in her stomach. Her whole body shook, but she finished the show. Afterward, she was rushed to the hospital, where she learned that her appendix had burst. The doctor advised her to take six weeks off; she went back to work after two.

The threat of serious injury lurked behind every step, but it was the garden-variety pains that preoccupied us: blisters, sore muscles, bruised toes. And our daily dose of pain soared when we began dancing on pointe at ten or eleven. (This rite of passage was reserved for girls; with a few exceptions—like the all-male drag troupe Les Ballets Trockadero de Monte Carlo, which performs satires of classic ballets—men don't dance on pointe.)

My ballet classmates and I were, in almost every way, extremely obedient. But there was one rule many of us violated: before our teachers had deemed our feet strong enough, we went to Capezio or Bloch and got fitted for our first pointe shoes. We couldn't wait.

I don't remember buying my first bra or trying my first drink, but I remember the thrill of easing my feet into pointe shoes for the first time; of learning how to crisscross the ribbons over my ankles and tuck in the knot so it didn't show—it might cut into my ankle, but at least it wouldn't disturb the smooth line of my leg. I remember how elegant it looked and how the pain, when I stood up, was shocking. I would perform this ritual countless times in the coming years, but I would never get used to it; the pain was fresh every time. According to Leigh Cowart's *Hurts So Good: The Science and Pleasure of Pain on Purpose*, the force of balancing en pointe on one foot is equivalent to letting the full weight of a grand piano fall on a single toe.

The basic look and structure of pointe shoes—from the peach-pink satin exterior to the leather shank and cardboard-and-fabric toe box—have barely changed in the past century: it would be hard to tell the difference between a pair of pointe shoes worn by Anna Pavlova and a pair on the shelf at Freed's today. They are still handcrafted in a painstaking process developed over a hundred years ago, and even custom-made shoes are delivered far from ready to wear. The dancer must break them in through a finicky process that may include, but is not limited to: shaving off parts of the shank; bending the arch with her hands; wetting the vamp and walking around; stomping on the toe; singeing the ends of the ribbons; and banging the shoes against a wall. In East Germany, according to Maja Landgsdorff's *Ballet—and Then?*, dancers softened their pointe shoes by cooking them in the potato steamer; even today, some prolong their pointe shoes' life by coating them in floor wax and baking them on foil-lined trays in the oven. ("Warning . . . the baking pointe shoes smell awful!" cautions a Redditor, on a thread in which users compare recipes— preheat the oven to two hundred degrees; roll up the ribbons so they don't melt; if you're in a rush, the microwave will do.) Even principals sew their own ribbons and elastics. After all this, pointe shoes break down after a few days or even hours of use; professionals go through several pairs a week. (Breaking down pointe shoes quickly was a source of pride—a sign of hard work and strong feet.) A pair of pointe shoes costs about eighty dollars; New York City Ballet's pointe shoe budget runs to over three-quarters of a million dollars a year.

In the 1990s, an ex-dancer named Eliza Gaynor Minden set out to disrupt the staid pointe shoe industry. Like most ballet students, she had gone on pointe as a preteen—but unlike most students, she had bristled against the expectation that she should be in pain from then on. She wondered why she was dancing on shoes that might as well be antiques, and after quitting ballet and graduating from college, she returned to the problem.

Gaynor Minden spent years tinkering with the traditional pointe shoe design, playing around with modern materials like shock-absorbent foam and polymer shanks. She took apart sneakers and studied orthopedic shoes. She wanted to create something durable, ready-to-wear, and—most taboo of all— comfortable. "I was outraged that dancers were expected to perform on such crummy shoes," she said. Gaynor Mindens went on the market in 1993.

By the early 2000s, rising stars like Gillian Murphy and Alina Cojocaru had ditched their Freeds for Gaynors. The gatekeepers, predictably, freaked out—so loudly that even the lay press picked up on it. "This newcomer shoe has kicked off a war," *The New Yorker* wrote in 2002. Both camps invoked the long-dead Balanchine, as feuding religious factions might invoke the spirit of God. The skeptics—led by Suki Schorer, a well-known teacher at SAB—didn't care that Minden's high-tech shoes might cut down on injuries. "Ballet isn't about health," she said. In the eyes of the audience, Gaynor Mindens are indistinguishable from traditional Capezios and Freeds. What the establishment really valued was stoicism.

When I was learning to go on pointe in the early 2000s, Gaynors were a lightning rod. I would never have dared to bring them in the doors at SAB, where Schorer and her like-minded peers reigned, but I could have gotten away with it at summer intensives and outside classes. Still, I stuck with my Capezios. If I was supposed to feel pain, then I didn't want to skimp on it. I wanted bunions, blisters, bleeding toenails, and I envied the girls who bruised more easily. If my feet looked whole, I felt like a fraud. As Toni Bentley wrote in the *New York Times*: "A bloodied toe inside her first pair of toe shoes is a welcome symbol of initiation for a young ballerina, just as it is considered a sign of good luck for a professional."

Pain is the body's warning system: nature's request that we stop what we are doing. But from an early age, dancers are inducted into a perverse relationship with pain. It isn't a sign that the body is under stress; it's a source of pride, a sign of progress—something to be ignored, if not outright relished. As students, we found ways to make it all more painful, just to show we could. We scraped our hair into buns so tight we worried about receding hairlines. We took pride in forgoing pads in our pointe shoes, in dancing on bruised toes. We learned to find our limits and then push past them; to ignore the thousands of nerves in our feet and legs and backs that screamed for us to stop. We were proud, too, when our teachers corrected us, even when the corrections took the form of insults or painful physical adjustments—yanking our leg above our ear or shoving our rib cage into our chest. We measured our status by the number of corrections we received: the more, the better—no matter how harshly they were delivered. ("Miss Ware gave me four corrections!" I would gleefully report to my mom, when she came to pick me up from class.) Withstanding emotional pain, even humiliation, was another badge of honor. "In this system, even anger is a kind of gift," wrote Suzanne Gordon. "Dancers worry if they are not chastised." We were never safe—not even onstage. I remember missing a cue in *The Nutcracker* and hearing the casting mistress's disappointed, disembodied shout coming from somewhere in the wings—"You missed it, Alice!" At least my cheeks had already been painted red. We rarely enjoyed our accomplishments, either. Once, I held a balance longer than I ever had, perching on pointe for several seconds. Maybe my pride showed on my face. The teacher looked at me. "People who can't dance love to balance," she said.

Dancers' pain, and their stoicism, are part of the spectacle. Tales of their offstage suffering are better known to the public than the components of good technique or the story of *Swan Lake*; the audience for TV shows like *Flesh and Bone* (whose protagonist, an ingénue at a New York ballet company, stabs herself with bobby pins, swallows glass, and beats herself with pointe shoes) and *Tiny Pretty Things* (which opens with an aspiring dancer pushing her teenaged rival off a roof) are exponentially bigger than the audience for live ballet.

Or take the movie *Black Swan*—which functioned, for many, as an introduction to ballet. While preparing for the film—in which she plays a lonely, bulimic ballerina whose quest for perfection mushrooms into full-on mania—Natalie Portman lost twenty pounds and dislocated a rib. By the time *Black Swan* came out in 2010, Portman had acted in twenty-nine films, starred on Broadway, and graduated from Harvard—but ballet, she said, "was more difficult than anything I've ever experienced before." Her costar, Mila Kunis, said the whole thing was "as close as I've ever come to just a complete mental breakdown." The movie is more interested in the masochism of ballet than in its beauty. The camera lingers over Portman's jutting bones, zooms in on her bloody feet. Her character starves, vomits, scratches her back until it bleeds, and denies herself any kind of pleasure—from sexual release to a bite of cake. Hollywood is a notoriously unforgiving environment for women. But—as Portman and Kunis so graphically explained—the movie business has nothing on ballet.

It is impossible to look at a dancer's body without thinking of the discipline and pain involved in shaping it—and that is part of the pleasure of looking. Even when we see images of dancers smiling onstage or leaping gleefully into the ocean on Instagram, we are aware of all the other dancers we have seen hurting and denying themselves on our screens. Susan Sontag observed in her 2003 essay *Regarding the Pain of Others* that our "appetite for pictures showing bodies in pain is as keen, almost, as the desire for ones that show bodies naked." Images of dancers in their skintight leotards offer both.

When I look at the picture of eleven-year-old Lily, kneeling in the second row of our class photo, I don't see the pain that has shaped her so much as I see the pain that is soon to come: the ankle that she will sprain the following year; the elbow that will break in five; the knee that will tear in ten. I see this pain haunting the future of a girl in a pale-pink leotard, crossing her arms in front of her chest in a gesture that might signify love, if her hands were a few inches closer to her heart, or death, if her elbows were a little bit straighter. But Lily doesn't know pantomime yet; she is still learning how to pas de bourrée. She has brown hair and brown eyes and tiny dark studs in her ears, and you probably wouldn't guess, from the photo, that she will eventually soar above most of the class: that she will survive the end-of-year culling again and again, until, at seventeen, she will be the only one left.

Lily was one of my closest friends, but after I gave up on ballet, our friendship faded. Maybe it had been based only on proximity, or maybe it couldn't survive such a divergence in our fates. While I was fretting over AP scores and college rankings, Lily was becoming more and more dedicated to ballet. The trek between Lincoln Center and her home in Astoria became a daily affair; in ninth grade, she left her local Catholic school in Queens for the Professional Performing Arts School in midtown.

It was around then that the injuries started. The first time she sprained her ankle, during a turning exercise in class, she felt like she might be in trouble. The teacher—an intense blond woman who seemed to be in a permanent state of having just downed several espressos—marched her down the hall to the front desk, dropped her off with the receptionist, and went back to class. Someone found Lily an ice pack and a boot and told her she would be fine. She could barely walk for weeks, let alone dance, but—in between physical therapy and Pilates—she was required to come to every class and sit on the floor, her foot in a cast, watching and worrying as her classmates pulled ahead. She felt like she was being punished—like she had done something wrong. She thought back to how, when we were eight or nine and sometimes lost our baby teeth in class, we were told to go rinse out our mouths and come right back to the studio. Our pain had never been met with any pity.

It's estimated that one in three professional dancers is forced into early retirement by injury. What is even more remarkable than the high rate of injury is how dancers deal with it: more than half, in one survey, said that they refused to rest. Their careers are so short, the competition so intense, that they will do anything to avoid losing time or looking weak. A student at the San Francisco Ballet School, who was secretly suffering from shin splints, explained to the writer Suzanne Gordon that if the director was teaching "and you can't jump because you're injured, you feel he's kind of disgusted, that he doesn't want to waste time with you." William Liebler, a doctor in New York, told Gordon how difficult it was to help his dancer patients. "Treating them is very hard because they get so worked up about taking time off or even taking medicine. If you want to give a girl with inflammation an anti-inflammatory drug, she doesn't want to take it because it will make her retain water. Or you tell a kid to take a pill three times a day with meals, and the kid says she doesn't eat three meals a day."

When Lily was thirteen, she received a devastating piece of news: her shins, according to a teacher who had known her since she was nine, were growing too long. Lily had little power over the development of her leg bones, but, she figured, at least she could control the flesh that covered them. By high school, she was tracking every calorie that crossed her lips and berating herself if the total passed one thousand. She left for school early so she would have time to look at "thinspo"—glamorous photos of anorexic women and advice on how to eat less—before her classmates arrived. At the end of the day, after ballet, she would take the train home to Astoria, lie to her parents that she had already had dinner, and retreat to her room for an extra, silent workout.

Hungry and weak, dancing for hours on little fuel, Lily was now hurting herself all the time: labral tears, stress fractures, herniated discs. She did her best to hide her injuries: she never forgot how invisible she felt when she and her first sprained ankle had been banished to that lonely chair at the front of the class.

But it was never enough. In her final year at the school, when her dream of joining the company seemed to be finally within reach, Lily was told to "tone up." One teacher suggested she add more Pilates to her routine—maybe the low-impact exercises would help her "lengthen." Lily knew what that meant: lose weight. She had given everything to ballet, and she wouldn't let her body hold her back now. She restricted her diet even more, and resigned herself to a life of feeling hungry and depleted all the time. When she brushed her teeth at night, she wondered if there were calories in toothpaste.

At seventeen, Lily's sacrifices looked poised, at last, to pay off: she was cast in a featured role in the workshop performance of Balanchine's *Valse Fantaisie*. (The graduation workshop is a crucial showcase for the students and an unofficial audition for the company.) For most of the ballet, Lily and three other girls were in constant motion, rising and falling, jumping and swirling like human confetti. Later, after the workshop, Lily learned that she was one of five in her class chosen for an apprenticeship with the New York City Ballet. It was the happiest day of her life. When I saw my old friend's picture above the *New York Times* workshop review, which praised the students for their "innocent" enthusiasm and "unfettered joy," I had no idea that she was secretly nursing a broken toe.

*   *   *

In 1995, a pair of British psychologists set out to explore how dancers experience pain. They invited fifty-three college students and fifty-two professional ballet dancers to their lab to take the "cold pressor test." First, each subject would submerge her hand in a bucket of comfortably lukewarm water and hold it there for two minutes. Then she would transfer it to a bucket of ice water and tell the experimenter when her hand started to hurt (indicating her pain threshold) and when it became unbearable (pain tolerance).

At both points, the dancers responded differently: they had a higher pain threshold as well as higher pain tolerance. The nondancer female college students complained after sixteen seconds, on average, and withdrew their hands after thirty-seven. The ballerinas, meanwhile, didn't admit they were in pain until forty-four seconds had passed, and kept their hands in the freezing water for a full ninety-five—more than twice as long as their nondancer peers.

Maybe, the researchers speculated, the dancers perceived pain differently; maybe they were somehow numb to it. But interviews revealed the opposite to be true: the dancers were actually more sensitive, consistently rating the pain as more intense. Ballet dancers are acutely in tune with their bodies, right down to the nerve receptors in their skin—but they are experts at pushing through.

If a masochistic streak might help ordinary women cope with pain, then imagine how useful such a streak would be for a dancer. It might even be a requirement. "In my experience, dancers tend to be masochists," Leigh Cowart writes. Cowart, a science reporter (who uses "they" pronouns), would know: they grew up studying ballet, moving away from home as a teenager to train at the North Carolina School of the Arts, and danced professionally in their early twenties. Now in their thirties, Cowart identifies as a "high-sensation seeking masochist": they often ask partners to hurt them in bed, and in their memoir recall episodes of sexual torture so gruesome I had to skim several pages. (Nonetheless, certain phrases jumped out: "wrought-iron stirrups," "industrial rubber bands," "I feel like I am dying.") They had always been intense. The first time they stood up on pointe, in the dusty back room of their local dance-wear shop, twelve-year-old Cowart almost passed out from the pain. But they refused to cushion their toes with the gel strips or lambswool that most dancers rely on, instead using only a square of single-ply toilet paper for padding. (My feet hurt just reading that.) Cowart's toenails turned purple and fell off, but they didn't care: dancing on pointe was the milestone that made them a ballerina—a member of this "very niche, very beautiful pain cult." Over the next decade, Cowart's body was battered by broken bones, torn ligaments, tendinitis, and an eating disorder; they suffered a spinal fracture and head trauma from being kicked under the chin onstage.

Cowart sees a clear link between their experiences in the ballet world and their adult appetite for pain—which they satisfy with activities ranging from the apparently erotic (being Saran-Wrapped to another person and hung from the ceiling) to the nonsexual (eating a pepper so spicy it causes hours of cold sweats and cramps). Perhaps, Cowart speculates, these pursuits are therapeutic, giving them a chance to relive the trauma of ballet, but this time in a position of control. Or maybe they're just wired to take pleasure in pain. "Did ballet make me a masochist?" they ask. "Or was I simply well suited to the grueling discipline of the art form because of something intrinsic to my core personality, the nebulous you-ness that becomes solid and nameable by kindergarten?" These are questions I've asked myself, too: when a man grabbed a fistful of my hair by the roots, triggering both a rush of blood and a vivid sense-memory of yanking my own hair into a bun.

And these are questions that I thought about as I read *The Surrender*, an erotic memoir by Toni Bentley, who made her name first as a dancer and then as a masochist.

Toni's relationship with ballet started off casually, when her mother—hoping the exercise would stimulate her tiny daughter's appetite—enrolled her in a weekly children's class in Bristol, England. But when the family relocated to New York in 1969 and her mother took her to try out for SAB—which she had heard about "at the laundromat or from a friend of a friend"—ballet became the guiding force in her life. The auditioners immediately recognized Toni's potential—her long limbs and preternatural flexibility—and they all gathered around as one lifted Toni's leg "to the front, the side, the back, higher and higher it went," she wrote in *Winter Season*, her first memoir. "The Russian eyebrows rose proportionately."

Toni started at SAB the very next day, and soon became obsessed with fitting into the "extremely competitive environment of beautiful young women." Her ambition grew as she climbed through the ranks—and so did her tolerance for pain. "Perhaps a certain tendency to masochism or at least the acceptance of both physical and emotional pain is a prerequisite for dancing," she suggests, echoing Cowart. In between ballet classes, she read "voraciously" about the lives of saints, and was so impressed by the stories of women starving, beating themselves with branches, and licking the open sores of lepers that she toyed with the idea of becoming a nun. But the stage was too seductive, and her potential too great. Willowy, dark-haired, and utterly devoted, she was a natural Balanchine dancer, and in her final year, she was cast as the lead in the graduation workshop performance of *The Sleeping Beauty*. It was the opportunity she had been working for since she was ten, and she made a promise to herself: if she could only get into the company, she would never ask for anything else, and would in fact be happy for the rest of her life.

For six months, Toni devoted herself to mastering the part of Princess Aurora. In one of her final rehearsals, with the performance just a week away, she launched herself into a pas de chat—a catlike leap, all knees and air—and felt herself slip on the way down. When Toni recalls this scene in *Winter Season*, she switches into the third person, as though—even after several years have passed—the emotions accompanying her fall are too intense to claim as her own. "She saw her performance, her Princess and her career disappear before her eyes," she wrote. "Her ankle turned black and blue and swelled. She sat for the last week of rehearsals in a chair, her foot packed in ice." But on the morning of the show, she pulled herself up and danced. Her stoicism paid off: the *New York Times* praised her delicacy and balance, and Balanchine offered her a place in the corps.

She was seventeen, and her upward trajectory seemed to

stretch out, limitless, in front of her. Right away, she was chosen to learn solo roles—"Big, grand ballerina things." But when she looked at the world-class dancers around her, she felt intimidated, unworthy, and she committed the gravest sin, in Balanchine's eyes: she held back. Her dancing, she realized later, was "too modest and fearful." But at the time, she didn't know why she stopped seeing her name alone, or why it started appearing with others. Still, her commitment to Balanchine, and her belief that he was right about everything, never wavered; New York City Ballet was the meaning of her life. Even as her career stalled, she took immense pride in being one of the seventy dancers in Balanchine's company; in representing her hero and sharing a stage with his stars.

Toni, who is an avid reader and lifelong journal-keeper, channeled some of her thwarted ambition into writing, publishing her first book when she was just twenty-two. *Winter Season: A Dancer's Journal* shows a young woman consumed with the daily grind—fighting for Balanchine's approval, analyzing the cast lists, maintaining her figure. "I went through years of neurotic eating when often each day began with the challenge to fast, to eat nothing," she confided. Although she had recovered, sort of—"I eat every day"—she still seemed to enjoy depriving herself. She limited the contents of her refrigerator to "diet soda, juice, skim milk, seltzer water, and cat food." Sometimes, when she was hungry, she took a perverted pleasure in skipping meals and feeding her cat instead.

Her main purpose in life was to please her ballet master. "Mr. Balanchine is our leader, our president, our mother, our father, our friend, our guide, our mentor, our destiny," she wrote, without a trace of irony. She describes how, when he entered the studio each morning, "his" dancers would automatically strip, peeling off the leg warmers and sweaters that kept them warm; how, at a meeting about the terms of their contracts, they shuffled toward him to sit, "childlike," at his feet. She asked Balanchine's permission before publishing *Winter Season* and, as soon as the galleys came in, dropped one off for him and waited anxiously for the "one review that really mattered." She recalls in a 2003 preface how she held her breath for a week, worrying what Balanchine would think of the book in which she says he "knows all, sees all, and controls all." (He liked it.)

Toni never stopped pushing herself, and by the time she was in her midtwenties, her body was beginning to fight back. The company was on a European tour in Tivoli when she suddenly found herself unable to lift her right leg, let alone dance. X-rays revealed that she had developed arthritis in her right hip and calcium deposits in her left, leaving the socket "looking craggy as Mount Rushmore when it should be smooth as Michelangelo marble."

Toni suffered through a "honey, it's all over" talk from the company doctor, then ignored his advice, dulled the pain with drugs, and clawed her way back. She eked out another year before her hips gave out for good, forcing her to turn "from the stage to the page." She published essays and reviews in *Rolling Stone* and the *New York Times*, wrote a coffee table book about the costume designer Karinska, and helped her idol, Suzanne Farrell, write her memoir. But her breakout didn't come until twenty years after she retired from professional ballet. In 2004, Toni released *The Surrender*, which lays out, in diaristic detail, her passion for anal sex. Years before *Fifty Shades of Grey* became an international phenomenon, *The Surrender* was a bestseller in four countries, landing on *Playboy*'s list of "sexiest memoirs of all time" and inspiring an off-Broadway play—as well as a feminist campaign against the author. "I got a lot of hate mail," Toni said at a conference called THiNK 2013. "One of them said I'd set back feminism a hundred years." The book's cover—a close-up of a woman's lace-fringed lavender panties—was too provocative for Barnes & Noble; the publisher compromised by adding a black jacket with a keyhole cutout.

If most women are squeamish about admitting their masochistic fantasies—if they hide *Fifty Shades of Grey* on their Kindle—dancers have more license to indulge their masochistic side publicly. "The Act"—as Toni calls it—represents, to her, submission, surrender, "an emotional and anatomical miracle." She writes rapturously of how her first experience of anal sex gave her "a profound sensation of freedom," even though—or perhaps because—it hurt. She carefully documented each subsequent tryst, luxuriating in the memories of her pain: "He was pushing into the fist in my gut and rolfing me from the inside," she wrote. "It hurt like hell but I didn't say a word. I just maintained the pain level just past bearable . . ." She reflects on how her decades in ballet prepared her—physically and emotionally—for this relationship. "I learned early how to transcend pain, deny pain," she wrote. "Learning to go past—way past—one's physical comfort level, and to love that moment of going past, is intrinsic to a dancer's training." And her submissive, all-consuming relationship with her lover—to whom she gives the moniker "A-Man"—echoed her relationship with Balanchine. "Dancing is about being in service to the choreographer, to the steps, to the music," she wrote. "Allowing this man into my ass reproduces this dynamic of service, of yielding to something greater than myself."

Toni became so obsessed with A-Man that she would dig his used condoms out of her wastebasket and display them as "a trophy" until his next visit. Throughout her life, Toni hoarded the detritus of her painful exploits—her anal adventures, her dancing, her hip surgery—the better to remember them by. When, twenty years after the injury that ended her career, she finally scheduled a hip replacement, she told her doctor she wanted to keep the bone, then asked a taxidermist how to preserve it. (The recipe he gave her—which involved soaking the bone and boiling it on her stove—reminded her of making chicken broth. "I drained the pot into a colander observing, I'm proud to report, very little fat on the surface of the liquid," she wrote in the *New York Review of Books*. "Less than with a chicken.") She stashed the dried and bleached hip bone in a wooden box painted with delicate flowers, next to the last pair of pointe shoes she ever wore onstage—"my fetishistic ally, my crown of thorns, my bed of nails."

✳   ✳   ✳

"Crown of thorns," "bed of nails": pointe shoes. There is no better symbol of the pain endured by female dancers. Lily strapped her broken toe into her pointe shoe and tried to ignore the ache: there was no time to rest. She had pushed through workshop with a stress fracture, and she had been rewarded with the chance of a lifetime—to dance three seasons with the corps, in a year-long audition for a full-time job. Just five years after Lily and I had stood in the wings in our soldiers' costumes, ogling the beautiful women warming up at the barre, she was one of them, dancing through the blue-gray snowstorm in *The Nutcracker*'s first act and the garden of enchanted flowers in Act II. I didn't know, as I lustily clicked through Lily's Facebook from my college dorm (that fuchsia tutu! that multitiered tiara!), that her ability to bask in the fulfillment of her childhood dream—*our* childhood dream—was hampered, somewhat, by the excruciating pain she had to conceal. I didn't know that she danced eight *Nutcracker*s a week on a broken foot, or that when—sick and vomiting with a 104-degree fever—she confessed at intermission that she might not be able to finish the show, an older dancer pulled her into a dressing room and offered her cocaine.

Lily's body, by this point, had been worn down not only by her grueling schedule—she often left the theater after eleven at night, only to return by ten the next morning—but by years of starvation: she fueled her dancing with fewer calories than a sedentary woman would burn. A few months into her apprenticeship, Lily reached a breaking point and ate a burger. She felt a surge of energy, and then of hope: maybe she wouldn't have to live this way. She gained five pounds, bringing her weight slightly above the anorexic range, and even got her period. But after a couple of months of more normal eating, Lily was called in to the ballet mistress's dark, cramped office. "You're getting a bit round," she told Lily, while Peter Martins nodded. Lily listened meekly and promised to do better. Afterward, she tried to make light of it. "I'm too fat, baby!" she told her boyfriend—a fellow dancer—when he asked her how the meeting had gone. That night, hungry and weeping in his arms, she bit his shoulder and pretended it was a burger. Over the next months, she starved herself back to her old, bony figure. She grew so malnourished that she passed out on the subway and woke to find a stranger spoon-feeding her grapefruit.

Once, an apprenticeship was practically a guarantee of a job. But in 2011, the New York City Ballet was facing a deficit. A dozen dancers had been let go, and the survivors faced a salary freeze and a reduction in sick leave. When it was time for Lily to find out whether she would be invited into the company, she and two other women were instead asked to spend another year apprenticing. (The two male apprentices, meanwhile, were offered full-time jobs on schedule.) Six months into her second year—her second year of treating every day like a trial; of acting like a company member but feeling second-class—Lily learned that she would not be joining the corps after all. She cried as Peter told her that he could not afford to keep her. "I was contemplating death when I heard those words," she wrote on her blog. In an instant, the dream that she had been chasing for over a decade evaporated. "All I've ever wanted was to dance in this company . . . I feel lost, like my identity has been stripped from me." She still had six months left in her apprentice contract: she would have to keep working for the boss who had fired her—as if she'd been dumped and had to keep living with her ex. Every day, she stood at the barre next to the men and women who had what she wanted, who were living the life that should have been hers. In between rehearsals, she looked up auditions and networked with directors, traveling to tryouts on her rare days off. Still, she couldn't help but hope that Peter might reconsider: maybe, if she worked even harder, he would realize he'd made a mistake. *This show is gonna change their minds!* she thought, as she threw herself into *Tchaikovsky Suite No. 3.*

At the end of the performance, Lily curtsied and ran offstage. The heavy, gold-fringed curtains went down. She took the elevator to the dressing room and unzipped the turquoise bodice of her costume. She waited for something to happen, but nothing did. She gathered up her makeup and hairpins, stuffed them into her bag, and walked out the stage door for the last time, into the chilly New York City night. Lily had grown up at Lincoln Center; she had thought of the place as her home. Now she felt like a commodity that had been used up and spit out. *That's it*, she thought. She was twenty-one, and she felt like her life was over.

It is easy to see a dancer's acceptance of pain as resignation— as a concession to a toxic culture. And it may be a symptom or a side effect of living and working in a system that endorses self-destruction. But the ability to endure—to tolerate enormous pain and keep going—can also be called resilience. That is the word that kept coming into my mind as I read about how Toni Bentley had reinvented herself as a writer; and as Lily told me how her life had unfolded in the years since she had posted those enviable *Nutcracker* shots on Facebook.

"Perhaps I can show the world that one defeat doesn't mean the end," Lily wrote on her blog, just days after learning that her lifelong dream had been crushed. "I am going to keep going. I am going to find a new job." As much as SAB and NYCB could be cutthroat, they had also been something of a cocoon: now she was out on her own, one of thousands of young dancers fighting for a few jobs. She booked auditions in Boston and Philadelphia, and sweated on the Bolt Bus up and down the East Coast. She celebrated the small wins: booking a modeling job with Discount Dance Supply and a guest artist gig in Canada; feeling happy for a day. She refused to wallow, even in the very recent past. "I am trying to focus on the future instead of dwelling on what was," she wrote.

The next phase of Lily's career was a hustle of hard work and false starts, punctuated by interludes of stability: a season or two with a troupe in New York; eight months here, with a body-positive startup in Portland; two years there, with a classical company in Antwerp. Ballet was the only constant as she started over again and again, in a new city, a new culture, a new language. When her work took her to Oregon, she got into nature and wellness, spending her weekends hiking and rock-climbing and hanging from silk scarves in an aerial yoga class. The new troupe she'd joined fell apart—the founder mysteriously disappeared; rumor had it that she'd changed her name and fled the country—so Lily decided to try her luck abroad. A friend lent her money for a plane ticket to Europe. *This is my life*, she said to herself, when she landed a job in the corps of the Royal Ballet of Flanders. *I'm Belgian and here I am, dancing.* She found herself a Belgian boyfriend and started learning Dutch. She could adapt to almost anything. In between jobs, she worked as a personal trainer and a Pilates instructor; she studied web design and learned to code.

Through it all, Lily was haunted by injuries: by the old ones that had never quite healed, and by the ever-present threat of another slip or tear. She had never lost the habit of pushing her body past its limits, of punishing herself for taking up space, for eating at all. In March 2016, Ballet Flanders staged *The Sleeping Beauty*—a grueling, all-hands-on-deck production, in which Lily danced five different roles. When she left the theater at the end of the run, which fell on a Sunday, her body was screaming for a break—but she forced herself back the next morning, for the optional Monday class.

Lily has a habit of twirling her wrists when she talks about her worst traumas, her voice rising and falling in a singsong rhythm. Her hands were spinning as she told me what happened next.

Lily fought her way through the barre, and then through adagio in the center. She was tired, but the class was almost over, and she thought she had gotten away with it again. And then, in the grande allegro—the final set of exercises—she launched herself into a sissonne.

We were children when we learned how to do a sissonne: how to slice the air like we had scissors for legs, sharp and clean, and come down neatly on one foot. A versatile jump, it could be a quick transitional step or it could be the centerpiece of a combination. Lily was twenty-five, and she had done thousands and thousands of sissonnes in her life. But that Monday in Antwerp, she was midair—legs taut, feet pointed as usual—and then she was on the floor. After almost twenty years of abuse, her muscles had finally rebelled. She had torn her ACL, her MCL, her meniscus—her entire left knee.

Through long months of rehab, surgery, and recovery, Lily did her best to stay upbeat. "Ballerina down for the count!" she wrote on Instagram, beneath a photo of her swollen knee, adding: "#sendhelp #andwine." A week after leaving the hospital, she posted a grinning selfie with her physical therapist and the caption "#kneepocalypse." She drew a smiley face on the sticky cotton tape that her doctor wound around her knee, holding her ligaments together. She posted a video of herself pedaling on a stationary bicycle at a glacial pace, with the cheery all-caps comment, "BABY STEPS!"

After spending six months working to rebuild her strength, Lily decided she was ready to go back to class. It was a catastrophic miscalculation. She had been back at work only a few weeks when it happened again: her left knee—the same knee that she had just spent half a year slowly healing—tore once more. She lay on the floor and watched those long, painful months of surgery and physical therapy and hard work go up in smoke. She didn't think she could do it all over again. "I'm kind of sick of being injured and hungry and fucked up all the time," she realized. It was time to reinvent herself again.

They Make You Feel Like an Hourglass

I'm in the third division at the School of American Ballet. My classmates and I are holding our hands in the telltale training position that, we have been told, Mr. B designed specially for the youngest dancers: we form an awkward circle with our index finger and thumb, our pinkies sticking out like lonely soldiers, and imagine that we are holding a rubber ball in our palms. (We would have to study for years before earning the privilege to separate our fingers into the graceful configuration the grown-up dancers used.) My leotard is that distinctive shade of Girls III pale pink, so translucent it could only be appropriate for girls of nine or ten. But in my dream, I am not nine or ten: I am twenty-one. I have been given a second chance, and I am determined not to squander it. I start to make calculations, as best as I can in the dream-state: if all goes well, I'll be twenty-three when I finish the children's division, twenty-eight when I'm ready to join the corps . . . So my career will last only a few years, but that's okay, it's something . . . And then the dream becomes a nightmare: I remember that I am already twenty-nine.

Timelines, deadlines, heart rate rising as I count the years closing in. I had been practicing this panicky math for so many years, it's no wonder I was able to do it in my sleep. As children, we were in an enormous hurry. If we were supposed to be company-ready by sixteen or seventeen, then every month mattered. (Even this was a relatively lenient timeline: Balanchine's earliest muses—his Russian "baby ballerinas"—had been discovered when they were only twelve.) While our peers in regular school slowly laid the foundations for a lifetime of work, looked ahead languidly to a future far away, we were mired in a constant state of panic. With so many milestones to hit—double pirouettes, triples, fouetté turns; summer programs attended, variations learned—it was easy to fall behind. And we already understood that a ballerina's career was cruelly brief: that even if we were among the very few who got jobs, we would be lucky to keep them until we were thirty. "They make you feel like an hourglass," Meiying said. "Time's running out!"

The casting directors preferred kids who looked young, so we yearned to stay as short and childlike as possible. I remember my brother, who didn't dance, waking up in the morning and running to the kitchen to stand against the measuring chart on the wall, eager to see if he had grown overnight. But I couldn't relate: I hated seeing those marks climb higher. (When Suzanne Farrell heard that growth takes place at night, she recalled in *Holding On to the Air*, she resolved to sleep curled up in a ball.) These are the conditions in which children feel like they are already over the hill. In which a seventeen-year-old SAB student interviewed by Suzanne Gordon saw herself as "a faded ingénue." (Men in ballet operate on a more relaxed timeline; they might start at the leisurely age of ten or eleven, joining a class of girls who have already been toiling away for several years, and their careers often last longer—whether because their feet aren't pummeled by pointe work, or because they are spared some of the grueling corps work, or because—with more job security—they can take time off to heal.)

Ballet is an ephemeral art. "Because it has no text, ballet dies every day, to be reborn as the next ballet," the critic Joan Acocella wrote in the *New York Review of Books* in 1994. Choreography is fragile and forgettable—stored in the bodies of repetiteurs, passed down in a delicate lineage of fallible dancers. Musical scores can be transcribed; books can be reprinted. But a dance performance is a living thing, involving countless accidents and improvisations, mistakes and spur-of-the-moment decisions. Its essence cannot be captured on camera or conveyed in writing. Many of the nineteenth-century masterpieces have been lost; before the advent of video cameras, choreographers relied on an imprecise system of "dance notation" to preserve their work, reducing complex movements to crude squiggles and arrows that, to the uninitiated, are as indecipherable as ancient hieroglyphs. Even film provides an imperfect record: it saps the energy from a performance, risks turning one dancer's quirks into doctrine. Suzanne Farrell hated seeing videos of herself dancing, and dreaded the idea that future generations might take them as an accurate representation of how she moved. "Any excitement of the moment was lost in the editing and splicing," she wrote. "I have often felt that if the choice were mine I would keep all filmed footage of my dancing under lock and key."

"There is no future; it is the present forever," Balanchine liked to say. Even toward the end of his life, he was reluctant to discuss his legacy, appoint a successor, or plan for his company's future.

The accoutrements of ballet, too, are fragile. If pointe shoes were a species, they would go extinct: their growth is too costly, their maturity too brief. The hours of work it takes for craftsmen to hand-make a pair of pointe shoes—plus the further hours the dancer spends sewing on the ribbons and

breaking them in—culminate in an hour or two of wear before they are, in dancer lingo, "dead."

Dancers receive flowers, perform with flowers, adorn their
hair with flowers—the universal symbol of fleeting beauty.
During *The Nutcracker*, our parents left so many bouquets
by the stage door that the vestibule looked like a florist's
shop. (The star dancers—but only the women—received their
bouquets onstage.) In some of the most beloved scenes in the
canon—from *The Nutcracker*'s Waltz of the Flowers to *Sleeping Beauty*'s Lilac Fairy—dancers impersonate or dance with
flowers. In the famous "Rose Adagio," Aurora accepts a long-
stemmed rose from each of her four suitors; in the "Garland
Waltz," villagers hold wreaths of flowers above their heads.
Ballet "is a woman, a garden of beautiful flowers, and man is
the gardener," Balanchine told *Life* magazine in 1965. When
pressed to expound on what his ballets "meant," he invoked
the same metaphor. "Dancers are just flowers, and flowers
grow without any literal meaning, they are just beautiful."

And, of course, ballet's primary instruments—women's bodies—
are in constant flux. As hard as we tried to stay physically
immature—breast-less, hip-less, premenstrual—we couldn't
fight time. Our bodies were always growing and shrinking,
tearing and breaking, getting older.

Perhaps this is why we infantilized ourselves: why we
clung too long to the accessories of girlhood. Why we pinned
ribbons and plastic pearls in our hair, and why my purple
dance bag had glitter on it when I was fourteen. Why Natalie
Portman's *Black Swan* character—a professional in her late
twenties—sleeps in a bedroom that would appeal to a six-

year-old (and to which it is impossible to imagine she has ever brought home a date), with stuffed animals on the bed and a tinkling music box on the nightstand. Some dancers take pride in their ignorance, play up the ditzy routine. In the same memoir in which she grapples with Nietzsche and Proust, Toni Bentley writes—performatively, I assume—"I really think we are the most ignorant paid people on earth." Her salary is barely enough to cover basic expenses, but keeping track of it or drawing up a budget would be too hard. After all, "Money is only to pay for the apartment, to buy a fur coat and ballet clothes." One renowned dancer wrote in her memoir that she sometimes needs to look in a dictionary to find out whether *New York Times* reviews of her performances were critical or not. (Until she looked up the definition, she wasn't sure if being called "saccharine" was a compliment.)

Perhaps this is why Balanchine's dancers felt comfortable in a prolonged state of financial dependence, subject to the whims of Daddy's largesse. One NYCB dancer bragged to Suzanne Gordon about her boss's generosity: one freezing winter day, she reported, Mr. B ran into one of his dancers trekking through the snow in wet, flimsy shoes. He asked her why she was so underdressed, and when she explained that she couldn't afford boots, he pulled seventy dollars out of his pocket and sent her to the shoe store. It did not, apparently, occur to the dancer that a more generous boss might try to make sure his employees could buy their own boots. Poverty, Balanchine once said, gave their dancing an edge. "Once girls get money and they can buy things, they tend to relax," one dancer remembered Balanchine telling a class of students. "The apprentices don't have money yet . . . so they have this drive. But the girls with money . . . they lost it." Attitudes have changed since Suzanne Gordon wrote, in 1983, "No one seems to feel that female dancers need to worry about making a living. When their demanding career is over, they are expected to find financial security in a husband." But even today, dancers are often unable to achieve financial independence, the hallmark of adulthood. The median salary for professional ballet dancers in the United States, in 2018, was just $30,000; even dancers in major companies often live with their parents or multiple roommates. In her first year as a professional dancer, Rachel survived in a major US city on $425 a week. She saved money by biking miles back and forth between the theater and the tiny apartment she shared with another dancer.

The circumstances of her life—a low salary and a strict routine—can stunt a dancer's emotional growth. But sometimes there's another person invested in keeping a dancer in her bubble. A stock figure in ballet media and movies—from the diabolical mother in *Black Swan*, who forbids her adult daughter from leaving the house and portions out her grapefruit for breakfast, to the catty mom in *Center Stage*, who works as a receptionist at Maureen's ballet school and snickers when she catches her daughter's rival eating pizza—the ballet mother, a subset of stage mom, is pushy, striving, ambitious; overinvolved in her daughter's life and overinvested in her career. Perhaps she herself once aspired to dance; perhaps she regrets the career she never had. (The mothers of *Center Stage* and *Black Swan* were thwarted by flat feet and pregnancy, respectively.) She knows where to shop for custom leotards and where to find the best private coaches. She organizes her life around her daughter's training. She might drive her daughter hours to and from class. She might leave her husband, and even her other children—she might say that this is temporary—to take her daughter to the best ballet school in London or San Francisco or New York.

The ballet mom may be a caricature, but she has some basis in real life. I remember the mothers who were always around, touching up their daughters' makeup, hovering in the hallways during class, peeping through the door if they could. Monitoring and criticizing, offering unsolicited corrections. Once, Emily and a group of friends were stretching and complaining about their bodies, as they often did on breaks. When one particularly emaciated girl piped up, a friend consoled her: "You're so skinny!" But the emaciated girl's mother overheard and scolded her daughter's friend: "Don't tell her that!"

Not so long ago, I interviewed a dancer who was my age exactly. This woman—a talented, experienced performer—shared a small apartment with her mother, who chaperoned her to our meeting. When I sent a message to the twenty-nine-year-old dancer's personal email address, I sometimes received a response from the mom instead.

These anecdotes are tame compared to the stories on the mothers-of-dancers message boards online. In these cesspits of parental anxiety, self-identified ballet moms air their fears about their children's futures, debate the relative prestige of different summer intensives, and compare notes on the best home ballet barres and cross-training programs (gymnastics? swimming? tap?). They offer nervous advice on threads like "Late bloomer at 11, what are her chances" and "By what age does she need to commit?" ("She," a fifth grader, is torn between a career in ballet and jazz.) The mothers often use a revealing pronoun when they talk about their daughters' activities: "We do Pilates twice a week"; "We are still pretty new to ballet"; "We weren't in the *Nutcracker* this year."

In language that wouldn't be out of place on horse-breeding forums, they fret over their children's changing bodies. "My daughter seems to be developing rather more quickly than I expected!" writes one worried mom. "We are both pretty skinny so I didn't expect this!" "My daughter has grown quite a bit, her breasts are bigger than her older sister's," writes another. "Won't this stymie her chances?" asks the mother of a Royal Ballet School hopeful who has recently started "developing." Another parent asks her to clarify: "Are we talking breast buds or more than that?"

In one of the most active threads, "Help! DD [darling daughter] is quitting dance for good," a desperate mother admits that her daughter's decision has threatened her own identity. "No more ballet slippers or pointes to sew, no more classes to watch," writes the mother—whose sixteen-year-old daughter had, in the previous year alone, endured tendinitis in her hip flexors and verbal abuse from her teacher, and had sought help from chiropractors, osteopaths, acupuncturists, and a psychologist—"I am in shock." She had unfollowed the ballet-themed Facebook and Twitter accounts that populated her newsfeed. She could no longer listen to piano music without crying. "You are not alone," wrote another mother—who had been in mourning ever since her own daughter quit. "I go in my sewing room and look at the tutus and costumes and pretty much grieve."

This mountain of maternal effort sometimes pays off: many of the most celebrated dance careers were pushed along by grade A ballet moms. Margot Fonteyn was only four, and still known as Peggy, when her mom, Hilda Hookham, took her to a local dance class in Shanghai. By the time Peggy was a teenager, Hilda was ferrying her all over the world in search of the best training. She left her husband in Shanghai—he eventually divorced her—and dropped off her son, Peggy's brother, at boarding school. "To me he was like somebody else's son for whom I was responsible," Mrs. Hookham wrote in an essay, "Recollections of a Dancer's Mother," which Margot included in her 1979 guidebook *A Dancer's World*. She escorted Margot to Paris, to study with famous Russian émigrés, and to London, to audition for Ninette de Valois's new ballet school. "It was Mrs. Hookham, you see, who was really interested," one of Margot's early coaches later said. She monitored Margot's progress and even her choice of friends. "We both learned together," Mrs. Hookham wrote, "so that I also knew what each movement should be." After class, she quizzed her daughter: "What is a plié?" "What is a grand battement?" She watched Margot's recitals from the wings and whispered corrections while she danced, reminding her to tuck her tongue in or to smile. Later, when Margot went on tour with the Royal Ballet, Mrs. Hookham found excuses to travel with her, carving out a place for herself as the company's unofficial costume mistress and all-around helper, running errands and sewing seams. It was not until she was a twenty-six-year-old star with a thriving career and a string of lovers that Margot would finally move out of Hilda's home.

"Mother was not a typical stage mother," Suzanne Farrell writes, generously, in her memoir. It was true that Donna did not stand in the doorway to watch class, or comment on Suzanne's technical flaws. She did, however, clean her daughter's ballet teacher's house in exchange for free lessons and relocate the family from Cincinnati to New York so that Suzanne could audition for SAB. (I find the story of the move somewhat inspiring, like one of those memes about "white man confidence":

a scout from SAB visited Suzanne's class and declined to offer her a scholarship, but suggested that—if she happened to find herself in New York—she might seek a second opinion in person. On the basis of that casual invitation, Donna sold all the family's furniture, packed a hot plate and an ironing board, and drove her daughters to New York.) Later, Donna forbade the teenaged Suzanne from seeing her age-appropriate boyfriend—better to stay open to Balanchine's advances.

Raising a dancer involves such a commitment that even a well-balanced parent may become excessively invested in her daughter's career and feel personally let down if she changes her mind. (A 2015 analysis by FiveThirtyEight estimated the cost of a ballet dancer's training—including fifteen years of class tuition, summer programs, pointe shoes, leotards, and tights—at over a hundred thousand dollars.) But I wonder how many ballet moms are foisting their own unsatisfied dreams onto the next generation. I see on Facebook a girl I knew at a midtier summer intensive—now in her thirties—posting old photos of herself dancing and new photos of her three-year-old daughter in a tutu. Before her daughter's recent dance recital, she posted a request: "Need a recommendation for lipstick for a 3-year-old!" I wonder how many are like a Canadian twentysomething named Piper, who had been turned down twice by an elite school and—when interviewed by the psychologist Tricia Sandham—said that she looked forward to one day having daughters and becoming a "dance mom."

For as long as she could remember, Tricia Sandham dreamed of becoming a ballerina. By the time she was a teenager, she had made significant progress toward her goal: she had performed in Alberta Ballet's *Nutcracker*, placed in dance competitions, and, at fifteen, attended the top summer intensive in Canada. When, at the end of the program, she was not offered a year-round place at the school, she felt the first flicker of a doubt about her future. But she pushed it away, continuing to train with single-minded focus, until, at eighteen, she conceded that her dream would not come true.

She drifted, defeated, from dead-end job to dead-end job until, at twenty-four, she discovered a passion for psychology. She finished college and started graduate school and felt lucky to have a new outlet for her ambition. But even as she approached the end of her master's degree at the University of Saskatchewan, ballet was never far from her mind. As part of her dissertation in 2012, she decided to interview other once-elite ballet students who had failed to achieve their dream.

Much had been written on how retiring professional dancers cope with the loss of their career, but the more common experience of adolescent failure had never been formally studied. How, Sandham wondered, had other girls coped with their heartbreak? Years later, had they succeeded in forging a new identity and finding new goals? And was there any room for ballet in their adult lives?

Sandham spent months interviewing her subjects—all women, mostly in their twenties—who had made it at least as far as professional ballet-school auditions. Although it had been years, and in one case decades, since they had resigned themselves to careers outside of dance, the women, like Sandham, still harbored deep attachments to ballet. Megan, who had just completed her first year of college, still took classes at a local studio, and was willing to live off canned pasta so she could afford to continue. Another woman brought two pairs of old pointe shoes—the first and last she ever wore—to one of her meetings with Sandham, and said that she would die if she ever lost them. Sam, a college student in her early twenties, taught ballet to children, and said it was the highlight of her week. She often told her students that she wanted to be them.

Sandham probed the women on why they had loved ballet— they cited friendships, tutus, and "beautiful and shiny" pointe shoes—and how they had coped with leaving it behind. One girl said she felt "useless" after quitting; another fell into a depression. When they tried to join the "real world," they felt like imposters. "I remember walking into college and feeling really really nervous because I wasn't a normal person, I was a ballerina," one woman said.

Some tried to deny their love for ballet. One retrained as a secretary and for years told no one, not even her husband, about her past. "The ballet world just didn't exist for me anymore," she said. Ella, who quit due to injuries, let her ballet friendships lapse, and struggled to connect with anyone else. "I think I lost a few years," she said. Without ballet, she didn't know who she was or what she might be interested in.

Others maintained a steady involvement in dance. After failing her end-of-year exam, Piper simply downgraded ballet from career aspiration to hobby, continuing to study and teach. And although twentysomething Megan was well past the age at which her old peers had turned pro, she still clung to her dream of becoming a dancer. She regretted giving up at seventeen and hoped to start training again. "I have to figure out a way to get back into it," she said.

The dancers' narratives of adjusting to the real world reminded Sandham of the framework for grieving set forth by the psychologist J. William Worden. Worden identified four "tasks" for the mourner to complete: she must accept the reality of the loss (or, in this case, recognize that her dream is not realistic); deal with the pain; adjust to an altered world (go to college, find a career, make new friends); and finally, as she embarks on a new life, find an enduring connection to the lost love (teaching, taking classes, going to the ballet).

For years, I was stuck on the first task. In 2004, I was expelled from SAB. Some of the most qualified teachers in the country, who had monitored my progress for years, had assessed me as without a future—but I refused to believe their verdict. I could not accept the reality of the loss. I told myself that they had made a mistake, and found a spot at a less prestigious academy. On my first day, I looked around at my new classmates, with their flat feet and their indifference, their messy buns and their barely concealed chatting during class, and wondered how I had fallen so far. When I was ignored there, too, I had to wonder if my SAB teachers hadn't been onto something. Still, at every juncture—meeting a new teacher, auditioning for a new summer program—I drummed up a flicker of hope. After all, even Margot Fonteyn hadn't been born with perfect feet; they had once been so flat that Frederick Ashton compared them to pats of butter. Maybe I had improved. Maybe this leotard made my legs look longer. Maybe I would be chosen.

Time after time, I wasn't. Eventually, the sting of accumulated rejections overtook the glimmers of hope. "I look at the girls in the class and I know I will never look like them and I wonder why I am wasting my time," I wrote in my diary, after a particularly dismal audition. "In the center, when I can fly and turn en pointe—that's when I love ballet, and I remember why I dance. But these moments, they are more and more rare." I passed the time in class by scheming to sneak a glance at the clock without getting caught: maybe when I tilted my head in tendu devant . . . but the momentary thrill of pulling this off was swiftly followed by disappointment: only a few minutes had elapsed since the last time I had done this. One winter, I stopped going to class.

I was fifteen the first time I skipped ballet. I puttered around after school, feeling like a truant or a criminal, wondering what I was supposed to do with this strange pocket of free time. I took the Degas poster off my wall and did my best not to think about ballet. *Maybe I'll discover talents I've never known*, I thought on good days. *Maybe I'm an athlete—a jock!* At ballet, I had been cautioned not to go for runs—my legs might get comfortable in the turned-in position—so, in an act of rebellion, I signed up for cross country. But I fell behind on long runs, ended up lost among the tourists in Central Park. I couldn't keep up, and I didn't really care. I quit after a few weeks. In the spring, I joined the track team, mostly because they took walk-ons, and decided my event would be the hurdles. Clearing a hurdle is a little like doing a grand jeté, I thought. (Only if you're doing it very badly, I learned.) I liked my weekly flute lesson, but sometimes I learned melodies I recognized from ballet—Bizet or Delibes—and I felt disoriented, like I had gotten lost in the wrong body. But I was no longer a dancer, I told myself. Ballet had nothing to do with me.

Of course, this attitude didn't last. My feelings toward ballet, in the following years, veered between longing and regret and feminist disdain. I would take open classes for a week, then swear them off forever. I would avoid the subject with a new friend, then decide that it was the most important thing for her to know about me.

My departure from the dance world may have alleviated some of the pressure around the passage of time—but I was still a girl. In high school, I studied the novels of Jane Austen and Edith Wharton, and saw the twentysomething protagonists worry about spinsterhood. My friends and I watched and rewatched *When Harry Met Sally*, and heard Sally, who was thirty-two, weep at the prospect of turning forty alone—the terrifying number "just sitting there, like some big dead end!" We read Nora Ephron, and learned that we had only until the age of thirty-four to enjoy wearing bikinis, and then another nine years to show our necks in public; after forty-three, we would have to wrap them up in turtlenecks and scarves. We started using "preventative" aging products in our early twenties; I don't think I've gone outside without sunscreen since college.

Not so long ago, a woman at a party—an acquaintance I'd met once or twice—overheard me mention my upcoming thirtieth birthday, crossed the room, and encouraged me to freeze my eggs. But I'd been hearing warnings about wasting my fertile years since practically before I got my first period. In the 2008 touchstone *Atlantic* piece "Marry Him! The Case for Settling for Mr. Good Enough," Lori Gottlieb, a forty-year-old single mom, offered herself up as a cautionary tale: if young women didn't want to end up overburdened and alone, like her, we should pick a subpar husband in our late twenties, while we still could. (A friend confided that she read the article at twenty-four and was so haunted by it that she committed to the next guy who came along.)

I may have had a head start at practicing the math of being a woman, but my peers in the real world have caught up. I had dinner recently with a friend who finds herself, to her surprise, single at thirty-one; growing up, she always thought she would be married by thirty. Now, whenever she matches with a promising guy on Hinge, numbers start running through her head. *The earliest I can be engaged,* she thinks, *is thirty-two. The earliest I can be married is thirty-three. The earliest I can have a baby is thirty-four. So if I meet a man tomorrow,* she thinks, *I might just skirt the "geriatric" medical label given to mothers who are thirty-five.*

At a party a few months ago, it came up that I had written a book about dreams, and a woman told me that she suffered from insomnia. She was thirty-three, she explained, and she was single. She kept herself awake at night doing math. She wanted her parents to know her future children, and she thought about how many years they might have left. That number was an anchor for the fevered calculations that came next: How many years until it was too late to have kids? How many until it was too late to find a partner?

My peers in ballet are approaching the age of retirement. My old classmate Beatriz Stix-Brunell left the Royal Ballet last year, at the age of twenty-eight. She had been dancing professionally since she was fourteen but "there are so many parts of me that I haven't discovered yet," she told the *Guardian.* Emily, too, has been working for most of her life: she got her first paycheck from the New York City Ballet at age eight, and her first full-time job at eighteen. When, at twenty-nine, she anticipated her next birthday, she thought: *Oh my God, my career is over.*

Some point to institutions like the National Book Foundation's "5 Under 35" list of "young" writers and complain that the literary world fetishizes youth. But to me, these lists demonstrate the opposite: I can still be young at thirty-four? How lenient are the standards of the literary world!

I turned thirty this year, and when I apply for residencies and grants, I don't hesitate to check the "emerging writer" box. I can reasonably hope that my professional peak is still years away. If I feel anxious about how my career is progressing, I can look at lists of beloved writers who debuted in middle age—from Helen DeWitt, whose first novel came out when she was forty-four, to Laura Ingalls Wilder, who found success only in her sixties. I can read about how Rachel Cusk—a terse, experimental writer lauded for reinventing plot—debuted thirty years ago with a novel so conventional it drew comparisons to *Bridget Jones's Diary*. I can browse *Bloom*, an online literary magazine that covers only writers over forty. I can read masterpieces written by Joan Didion, Vivian Gornick, and Janet Malcolm when they were in their seventies and eighties. Nor do physical limitations spell professional decline. The paralyzed scientist Stephen Hawking wrote several books letter by letter, blinking at a computer, raising his eyebrows or flexing a muscle in his cheek to indicate each character. The only real deadline, in my current career, is death.

In the summer of 2018, as I prepared for the release of my first book, *Why We Dream*, I set up a public email account and posted it on my website. Most of the messages I got were from readers requesting analysis of their dreams or old men who wanted me to know that they had read Freud in college. But one Sunday in November, an email caught my eye.

"Hello!!! from an old friend . . ." read the subject line. "Dear Alice," it began, formally, and continued, ludicrously, "I hope you remember me . . ."

Meiying and I lost touch after I left SAB. She wasn't on Facebook, and we had no mutual friends. Over the years, she occasionally appeared in my dreams, from which I woke with a hazy feeling of inadequacy.

I read her email as fast as I could, my eyes flitting around the screen, trying to take in all the text at once. She had seen a review of my book, she said, and she was happy to see my name again after all these years. She reminisced about trick-or-treating together and promised to come to my book launch the following week. "Sending you lots of love and congratulations," she signed off.

One afternoon, about a month later, we arranged to meet in a coffee shop near Union Square. When I walked in, a few minutes late, she ran to the door and we hugged like long-lost sisters. I noticed immediately that we had dressed and styled our hair almost identically, with bangs and small hoop earrings and messy buns. We had each left a few strands hanging loose in front of our faces—the kind of "wispies" we'd once have been scolded for. At one point, Meiying shook out her hair—it was, as I remembered, long and thick and wavy—and I felt a rush of familiar envy.

We talked for more than three hours. Customers came and went around us and our coffee got cold as we talked about college and therapy and art and our careers; about how we had suffered from ballet and how we had suffered from its absence.

In a startlingly frank conclusion for an academic paper, Sandham admits that her project stirred up some unscholarly sentiments in her. She felt jealous of the women who had made it farther than she did in the ballet world. All these years later, she still felt "a great sadness" at not achieving her dream. But her discussions with other ex-dancers also led her to an important discovery: there was no point in ignoring ballet or pretending that she had moved on. The happiest women had found a way to keep ballet in their lives, and she would have to do the same.

Brains in Their Toes

I do not recommend eating a breakfast burrito an hour before a hot yoga class, but if you do—if you turn up to the studio, change into your skintight leggings, and realize that you have made a grave mistake—I hope that you are in Flora Wildes's class. Her presence makes you feel like everything will be okay, even exercising in a 105-degree room on a stomach full of eggs and potatoes. If you saw her on Instagram, you might be intimidated by her movie-star looks and waist-length blond hair—she signed with Elite Models at the age of thirteen—but in person, she radiates the kind of Zen acceptance and presence in her body that you want to bask in, in the hopes it might rub off on you.

When I opened the door to the studio, I reeled: the heat and humidity hit me like a physical force. I've never lingered in a steam room or sauna; I have little tolerance for high temperatures. I reminded myself that Flora spends up to five hours a day in this dimly lit room, teaching and practicing "26 and 2." (Formerly known as Bikram yoga, the practice was rebranded after its namesake, guru Bikram Choudhury, was accused of sexual assault.) Still, I had to fight every instinct for self-preservation as I marched myself onward into the heat, joining a handful of men and women of various ages, body types, and states of undress, most of them already stretching on their yoga mats and looking supremely prepared for whatever was about to happen. I, meanwhile, sought refuge in the slightly cooler bathroom until the last possible moment. When I saw Flora open the door to the studio, I reemerged—bowled over again by the heat—unfurled my yoga mat, and lay down.

As soon as Flora started teaching, though, I relaxed: I felt as if I had entered a trance. Her voice rose and fell like a hypnotist's as she led us through gentle stretches, breathing exercises, and poses with names like "rabbit," "cobra," and "camel." We balanced on one leg, and Flora told us to feel time slow down— to embody what it is to be a tree. When she demonstrated, she looked like a dancer: I could see her, in a flash, in a leotard and tights, at the barre where we met nearly two decades ago. Mostly, though, she guided us with her voice: she wanted us to listen to our own bodies, rather than striving to look like her. She wanted us to feel the breath in the body, and to feel the body in space. To feel how our bones were stacked on top of each other, how the spine was like a column. She implored us not to compare the way our body was working today to the way it worked yesterday or last week or last year: to let go of our goals, and honor the body as it is. At the end of the sequence, we rhythmically inhaled and exhaled to the beat of Flora's clapping.

The hour was up, and the spell was broken. The few drops remaining in my recently cold water bottle could by the end be used to make tea. I sweat so much I felt like my eyeballs were dehydrated. I also felt loose, limber, and blissfully present: like I was inhabiting every inch of my body. We were a world away from where Flora and I began—and yet, in the way she guided us to feel our bodies from within, I could see the influence of ballet in Flora's class.

Flora followed her older sister to SAB when she was eight, and it was there, she says, that she began "building the bridges between brain and muscle." The ever-present mirrors sometimes got in the way, but she still traces her current body awareness back to that early training. Flora's stage presence and natural charisma helped her win lead roles in the children's repertoire, and she discovered that she loved performing: she loved how a feeling or a line of music would reverberate throughout her body—starting in the orchestra pit and showing up in the way she held her fingers or arranged her face onstage. But after a few years, she was told that her turnout might hold her back. She followed her teachers' advice to watch TV while holding a frog stretch every day—ignoring the pain in her hips as she lay on her stomach, her legs in a rhombus on the floor—but it wasn't enough. At thirteen, her turnout was deemed inadequate, and she was expelled. (To this day, the old hip pain still flares up in times of stress.)

At first, Flora fled from anything that reminded her of ballet. She threw away her pointe shoes, bought a drum set, and stopped exercising. Quitting ballet mostly felt like a relief, but she missed the stage—until she discovered that acting could fill that void. She enrolled in a performing arts academy for high school and then a drama conservatory for college. It was there, as an undergraduate, that she rediscovered dance, this time without the pressures of SAB. She fell in love with Balinese mask dance—a dramatic, improvisational art form in which performers hide their faces behind heavy painted masks—and spent a month in Indonesia learning from a master. Instead of drawing attention to her beauty, as she had at SAB, she covered up her face with a clown mask and let her emotions guide her movement.

It was in college, too, that Flora, on a whim, signed up for a class at Yoga to the People. Still wary of the studio environment, she was surprised by how comfortable she felt. The room had no mirrors, and the teacher encouraged the students to close their eyes. "They made a space where you could be anonymous. You could go in a corner, lie down, and just breathe for an hour," Flora said. "That was a profound way for me to tune inward, and let the outer movements stem from within." Instead of staring at her own image, she was able to focus on her physical and mental responses, and to feel the strength that was steadily building. She fought against the mentality—a holdover from ballet—that physical activity had to have an objective, and tried to accept yoga as a practice, a meditation. After all, she reminded herself, she wasn't trying to join a yoga company or win a certain role. She wasn't trying to compete with anyone else. She was only trying to be in the moment. Even as she was fighting against certain habits she had cultivated at ballet, she also realized, as she reconnected with her body, that she was tapping into a foundation she had built there.

Today, as an actor and yoga teacher in Los Angeles, Flora's body is her livelihood: it's her tool for connecting with her students and for communicating with an audience. It's also a conduit to her past, a map of old traumas and joys: she said she can point to the precise muscles in her body where different memories are stored. "I feel that I have a connection to my body in a very unusual way," she said. She is "profoundly physically sensitive"; if she so much as stubs her toe, she can sense the pain traveling up her leg, up her spine and neck, and arriving as a grimace on her face. Her physical awareness extends to other people, too, helping her understand her yoga students' individual needs. "You can look at a person and you could tell a story based on how they carry their body—where they're tight, where they're soft, where they're pushing out," she said. "I try to pull the tension out and replace it with support."

Since moving to LA four years ago, Flora has acted in a Marvel TV show, an HBO period drama, and a dozen independent films. She recently appeared on *Law & Order* as a twitchy van-life influencer who happens to be friends with the vlogging murder victim. Embodiment and sense memories are a crucial part of her process. If she has an intimate scene with a stranger, she might will herself to call up the particular scent of a lover, or the feel of a boyfriend's hair. If she succeeds, the awkwardness dissipates; she has an entry point to intimacy, and her scene partner no longer feels like a stranger. Success comes most easily when she is on top of her yoga practice and in tune with her body.

Our modern lifestyle allows for an unprecedentedly disembodied existence. We spend our days hunched over the computer, moving only our fingertips, ignoring our bodies until our limbs go numb. Through two-dimensional avatars, we talk without opening our mouths, send virtual hugs without touching. "Human flesh no longer exists, except as an incept of the wireless world," a digital theorist argued as early as 1994. More Americans than ever work at a desk—only about twenty percent have physically active jobs, according to the journal *PLOS One*, down from half in 1960—and the average office worker spends three-quarters of her waking hours sitting down. During the Covid-19 pandemic, we became even more estranged from our physical selves. "Screen time" became synonymous with "awake time" as we adjusted to holding everything from happy hours and celebrations to museum tours and meetings online.

From our earliest years, the mind-body divide is built into the fabric of daily life. (We might blame the seventeenth-century French philosopher René Descartes, who drew a binary between the animalistic body—the site of base instincts and desires—and the uniquely human, rational mind. According to him, the body was merely a machine whose most important function was to cart around the intelligent mind.) "We talk about 'having bodies' but rarely 'being bodies,'" wrote scholar Dennis Proffitt and journalist Drake Baer in *Perception: How Our Bodies Shape Our Minds*. Proffitt and other psychologists in the growing field of embodied cognition are discovering, contra-Descartes, how our perceptions of the world—how steep a hill looks; how fast a tennis ball is coming toward us—are not just a function of our brain, but of our bodies and our physical abilities. (The hill looks steeper to a hiker with a heavy backpack; the ball seems to have been traveling faster if we miss our swing.)

The psychologist Paul Bloom has observed that even young children say that they use their brain for certain things, like doing math, but not others, like loving their family. At school, having a body often felt like the elephant in the room, as we were herded from classroom to classroom—from forty-five-minute block of sitting and thinking to forty-five-minute block of sitting and thinking about something else. Then—at a time determined not by the rhythms of the body but by the availability of the sixth-floor gym—we would suddenly become, for another forty-five-minute stretch, bodies: bodies performing push-ups and crunches on command, clenching our biceps and counting down sets of ten until we were sent back to the locker rooms to change back into our uniforms and back into brains.

When we work out as adults, it's as compartmentalized, often, as it was in gym class: a YouTube yoga session between Zoom calls; a quick run and then back to the desk. (That is, if we do it at all: more people than ever—an estimated 50 million Americans, according to the American Psychological Association—are considered entirely sedentary.) During the Covid lockdown, I downloaded the Strava app and joined 100 million users in tracking our bike rides and runs, analyzing detailed graphs of weekly distance and average mile times. Thanks to the app, I spent my runs staring at the pacing calculator on my phone, jogging in place at red lights and speeding up at the end of each mile, no matter how badly my body wanted to slow down or take a break. Even when we play more spontaneous sports and games, we tend to focus on our surroundings—rackets, balls, nets, opponents—rather than on the muscles and bodily processes allowing us to move. The philosopher Drew Leder gives the example of a tennis player: a ball flies toward him, and as he prepares to return it, he is aware of the court, the other player, the force of the wind. His body is almost as irrelevant as when he sits at his desk and thinks.

The cerebral narrator of Megan Nolan's novel *Acts of Desperation* calls her body an "unmanageable thing that has basically nothing to do with me, is not really any of my business at all." Nolan's contemporary, the novelist Sally Rooney, who has been called the voice of my generation, confided in an interview that, growing up, she fantasized about being "a brain in a jar." Her characters—especially her young women—have a remarkably high tolerance for sitting. They read in the library or lie in bed all day, forgetting to eat or tend to their bodies. Rooney is often praised for writing such relatable characters.

Women are especially prone to feeling detached from our bodies. We learn early to see ourselves from the outside, to always think about how we come across. "Men act and women appear," the art critic John Berger wrote in 1972. His words have resonated with generations of women, repurposed for chapter epigraphs and Instagram grids. "A woman must continually watch herself," he wrote. "She is almost continually accompanied by her own image of herself. Whilst she is walking across a room or whilst she is weeping at the death of her father, she can scarcely avoid envisaging herself walking or weeping. From earliest childhood she has been taught and persuaded to survey herself continually."

After a few stabs at change—second-wave feminists picketed Miss America and dumped fake eyelashes into a "Freedom Trash Can"—women, for the most part, have resigned ourselves to the status quo. Today, Miss America is broadcast to millions, and Sephora offers fifty-one kinds of eyelash extensions.

Structural change can feel impossible; it's easier, for many women, to just go numb, to distance themselves from their bodies—to pretend they don't have a body at all. In a recent *BuzzFeed* essay, millennial writer Emmeline Clein described a trend she had noticed among popular female characters—on TV shows like *Fleabag*, in the viral short story "Cat Person"—as well as among her own friends. They cope with the pain and indignity of modern womanhood, of Brazilian waxing and "certain types of sex" (the kind that a woman "does not want to be having"), by simply shutting down, sometimes with the help of benzodiazepines or booze. "Aspirationally dead inside feminism," she called it. "The smartest women I know are all dissociating." Along with discomfort—even squeamishness—with our bodies comes a distaste for our own pleasure. In the 2009 National Survey of Sexual Health and Behavior, which included nearly two thousand American adults, ninety-one percent of men—compared with only sixty-four percent of women—said they had orgasmed during their last sexual encounter. Another study of eight hundred college students found that only thirty-nine percent of women—but ninety-one percent of their male peers—"usually or always" climaxed during sex. The "orgasm gap" can't be explained by anatomical differences alone.

On a certain level, I related to these young women, to their insecurities and struggle to find their place in the world. I enjoyed watching and reading about them. But on another, I did not relate to them at all. When Clein writes of learning to decouple her "consciousness from . . . [her] immediate bodily and emotional experience"; when Margot of "Cat Person" "imagined herself from above" during sex; I felt blissfully exempt from the detachment that, for my real and fictional peers, was apparently the norm.

At ballet, I had learned not only to think about how my body looked from the outside, but to fully inhabit it from the inside. As much as I obsessed about my reflection in the mirror, I thought even more about how my body felt: how my chest felt open if I imagined teacups on my shoulders; how my legs felt light if I lifted from underneath (striving to engage muscles that, looking back, might have been more of an idea). How every nerve and joint and tendon felt alert, alive.

I can't remember ever being shown a two-dimensional diagram at ballet, or hearing about the disembodied quads or abs our gym teachers shouted about. The whole process of becoming a dancer was a deeply embodied one: we learned not by sitting and reading, but by imitating, trying, falling, adjusting, trying again. We understood our bodies not through anatomical labels, but through luscious metaphors of food and nature and everyday life. I didn't know what muscles were involved when I held my foot in front of me in the air—but I knew that my leg should be so steady and turned out that I could balance a glass of water on my heel. I didn't know what mechanism was at work when I prepared to take off for a leap, but I knew that I would jump higher if I pictured a cat getting ready to pounce. When I lifted my arms, I didn't think about flexing my biceps; I thought about how my fingertips would feel if they were brushing against a velvet curtain.

Even the pain of ballet could enhance our awareness of the body. Pain disrupts the cycle of bodily neglect, intruding on our consciousness and forcing us to remember that we have a physical form. Drew Leder continues his example of the body-oblivious tennis player: thinking only of his racket and his opponent, he swings—and feels a pain in his chest. In an instant, the game falls away, and his body appears; it has spoken up, demanded attention.

On the therapist Esther Perel's podcast *How's Work?*, a successful model explains how, from the moment she was scouted at fifteen, she had been subjected to a constant barrage of objectifying eyes and hands—from the agents and designers who appraised her looks to the hairdressers and stylists who treated her like a hanger. She had to find a way to deal, too, with her discomfort on set—painful shoes, revealing clothes, extreme heat and cold—and so she taught herself to vacate her surroundings and imagine that she was off "somewhere in a cloud." She got so good at this trick that she ended up unable to feel much at all—even pleasure. But the anonymous model's voice takes on a sudden confidence when she explains how dance classes led her back to herself, helped her rekindle her relationship with her body and her senses: with, as Perel put it, "movement that is not about performance, but about experience."

Sports and exercise can blunt the dark forces alienating women from themselves: striving for and achieving athletic goals can help women appreciate their bodies as more than just aesthetic objects. The writer Caroline Knapp's early twenties were ruled by her obsession with weighing as little as possible. What started as an impulsive dorm room experiment—how long could she survive on rice cakes and cottage cheese?—escalated into a life-threatening case of anorexia. Over the years of her illness, she sought help from her therapist and her parents, but it was only after she signed up for a summer rowing class at the age of twenty-five that the symptoms of her eating disorder began to recede. Inspired by the power and grace of the more advanced rowers, Knapp finally had a physical goal other than to eliminate herself. At first, she "flailed on the water, jerked and teetered, held the oars in a blistering death grip." But slowly, over the course of hundreds of outings on the Charles River, she grew more confident on the water—and for the first time in her life, she understood her body as "responsive and connected to the mind," and as "a worthy place to live."

When Knapp took up rowing in 1985, women all over the country were discovering the pleasures of exercise. Jane Fonda's *Workout* tape was released in 1982, soaring to the top of the sales charts and introducing women to the joys of Jazzercise, aerobics, and brightly colored leg warmers. (Fonda's *Workout* remains the bestselling VHS of all time.) Two years later, the Olympic committee caved to years of feminist campaigning and added a women's marathon to the summer games. (Men had been competing in the marathon for nearly a century.)

As recently as the 1960s and '70s, according to Danielle Friedman's 2022 book *Let's Get Physical: How Women Discovered*

Exercise and Reshaped the World, women were systematically excluded from most forms of exercise. Doctors believed it was dangerous for women to exert themselves, especially when they were on their periods; rumor held that vigorous exercise could even cause a woman's uterus to fall out. Sweating in public was considered unladylike, as were visible muscles. When a talented female runner snuck into the Boston Marathon in 1967, a race director spotted her around mile four, jumped onto the course, and tackled her. (She reached the finish line anyway.)

The boomer women discovering their strength through these newly acceptable workouts might not have known that they owed a debt to ballet. For decades, when exercise was seen as unfeminine, ballet was the exception: a vigorous workout that did not risk turning them into men. In the 1960s, when women were prohibited from running in races longer than two miles, women in Balanchine's classroom were heaving and sweating and pushing themselves to the brink.

Ballet dancers and ex-dancers were the mothers of the women's fitness movement. The visionary Bonnie Prudden, who opened one of America's earliest fitness centers in 1954—a time when, according to a *Sports Illustrated* article cited in Friedman's book, "the mere mention of formal exercise [was] enough to bring a shudder to the average American spine"— first discovered the magic of moving her body at the age of four, when her parents enrolled her in a local ballet class. A few years later, in 1959, the German-Jewish modern dancer Lotte Berk rented out an old hat factory in London and opened the world's first barre studio. Berk's class—featuring a combination of ballet- and yoga-inspired stretches, lunges, and lifts— developed a loyal following of celebrities and society women, and when it was time to hire more instructors, Berk chose lithe dancers like herself. (Barre remains one of the most popular workouts today, with more than 850 studios in the United States and hundreds of thousands of devotees.) Even Jane Fonda considered ballet an integral part of her routine: from her early twenties on, she sought out ballet studios all over the country, wherever her acting jobs took her—sometimes waking up at four a.m. to fit in a barre before her call time. Ballet gave her a way of "keeping at least a tenuous connection to my body," she wrote, even as she struggled with eating disorders and an obsession with staying thin.

"Our spirits, our souls, our love reside totally in our bodies, in our toes and knees and hips and vertebrae and necks and elbows and fingertips," Toni Bentley wrote. Dancers "have brains in their toes." I used to feel this sense of embodiment all the time, even when I wasn't dancing. I would lie in bed or sit in class, my legs folded into a hard plastic chair, and I would sense my muscles brimming with potential energy; I felt powerful, knowing what my body could do. I felt like my body was different.

If I had been x-rayed, I probably would have learned that it was—not just in the way my muscles were built, but in the way my bones and even my brain were shaped. When a group of radiologists in Ohio scanned the lower extremities of fifty-two ballet dancers, they found a "unique and consistent" bone pattern: the dancers had enlarged metatarsals, ankle spurs, and thickening of the thigh, shin, and calf bones. Another study, this one by doctors at Imperial College in London, found a neurological anomaly: the area of the cerebellum that receives signals from the "balance organs" in the inner ear and converts them into feelings of dizziness was visibly smaller in ballet dancers. Through years of practicing turns, they had trained their brains to suppress the sensation of dizziness.

In 2003, the medical anthropologist Caroline Potter—hoping to learn about how dancers experience their bodies—enrolled in an elite dance academy in London. She spent her days training and her nights socializing with her classmates (and slyly taking notes on their conversations). Dancers, she came to believe, occupy a "shifted sensorium" featuring an "interconnected, bodily-grounded sense of cultural identity." They develop a heightened awareness of gravity, of the weight of the air and the resistance of the ground.

I remember being told to feel the floor, use the floor, strike the floor; that the floor was my friend. To piqué like the ground was hot and to dégagé like I was moving through water. When I struggled to balance en pointe, my teachers repeated Balanchine's advice: "Just hold on to the air." We thought continuously about the relationship of our bodies to space, and to each other. We learned to dance in straight lines without turning our heads; to sense each other's locations from the sound of our breath or our feet on the Marley floor.* We strove to keep our hips "square," according to an imagined geometry, and our shoulders "open" or "closed."

Potter was struck, too, by how dancers prioritized their sense of touch. In most settings—in public, in school, at work—touch is carefully regulated, but for dancers, physical contact is so ordinary that it sometimes "became difficult to distinguish between sensations of touch versus kinesthesia" (the sense of where the body is located in space). She noticed that "ways of touching as permitted within the School varied

---

* A type of vinyl dance flooring designed to prevent slipping and absorb shocks.

markedly from conventions of touch . . . that were followed outside of the studio."

That's putting it mildly. My classmates and I took turns lying on our sides and pushing each other's legs up to our ears; straddling the ground and pushing each other's backs into the floor. We sat on each other's feet, using the weight of our bodies to stretch each other's arches. We were experts at nonverbal communication—at talking with our bodies. We weren't allowed to speak in class, but we smiled and nodded when the teacher gave a correction, giggled when she imitated an incorrect move. When she demonstrated a combination, we "marked" it with our hands to show we understood—wiggling our fingers in a circle if the exercise included a pirouette, flexing the wrist if we would lift our leg to the front.

Our personal boundaries were so fluid as to practically dissolve. We stood in line and massaged each other's bare shoulders. Backstage, we twisted each other's hair into buns and pinned them to the back of our heads, whispered *merde*, and kissed each other on the cheeks.

Boundaries don't suddenly appear once dancers turn pro. When the Swedish anthropologist Helena Wulff embedded with ballet companies in London, Europe, and New York, she initially assumed that the men and women fondling each other during breaks and sitting in each other's laps were lovers; eventually, she realized they were just colleagues and friends. "I have never worked in an office," NYCB soloist Georgina Pazcoguin wrote in her 2021 memoir *Swan Dive*, "but I'm fairly sure that if you walked in on a naked coworker with her leg extended, her foot stretched up to her face (rendering her lady business 100 percent visible) in order for her to get a better look at the foot corn she's cutting out, it would be considered inappropriate." In her early thirties, Pazcoguin—

who had spent her entire adolescence and young adulthood
ensconced in the insular world of ballet—took a job dancing
in *Cats* on Broadway. On opening night, she and her cast-
mates were offered bathrobes, and Pazcoguin couldn't figure
out why. Finally, another dancer explained: "It's so everyone
doesn't have to see you naked." What a courtesy: Pazcoguin
was blown away.

As Caroline Potter carried on with her training, she noticed
profound changes not only in the way she danced, but in the
way she inhabited space outside the studio. She no longer perceived the world through the five senses—sight, sound, smell,
touch, taste—that she had grown up with. Her world, she
wrote in the journal *Ethnos*, came to revolve instead around
"a dynamic sense of constantly shifting one's body in space
and time."

*   *   *

No ballerina more dramatically illustrates how dancers tran-
scend the five-sense model of perception than Alicia Alonso.
She was just hitting her stride as a member of Manhattan's
Ballet Theatre when she began to go blind.

Born Alicia Martínez in 1920, to an army officer father and
an artistically minded mother, she grew up in a large apartment in a leafy neighborhood of Havana. The youngest of
four, Alicia was an energetic child. "Mama used to put me in
a room with a phonograph and a scarf," she told *Dance* magazine in 1953. "That would keep me quiet for a few hours,
doing what I imagined was dancing." Alicia attended her first
formal ballet class at the age of nine, at a scrappy school
where well-off girls were sent to improve their posture. There

was no professional ballet in Cuba, and back then, "dancing and showing your legs was a taboo," Alicia said. But she loved her lessons at the Sociedad Pro-Arte Musical. She wore street clothes and sneakers and studied with a Russian émigré who, like Balanchine, had fled the revolution in 1917.

Before long, Alicia had lost interest in her old hobbies. She stopped caring about roller skating and horseback riding. "I said to myself, 'I want to be a dancer!'" she told a documentarian in 2015. "Are you sure you want to show your legs like that?" her conservative father asked. "I insisted: 'I want to be a dancer!'" Alicia was doted on by her teachers and cast as the lead in every recital, but by the time she reached her teens, she knew she had outgrown Cuba's small ballet scene.

So, at the age of just fifteen, she set sail on her own for New York. Her soon-to-be husband, Fernando Alonso, another aspiring dancer, had gone on ahead of her. They traded in the airy villas of upscale Havana for a one-room rental in Spanish Harlem where, Fernando later wrote, they faced "racial prejudice and miserable living conditions." But the heady dance world they discovered made their sacrifices worthwhile. They learned about modern dance and the avant-garde and took twenty-five-cent ballet classes in a church basement. Alicia understood little English, but she learned by watching and by practicing with Fernando at night. Not long after arriving in America, Alicia gave birth to a baby girl, but her ambition left no room for child-rearing. She sent the child home to Cuba to live with her grandparents and was back in the studio a month later.

Alicia's first jobs in New York were in the chorus lines of Broadway musicals, sometimes alongside her husband, but she never lost sight of her true calling: ballet. She won a scholarship to Balanchine's nascent School of American Ballet and, in 1939, joined his American Ballet Caravan for a cross-country tour. She started off in the ensemble but, by the end of the two-month stint, had been singled out for her technique, her work ethic, and her beauty.

Alicia had long black hair and huge dark eyes, made even more prominent with thick rings of kohl. Hers wasn't the delicate, vulnerable beauty of Gelsey Kirkland or Margot Fonteyn; her looks were showstopping, formidable. There was something haughty in her high cheekbones, something aggressive about her gaze—perhaps exacerbated, in photos, by a tendency to sneer. She was not the stereotypical sylphlike ballerina but "dramatically forceful and very much human," as the *Daily Express* put it. In videos, her upper body appears almost casual, impervious to the labor of her legs and feet. Her movement has a regal, maximalist quality, which lent itself to dramatic roles like Carmen and the Swan Queen.

In 1940, Alicia joined the corps of the fledgling American Ballet Theatre. Within months, she had once again worked her way up to solo roles. "She radiated a sense of sun, a kind of full-blooded honesty," said the choreographer Eugene Loring, who created two roles for her in 1940. Critics buzzed about the striking Cuban up-and-comer. "Here is a young artist . . . who is eminently worth watching," one reviewer wrote in 1941. When she debuted in *Pas de Quatre* that same year, she received seventeen curtain calls. Her ascent to stardom seemed inevitable.

Alicia was still in her first year with Ballet Theatre when she started bumping into furniture at home. She noticed, too, that she could see her dance partner only when he was standing directly in front of her. She wondered if there was something wrong with her eyes, but it wasn't until she was onstage one night that her increasingly hazy eyesight reached a point she could no longer ignore. She grew dangerously dizzy while dancing and saw dark patches clouding her field of vision. After the show, she was rushed to the hospital, where she learned that the retina of her right eye had detached. She needed urgent surgery, but her first reaction was denial: she postponed the operation until she could finish the season. By the time she went back to the hospital, the day after dancing a full program, she could barely see.

A Spanish ophthalmologist performed the delicate retina reattachment, and warned Alicia that the recovery would be slow. She would have to lie still in her hospital bed for three months: any movement might disturb the newly placed membrane. She tried to maintain her technique by covertly stretching and pointing her feet beneath the sheets, and she returned to class as soon as she could—only for the retina that had just healed to detach once more. After another painful operation, she went home to Cuba to rest.

In Havana, Alicia was given strict instructions not to chew too hard, move her head, cry, play with her daughter, or even laugh. Dancing was out of the question—for now, and maybe forever. For more than a year, Alicia lay immobile in bed, with bandages over her eyes. "It was torture for me to lie still, feeling my body gain weight and become flabby," she recalled. But she refused to consider that her career was over. "I danced—I danced inside of me," she said. "I danced with my eyes closed." She spent her time memorizing the steps for her dream role, Giselle, listening to the music and marking the movements with her hands, pretending that her fingers were legs. "My mental dancing became so real that I could watch my own performances and criticize them."

When asked which of the five senses they would be least willing to give up, an overwhelming majority—seventy percent, in one survey—choose sight. (Only three percent would save their sense of touch.) Most of us experience the world through our eyes. But dancers are different.

By early 1942, the bandages were off, and Alicia, now twenty-one, was eager to get back to work. Her doctors had only authorized her to walk, but she found an empty studio at the Pro Arte theater and began practicing in secret. The transition was harder than she had anticipated. Not only had her muscles wasted away; she had to find new ways to navigate space. With partial sight in one eye and no peripheral vision in either, she could no longer rely on her eyes for information. She would have to relearn steps that she had long since mastered. Pirouettes and fouetté turns left her dizzy: "spotting"— the trick dancers use to steady themselves by training their gaze on a single point—was no longer possible. But Alicia was stoic as she adjusted to her new reality. She learned to rely instead on an internal center of balance, focusing on the way her body felt as she spun.

"Proprioception" is the term scientists use to describe our knowledge of where our body is situated in space; it's what allows us to conjure a mental map of our limbs, to visualize their location with our eyes shut. (People with a damaged sense of proprioception may be unable to walk without watching their feet, or find their own nose in the dark. Two sisters born without the receptor that carries touch into conscious awareness grew up to need wheelchairs; they explained in a Vox profile that, due to their poor proprioception, they were liable to fall down if the lights went out, or to grow disoriented if a strand of hair fell in front of their face.)

Dancers, meanwhile—who strive to control even involuntary muscles, to feel all twenty-six bones of the foot—develop a superior sense of the body in space. In one study, doctors had a group of ballet dancers and a group of adults without dance training stand on one leg with their eyes closed. A researcher then arranged each subject's legs and ankles in different positions, returned them to standing, and asked them to re-create the pose. Ordinary people struggled, but the dancers had no trouble.

Dancers have a heightened sense, too, of the invisible inner workings of the body. "Interoception" is the sense of our own internal states—our awareness of the physical signals that travel from body to brain, telling us when it's time to eat or drink or empty our bladder. Scientists measure interoception by administering the "heartbeat detection task," which asks subjects to guess—without touching the wrist or neck or any other pulse point—how many times their heart beats in a given period of time. Professional dancers excel at this task.

In the fall of 1943, Alicia was ready to go back to New York. The Ballet Theatre she returned to was bigger and more professional than the one she had left behind two years earlier. A new hierarchy had formed in her absence, and at the top of it was the English dancer Alicia Markova. (Born Lillian Marks, she changed her name in the 1920s—a time when Russian heritage would confer legitimacy on an aspiring ballerina.) Markova's signature role was Giselle, but that season, she had to pull out of a performance at the last minute. Markova's partner needed a replacement, and Alicia seized her chance. She would have only a few days to learn the role, but she had practiced for months on her fingers. Her debut as Giselle was a triumph—"One of the most distinguished performances of the season," according to the *New York Times*. "Miss Alonso acquitted herself with brilliance."

Onstage, Alicia used the heat of the spotlights, and the vibrations of the music, to navigate space. She arranged to have two colored spotlights trained on the front of the stage; if she got too close, she knew she was in danger of falling into the orchestra pit. Pas de deux posed new risks, too, as she blindly leapt into men's arms or reached out for an unseen hand. She asked her partners to whisper, click, or cough, and danced toward the sound. "It's as if we were to take the camera and move it out of focus slowly," she said, explaining how the world looked, "until you can just about make out a face, but you can't distinguish the color or shape of the eyes, the mouth or the hair. It's like a figure moving between clouds."

In the 1940s, Alicia's fame spread beyond the dance world. She appeared in *Newsweek* and *Life* and, in 1946, was named a woman of the year by *Mademoiselle* magazine. Cuba anointed her a *Dama* and issued a postage stamp with her portrait on it. Choreographers—from the neoclassical Balanchine to the prim Antony Tudor and the folksy Agnes de Mille—clamored to work with her. (At one point, Tudor and de Mille were competing for her attention as she learned new ballets by both of them at the same time.) She could master a new role in a few hours and had, according to de Mille, "the fastest feet in the business." Her work ethic was relentless: instead of retiring to her dressing room after a show, she would return to the darkened stage and go over any steps she thought she had missed.

Alicia had enough confidence and grit to make up for her

impaired vision. After three days of back-to-back rehearsals
for de Mille's *Fall River Legend*—a ballet based on the story
of Massachusetts ax murderer Lizzie Borden—de Mille told
Alicia that she wasn't sure if she would be ready for opening
night. "I open," Alonso countered, and she did. When de Mille
told Alicia that, for political reasons, she would have to let a
less distinguished rival take one performance, Alicia tried to
talk her out of it. "You are a fool," the twenty-seven-year-old
Alicia said to the renowned choreographer. "You ruin your
work."

That spring, Ballet Theatre ran into financial trouble and
canceled the following fall season. De Mille recalled in her
memoir how ABT's founder, Lucia Chase, "sat at her desk
and sadly informed the eager dedicated children that she had
not the faintest idea how they were going to feed themselves
for the coming year." Fernando and Alicia were devastated.
"It will be approximately nine months lay-off by the time we
start again!" Fernando wrote to Chase. "That is terrible!"

But instead of waiting for Ballet Theatre to reopen, Alicia
and Fernando decided to pursue a long-held dream of their
own: to move back home, where their daughter was being
raised by Fernando's parents, and open a new, Cuban ballet
company. Cuba still lacked a serious ballet scene; ambitious
students had to leave the island if they wanted to dance and
train professionally. The Alonsos had no backers, capital, or
business experience, but they had connections and fame. They
persuaded the Pro Arte theater to lend them scenery and costumes, recruited a dozen of their laid-off Ballet Theatre colleagues, and used money from advance ticket sales to cover
the cost of the flights. The "Ballet Alicia Alonso" debuted in
October 1948, with a cast of thirty dancers—most of them

foreigners—and an auditorium packed with socialites and government elites.

After a few nights in Havana, the Alonsos embarked on an ambitious tour across Latin America and the provinces of Cuba. They continued to struggle with the costs of production and travel; once, short on money for fabric, Alicia performed in a tutu stitched from a stolen hotel curtain. She poured her own savings into the company, flying back and forth to New York for gigs, reprising her old roles with the resurrected Ballet Theatre and funneling her earnings back into the troupe.

In 1950—hoping to one day fill the company's rosters with Cuban dancers—the Alonsos added a school. They drew on elements of all the different styles they had learned—French elegance, English precision, American speed—as they developed a new, Cuban ballet. Within five years, the company was made up almost entirely of homegrown dancers, and was renamed the National Ballet of Cuba.

While Alicia was directing, coaching, and choreographing, she was also continuing to perform all over the world. In 1957, she was the first Western ballerina invited to dance in the Soviet Union; her tour was such a success that it was extended from the planned three weeks to two and a half months.

But the constant travel and grueling work took a toll on her fragile eyesight. In her thirties, she developed cataracts, and underwent two more surgeries. With every fluctuation in her vision, she had to readjust her sense of balance; even improvements could be destabilizing. Ever the stoic, she tried to hide her blindness, but she sometimes slipped up. She fell down in rehearsals. Once, she went onstage facing the wrong direction, and danced with her back to the audience.

The fortunes of the National Ballet of Cuba, meanwhile, were improving: in 1959, Fidel Castro rose to power and gave Fernando $200,000 in exchange for a promise to build "a good company." Ballet—which originated in the royal courts of seventeenth-century France—has, paradoxically, thrived under communist regimes. Castro deployed ballet to impress foreign dignitaries, and Joseph Stalin, who had his own bulletproof box at the Bolshoi, commissioned dances celebrating the state; the ballet stage was a site of Cold War competition, along with the Olympics and outer space. (In one Soviet ballet, dancers portrayed factory workers and wielded giant hammers.) "No matter its Imperial roots, [ballet] was a universal language accessible to anyone from barely literate workers to sophisticated foreign ambassadors," Jennifer Homans wrote in *Apollo's Angels*. "Of all the performing arts, ballet was perhaps the easiest to control . . . Their work was by nature public and collaborative." Whereas other artists—writers, composers, painters—could work in private, with relatively few resources, dancers and choreographers could not. And, for citizens, a ballet career offered one of few paths to stability and prestige.

With funding from Castro's government, the Alonsos eliminated tuition fees for the National Ballet School and embarked on an exhaustive talent search. "I was all over the island, to every one of the tiny mountain villages, to find children who wanted to dance," Alicia recalled. "In Cuba, we don't miss one single person with a flair for dancing." She and her company continued to tour all over the country, in rural villages and fishing towns, leaving new ballet lovers—peasants and farmers and factory workers—in their wake. They rode in jeeps to the mountains and set up portable stages outdoors.

One free performance in Havana drew thirty thousand rowdy fans, fighting for seats and squatting on the grass around the stage. Even when the troupe performed at the Gran Teatro opera house, tickets cost only a single peso. Ballet, Alicia believed, wasn't just for the elites to admire, or for gifted pupils to study; it was for the masses to enjoy, both as spectators and as participants. She designed ballet curricula for nursery schools and offered classes for amateur adults. "One forgets how wide awake the people are," Alonso told the *New York Times* in 1964. "They're interested in the craft of dancing; they ask how it's done, what a dancer's life is like."

In the following decades, Alicia built the school and company into world-class institutions, drawing passionate audiences from all walks of Cuban society. Cuban dancers became celebrities at home and political emissaries abroad. ("Cuba has three chief exports: cigars, sugar, and Alicia Alonso," Agnes de Mille wrote in 1990.) When, in 1975, Alicia danced at Lincoln Center, her performance was greeted as a sign that US-Cuba relations had thawed. Graduates of the Alonsos' school were sought after all over the world, and Alicia—the woman behind it all—was the pride of the island. Castro gave her a lavish home, a car, and a chauffeur. Cubans celebrated her in the street, shouting "Viva Alicia" as she went by.

Alicia performed into her midseventies—at one point partnering her own grandson onstage—but even after she could no longer dance with her feet, "I dance with the hands," she told the *New York Times* in 2010. "I dance with my heart actually more. So it comes through my body." After watching footage of her speaking, I knew what she meant. In one clip, she wears dark glasses and sits on a tassel-fringed sofa, her ankles crossed demurely in front of her, but she seems to vibrate, nonetheless, with kinetic energy: her shoulders tilt, her back sways to and fro, her hand flutters up to her cheek and then down to perch delicately on her thigh. "She spoke in true dancer fashion by using her body," wrote the historian Elizabeth Schwall, who met Alicia in 2015 while researching her book *Dancing with the Revolution: Power, Politics, and Privilege in Cuba.* "Her long fingernails tapped, and her fists hit the desk to emphasize certain points; her head moved constantly up and down, side to side."

Alicia presided over the National Ballet as an authority on casting, promotions, and programming until her death in 2019. (She lived for almost a century, falling short of her goal: she often told journalists that she planned to reach two hundred.)

Alicia wore powerful binoculars to watch TV and judge auditions, but otherwise made few concessions to her blindness. Yet her vision may have been even worse than she ever admitted. When a journalist for the *Daily Telegraph* met her in 2004, she reached out her hand to shake but offered it instead "to the empty space to my side," he recalled, "before swiveling around at my voice." Alicia's world, and her extraordinary accomplishments—dancing and directing, choreographing and campaigning—sprung from her body; from her relationship with motion and sound and space. She inhabited her physical self so fully that she transcended the need to see.

Dancers cultivate a sense of otherness, consciously drawing a line between themselves and "civilians," "pedestrians," even "people." Nondancers, too, have remarked that dancers resemble a "different species." The reason, I think, that you can spot a dancer from across a room is not her hairstyle or her makeup or her thinness; it's her ineffable presence in her body, her superhuman awareness of space and herself. It's her presence in every movement, whether a grand jeté or a tilt of the head or nothing at all; her stillness, too, is deliberate, is pregnant with potential movement. Even a dancer's headshot—a close-up of just her face, perhaps her neck—conveys the possibility of motion: she seems poised to leap out of the playbill, jump off the page. And it's that quality—more than her beauty or her fragility—that makes her so magnetic.

Reverence

After she dropped out of college, eighteen-year-old Meiying puttered around at home in New York, watching her high school friends post Facebook updates from raucous college parties and scenic New England campuses. Finally, her mom—remembering how Meiying had loved drawing as a child—signed her up for an art class at Parsons. And in that classroom downtown, something inside her, something that had been dormant ever since she quit ballet, woke up. Experimenting with watercolors and pastels, she felt alive in a way she hadn't since she had danced onstage. Without telling anyone, she began putting together a portfolio and downloading art school applications online. The next fall, in 2011, she started her freshman year at the Maryland Institute College of Art.

Stepping into Meiying's studio on Duane Street feels like falling into a dreamworld. Her paintings are exuberant—flush with romantic pinks and reds, flaming yellows and oranges, and big, confident brushstrokes. She paints festive cafés and coy party girls and moody women waiting by the phone; but most of all, she paints dancers. In *Backstage Sisters*, a dancer in a marigold-yellow tutu leans over to adjust the bodice of her friend's costume. In *Paris Girls*, a dancer closes her eyes as if stealing a private moment amid the frenzy backstage.

She leans back in an invisible chair and lets the full weight of her head fall into her friend's hands, like a baby supported by her mother. I have a framed print of this painting on my wall: a reminder, as I read about Peter Martins's abuse and Balanchine's paternalism, of the intimacy and trust that still blossom between women in ballet.

"Ballet informs everything that I do," said Meiying. "I take the romanticism of the ballet world and put that in my paintings." I see, in her work, the influence of Degas's classroom scenes and Chagall's stage sets, of Karinska's costumes and Balanchine's Land of Sweets. A pair of pointe shoes hangs in her studio beside her paintbrushes. Sometimes, she holds a brush against a canvas and lifts her arms in port de bras; her performance—which she captures on video—is as much a part of the work as the striking marks that appear on the canvas. (Meiying began reconnecting with movement in college, giving herself ballet barres in the deserted art school gym; at the insistence of a therapist, she also added yoga to her routine. She credited Flora's Zoom yoga classes with helping her through the pandemic.)

As an artist, Meiying found her voice first through ballet. "I was a bunhead, but that was just because that was my only version of what a professional artist was, at that point," she said. In her early self-portraits, Meiying often painted herself holding a fan that obscured her face. More recently, the fan has migrated farther from her body, leaving her face exposed.

As an up-and-coming visual artist, Meiying appreciates her industry's more relaxed approach to time. At thirty, she said—a note of amazement in her voice—"I'm considered very young." She works at a contemporary art gallery downtown, and in 2021 had her first solo exhibition at a gallery in Chelsea. At her triumphant opening—packed with so many friends and fans I could hardly move—two musicians from the New York City Ballet orchestra performed a new piece inspired by her work.

One of the happiest guests that night—whose moving image was also projected on the wall, in a lyrical dance duet she filmed with Meiying—was Emily. After years of auditioning, she had booked a full-time job with the innovative female-led ballet troupe MorDance. In a decade of dancing with regional companies along the East Coast and the Metropolitan Opera in New York, MorDance's founder, Morgan McEwen, could count on one hand the female choreographers she had worked with. Tired of having only male bosses, she launched a Kickstarter campaign in 2013, raising thirteen thousand dollars to build her own company. Almost a decade later, MorDance's eight talented dancers regularly perform her choreography at prestigious venues around New York.

Morgan uses her balletic vocabulary to address issues like climate change, mass consumerism, and misogyny. A few years ago, she choreographed a feminist retelling of *Romeo and Juliet,* featuring sword-fighting women villagers and an independent Juliet with a best friend instead of a nurse. She is planning a collaboration with an artist who studies the effects of plastic waste on birds. "It's not women in tutus that need to be saved by a prince," she told me.

It's Valentine's Day when I go to see MorDance rehearse on the Upper West Side, and all of the women are wearing red. You wouldn't know, up here on the ninth floor, that it's freezing outside: the air is hot with sweat, and late-morning sunlight streams in through the window, turning the Marley floor into a checkerboard. Emily wears a baggy tracksuit over her burgundy leotard, and her hair—short now—is pulled into a low ponytail. Her nail polish is bloodred, and her face mask is black. She makes me think of Mila Kunis's entrance in *Black Swan*—the strutting cool girl dressed in black, the foil to Natalie Portman's bunhead in pink.

The group is learning a new dance set to a postmodern piece of piano music. They walk through their places while the music plays, searching out the rhythm in the fragmented score, and then it's time for "full-out." As soon as they start dancing, the troupe seem to have multiplied into many more than eight, as they weave in and out of diamonds and lines, fusing and dissolving. One moment, the dancers are holding an arabesque on pointe, looking like they're posing for a ballet company brochure; the next, they're on their hands and knees, crawling on the floor. Occasionally, they look like they're in a 1980s aerobics class; one move reminds me of a sit-up, if a sit-up were beautiful. Particularly arresting are the partnering sequences—playful and mutually supportive. In one duet, a man and a woman stand back to back, resting gently on each other, and—as if they're doing a balletic version of a summer-camp trust exercise—take turns leaning back and letting their partner support them. The group rarely moves in simple unison, though the dancers never lose track of each other; a viewer could just as happily pan out and take in the whole bustling scene as zoom in on a single dancer.

The dancer I zoom in on, of course, is Emily. When Emily was invited to join MorDance, it had been almost a decade since she had performed on pointe. But I would never have guessed she had retrained in just a few weeks: she moves in her pointe shoes as though they're an extension of her body. She and a young dancer named Cemiyon take center stage for an acrobatic duet, most of which she spends off the ground—balancing on his back with her legs in a split, swept through the air like a ballroom dancer. Even in rehearsal, with her "lines" obscured by baggy warm-ups, her dancing casts a spell. Every gesture—a flick of the wrist, a slight lift of the arm—is full of pathos; her fingers are more expressive than some people's faces.

Morgan's mission is "to influence a new normal for the ballet world." She is adamant that dancers should be treated with respect: after all, she points out, they are professionals with as many years of training as lawyers. She addresses the dancers not as "girls," but by their names. The atmosphere is collegial—focused but relaxed. In idle moments—when Morgan is working out a tricky diagonal with one dancer, or refining the angle of another's arabesque—the others chat comfortably or massage their legs on foam rollers. One of the women wears running shorts over bare legs; another wears a T-shirt with the word "fun" spelled out in Popsicle sticks. But it's still ballet. "Don't look at my feet," Emily warns me, as she walks over to me, barefoot, on a break. I do, of course, and then I catch a glimpse of blood and wish I hadn't.

Emily once assumed that her career would be winding down by the time she was thirty. Instead, her years of anonymous toil are finally paying off. Shortly after the MorDance season ended, she booked her biggest job ever: in 2023 she will dance with the Metropolitan Opera at Lincoln Center.

"Don't you find it really liberating that it doesn't fucking matter what you look like as a writer?" Meiying asked me recently. Emily, Meiying, and I were talking about body image over, ironically, a dinner of pasta and sangria on the Lower East Side. We had all dressed and done our makeup similarly, with dark eyeliner and mascara and small gold earrings.

Emily and I looked at each other. I wished I could say, simply, yes. For Meiying, art school was the antidote she needed. She finally felt free to focus on her craft; she even relished criticism, because it targeted her work and not her weight. "They'll say this painting sucks, you're not good at this, this is unsuccessful. I'll get ripped to shreds in a six-hour critique, but at no point is someone gonna be like, 'You're fat.'"

Lily, meanwhile, is working to change the system that hurt her. In the five years since she stopped performing full-time, she has opened a ballet school in Antwerp, moved back to the United States, and mentored young dancers around the country. (She attributes her soaring energy levels to finally allowing herself to eat.) She urges her students not to worry about the way they look and to focus on the way their bodies move. "Ten pounds is not going to break your career," she tells them. "Just try to be healthy." When her students are injured, she tells them to rest; she does not let them come back to class until they are fully recovered. A few years ago, Lily was hired to start a new dance program at a West Texas Christian university so conservative that, until recently, dancing was forbidden on campus. It was an unlikely proposition—but, against all odds, Lily built the department into a local magnet, drawing students from as far as London and California. She has also been exploring her academic interests, studying toward an English degree at the university. "I wake up excited every morning," she told me. In 2022, she started an even bigger job as the assistant director of an established preprofessional ballet school in Lubbock, Texas. She is helping to revamp the school's curriculum—and she is implementing a Balanchine-centric program. I asked her why, after everything she has been through, she would choose to do this. She clarified that she teaches "Balanchine, but healthy." She never forces her students' turnout or pushes their legs higher than they are ready to go. One of her favorite classes is her ten-year-olds; she loves how inquisitive they are. "They are allowed to ask questions?" I asked. This is still, somehow, difficult to imagine. "I don't yell at them when they breathe too loud," Lily said.

The stress fracture she incurred at twelve—the one for which she was banished to the front of the room, and from which she never had time to heal—has continued to haunt her. Years after she retired from dancing, her metatarsal still hurt most of the time. When it went numb a few years ago, she finally went to the doctor, who told her that her bone was decaying. If I were diagnosed with a necrotic toe, I would Google Image it before I was out of the waiting room, see the pictures of blackened toes and dead flesh, and hail a cab to the emergency room. But Lily still has a dancer's approach to pain. "If I've waited this long, I can wait longer," she figured, and went back to a busy semester. Other scars, she has simply adapted to. In a concession to the labral tears in her hips, she rarely lifts her leg higher than ninety degrees. Her knees "will never be quite what they used to be," but she's grateful that they no longer hurt.

Rachel was back at home in 2012, wondering what she was going to do with her life, when a friend suggested she sign up with Central Casting: anyone could be an extra, and she was already comfortable on sets. Soon, Rachel had steady work as a stand-in. Her job, she explained to me, was "to be a mannequin"—to walk through scenes before the actors arrived, giving the camera and lighting crews a chance to rehearse. She says this work is empowering. She feels more respected than she ever did at ballet, and she makes more money. She has opportunities to travel; she spent six months working on a TV show in Morocco, and another half a year living in London and working as a stand-in for a celebrity she resembles. "To say it's been more fun is possibly the biggest understatement of my life."

Rachel's confidence has soared since she quit ballet, and she has had boyfriends and even, for a while, a fiancé. But she still has trouble recognizing romantic cues and accepting that men are interested in her. Rachel long ago lopped off her long, regulation dancer hair in favor of a stylish bob, but she still moves with the telltale poise of a dancer. She says she wants to find love, and has downloaded the usual array of dating apps, but she rarely replies to men's messages, let alone starts a conversation. Rachel is thirty and could pass for a teenager, but she refers to herself as a "granny," as though preemptively removing herself from the dating pool.

Sometimes, on set, a cameraman will ask for permission before moving her body. Rachel can't get over it. "Yes," Rachel responds, and thinks: *Why are you asking?* Recently, her therapist—who has been trying to teach her to set limits—asked her to reflect on her physical boundaries. "I don't know what those are," Rachel says. She sounds bewildered as she recalls a question her therapist asked: "'Do you feel you've been taken advantage of in a physical boundary?' I don't know." Growing up, she never had a choice about being touched. "Have I just been trained to let whatever it is happen?" she wonders.

*   *   *

Several years ago, the novelist Sigrid Nunez spoke with the literary magazine the *Morning News* about her latest book tour and her evolution as a writer. Nunez was in her fifties then, and she had the kind of success that I once imagined would lead to happiness, or at least contentment; I imagined that a person like her—with five books published to critical acclaim and teaching appointments at Ivy League schools—would look back on her career and feel pretty great.

And yet, Nunez confessed, she was still haunted by her childhood dream. "I wanted to be a dancer when I was young," she said. "And I failed at that. I have never gotten over that. I'll never get over that." The interviewer—a fellow writer—seemed confused. "Meaning you feel badly about yourself?" he asked. I imagine Nunez testy as she repeated herself. "I don't know how else to put it except to say that I wanted to be a dancer and I failed at that and I'll never get over that," she said. "I don't think it's a terrible thing that I will never get over it. I don't see why I would get over it." So did that failure weigh her down? the interviewer pressed. Nunez tried again. Imagine you were young and you fell in love, she said, and then you broke up. "Though you move on you don't ever completely get over it. That loss is part of your life and who you are forever."

I came across this interview shortly after reading Nunez's novel *The Friend*, in which a staid New York writer reluctantly inherits a late friend's needy Great Dane. I had been thinking a lot about dogs at the time: like Nunez's narrator, I had recently acquired my first canine roommate, and the novel spoke to me so intensely I imagined it had been written for me alone.

After turning the last page, I began reading through Nunez's back catalog, with the same sense of pleasure I might take in getting to know a new friend. When I had worked my way back to Nunez's first book—a thinly veiled memoir about growing up in the projects of Staten Island—I was stunned to learn that she had spent much of her childhood riding the subway back and forth to Manhattan for ballet classes. She even seemed to understand my own original attraction to ballet: "The dream of being a ballerina begins with the dream of being beautiful."

So when I read that Nunez, more than thirty years after quitting ballet, still hadn't recovered from the loss, I felt vindicated. Of course I had not gotten over it; even Sigrid Nunez had not gotten over it. Like me, she still ruminated on what might have gone differently, looked back on her career like a coach rewinding the tape of an athlete's latest game. Except, of course, there would be no redo; the season was over.

But I also felt hopeless: if Sigrid Nunez, with all her talent and literary success, still regretted her failure in ballet, then what chance did I have? It dawned on me that I would live with this for the rest of my life, that this scar might never disappear.

"By age twelve any girl left at the barre wanted to be Margot Fonteyn and believed she could be," wrote Adrienne Sharp, a novelist and onetime dancer who in her fiction returns, again and again, to ballet. "Quit at this age, or at fourteen or fifteen or sixteen, and you'd be haunted by dancing the rest of your life."

I am thrilled to have a career as a writer. I am often amazed at my own good luck.

And yet.

"One of the most significant facts about us," wrote the anthropologist Clifford Geertz, "may finally be that we all begin with the natural equipment to live a thousand kinds of life but end in the end having lived only one."

The litany of counterfactuals is loudest after taking a class or going to see the ballet. If only I'd gone to Miami that one year I got in. If only I'd had a different coach. If only I hadn't given up.

"You stop dancing and your body tightens," wrote Sigrid Nunez. "You feel like a piece of clothing that has shrunk in the wash. A sensation worse than any muscle ache." Almost every night, before bed, I stretch. I stretch the way you're not supposed to, sitting down into a split without warming up. With my right leg in front, I count to five; I bend forward and back, switch legs, repeat. I've been doing this for fifteen years, ever since I stopped going to class: I was determined not to lose this ability. I was determined that my body would remain different—special. Marked. I catch myself practicing in quiet moments, too—pointing and flexing while I'm on the phone, absentminded fondues while I brush my teeth.

Children dream of being baseball players and movie stars and astronauts. Most of us, at some point, must face our limitations. But the closer we come to making it, the harder it is to accept our failure—at every level. Athletes who come in second feel worse than those who finish third. (A 1995 analysis by Cornell University psychologists found that Olympic silver medalists looked less happy on the podium than those who had won bronze, and were more likely to speak in postgame interviews about what "almost" happened.)

Some of my old classmates rigorously avoid ballet—watching it, doing it, talking about it. Some of them didn't want to participate in this book. They find it too painful: a reminder of all they have lost.

The Canadian artist Leanne Shapton spent her youth as a competitive swimmer, making it as far as the Olympic trials but not quite qualifying for the national team. Twenty years later, she published a memoir, *Swimming Studies*, in which she grappled with the role swimming had played in her life. She was in her late thirties then, with an enviable career—she had written several books and been an art director for the *New York Times*; her textile designs had appeared on high-fashion runways—and yet she still defined herself by her "brief, intense years as an athlete." As a young woman, she fell into all-consuming relationships with male bosses and lovers that reminded her of the dynamic she'd once had with her coach. As an artist, she drew on the discipline and self-awareness she had developed through training. She knew, intuitively, how to gear up for a deadline or a big event; when to rest and when to push on. And even after she stopped training formally, she never stopped swimming. "I'm drawn to swimming pools, all swimming pools, no matter how small or murky," she writes. She plunges into the freezing Ladies' Pond in London's Hampstead Heath, swims compulsive laps in hotel pools, follows the naked locals into a swimming pavilion in Sweden. But her laps are tinged with regret. "When I swim now, I step into the water as though absentmindedly touching a scar." Unsure of "what to do with something I do well but no longer have any use for," she sometimes competes with recreational teams—setting early alarms for practice and carbo-loading before meets, resuming her old habits like "an outgrown winter coat." Three nights a week, she dreams about swimming.

I dream that I'm auditioning for the Bolshoi. I know it's unusual that they would consider me at the advanced age of twenty-eight, but I'm delighted to find that I can still execute all the steps. *I've had ten years off*, I think, *but I'm back.*

I dream that I have been cast in *Serenade*—one of my favorite ballets, a moonlit Balanchine masterpiece. I don't feel confident that I know my part—in fact, I am trying to learn it from YouTube as the curtain rises—but I decide not to worry about it too much: this is the best moment of my life.

I dream that I attend an SAB fundraiser and afterward have sex with Balanchine, who is eighty-five years old. He mentions his girlfriend. I hope he will leave her for me.

I dream that I have been cast as Marie in *The Nutcracker*. I wonder if it will look odd that I'm so much bigger than the prince; I am thirty, after all, and he is eleven. Or that it will be a problem that I haven't been to any of the rehearsals and don't know the part. But the casting mistress is unconcerned. "Just make something up," she suggests.

I dream that I'm wearing a leotard with a number pinned to the front, and I'm dancing: piqués across the floor, pirouettes en pointe. A man sits at the front of the room with a clipboard, watching. I am both twenty-seven and seventeen, and I am auditioning for SAB. I feel so lucky to have a second chance, and I'm determined to make it count. I'm dancing better than ever and I know I'll be chosen.

The details don't matter. What matters is this: the euphoria, the relief, as I discover that it's not too late, after all. The exquisite pain of waking up, of remembering that it was just a dream. That I am not a dancer after all.

I read *Pointe* magazine's "Five Tips for Mastering Your Double Pirouette" and "What Are the Best Preperformance Snacks?" and imagine that they are relevant to my life. I travel with my ballet slippers tucked in the zipper pocket of my suitcase; I look up the local studio in foreign cities. I open my calendar and pencil in the classes I might attend. I usually don't, but I like knowing that I could.

Sometimes, when I'm in an open class, I catch myself day-dreaming that the teacher stops me on my way out to ask me who I am, what's my story, how did someone with so much talent end up here? Out of loyalty to Balanchine, I keep my fourth-position back leg straight as I prepare for a pirouette. (Classically trained dancers take off from two bent knees—an easier position from which to push off the ground—but Balanchine dancers pride themselves on the ability to spring up from an off-kilter pose.)

When I read that Balanchine chose Guerlain's "L'Heure Bleue" for his then-muse Maria Tallchief, I looked up the fragrance online. I saw that it was still being produced—the website said it had notes of iris and vanilla—and I ordered it. The liquid inside the bottle was golden yellow, and the top resembled an old-fashioned glass stopper. My first thought, when I sprayed it in the bathroom, was that it would be a good choice for keeping track of someone's whereabouts in the theater—the smell is overwhelming. It's loud and sweet and a little fusty; it makes me think of apothecaries and leather suitcases and the orgy scene in *Eyes Wide Shut*. All day, I kept sniffing my wrists, feeling both glamorous and creepy.

I think about how my early immersion in the legend of Balanchine shaped my own beliefs about creative work. My appreciation for his pragmatism has only grown as I have fought to establish a writing routine. I think about how he used constraints—the dimensions of a borrowed stage; the shortcomings of a particular dancer—to spur his creativity. (When NYCB moved from City Center to the much bigger Lincoln Center, the size of the dancers' steps increased accordingly.) I think about how he found inspiration everywhere, from Greek mythology and Bible stories to orange groves and commercial airline jingles. About how he shrugged off bad reviews. I force myself to sit down at my desk even when I'm afraid I have nothing to say, and I think of Balanchine's motto: "My muse must come to me on union time." I want to give up, and I hear Carol channeling Balanchine: "What are you saving it for? Do it now!" I feel like I'm choking on my own ambitions, and I think of his modesty. "If you set out to make a masterpiece," he once asked, "how will you ever get it finished?" His humble approach was much more effective. "Today, I think I'll make a little something," he said one day, and began arranging his seventeen students into a double-diamond configuration—the iconic opening of *Serenade*.

A group of women has gathered in a friend's living room. Coats and shoes come off; feet go up on the coffee table. Reflexively, I appraise my friends' socked arches. I feel like a lecherous man giving women on the street a once-over, but I can't help it. B's are almost flat, but I doubt it's ever bothered her. K's are high—so high that, if she just stood up, she would be halfway up to pointe. I'm jealous of her. *What a waste,* I think. *She doesn't even know how lucky she is. I doubt she appreciates her feet; I wonder if she has ever even noticed.*

A few weeks ago, I ate a big dinner and then I went to the ballet. When the dancers started moving, I thought, *Oh no: I'm too full.*

I'm not sure what I wanted to find when I went digging for old photos in the storage boxes beneath my childhood bed. Did I want to see confirmation of what I suspected—that I'd never been very good at ballet? Or did I want to find evidence that I'd been better than I remembered—that those years of devotion hadn't been totally deluded?

Digital cameras were not yet in everyone's pockets in the early aughts, and my parents shot few home videos. If there were Polaroids, they have been lost to time or periodic bedroom purges. I turned up a few grainy VHS tapes of summer-program recitals, but I couldn't pick myself out of the pixelated lineup; I was one of many indistinguishable figures in the back.

It was in my old, defunct email inbox ("sugarplumfairy54" at yahoo) that, after guessing the answers to a few ancient security questions, I found them: the audition photos I had submitted to summer programs at thirteen. I wore a plain black leotard in front of a blank studio wall—costumes or busy backdrops would have been frowned on—and struck a few basic poses: my legs crossed demurely in fourth position on pointe; one leg raised in a shallow V in attitude derriere.

I look different than I'd imagined. My feet look decent, although I suspect I wore broken-down pointe shoes to make my arches look more pronounced. My placement is passable, if my back is a bit too bent. But the biggest surprise is my body. My hips are not the monstrosities I remember. The problem is the opposite: I look weak. My arms are droopy and my balance looks precarious, as though my stringy legs might not be strong enough to hold up the weight of my body: I don't appear to be dancing so much as clenching my muscles and hoping I don't tip over. I wonder if I fell off pointe as soon as this photo was snapped. The tendons in my neck are popping, and my lips are pursed. I look miserable.

Sometimes, Meiying asks herself if she would enroll a daughter in ballet. "My thought is always, *No, I would not,*" she told me. "I don't want her to hate herself." She would like it if her children played an instrument or a team sport.

Even the most successful dancers tend to say they wouldn't let their own daughters follow in their footsteps. "Mother discouraged me from going into dancing, because of the rigor and confinement of a dancer's career," Alicia Alonso's daughter, Laura, told the *Washington Post* in 1979. "She wanted me to have a different life." (Laura defied her mother's wishes; in her mideighties, she is still teaching and staging ballets.) "When I have a daughter, I too will keep her clear of competitive ballet schools," Toni Bentley wrote in *Winter Season*. Are they just posturing—bragging about the difficulty of their lives? Or do they mean it? Do they regret their choices—do they want to save future generations from the pain of ballet?

"After I turn in my book, I need a long break from thinking about ballet," I texted a friend recently. In the same thread, we made plans to see the all-Balanchine program at New York City Ballet.

On a recent weekend trip to Seattle, my friend E and I found ourselves with a free afternoon. E hadn't been to the ballet in years, and I suggested we catch a matinee of Pacific Northwest Ballet's *Swan Lake*. I have known E—a voluble writer in her thirties—for almost a decade, and I had never seen her lost for words. But at the end of the ballet, she was speechless. "It was so beautiful," was all she could say.

And it was. What we had witnessed together was nothing short of a miracle. We had been swept away to an ancient palace and an enchanted lake. There had been raucous court dances and moonlit communions; we had seen doomed maidens dance with desperate joy and watched a wayward prince fall in love. We had heard a live orchestra perform the spectacular Tchaikovsky score. Dumbstruck awe was really the only appropriate response.

And yet when E asked me what I thought of the show, the first thing that came to mind was that the dancer playing the Swan Queen—a role so intense that just learning it drove Natalie Portman's *Black Swan* character to madness—had fallen out of her fouettés in Act III. The sequence of thirty-two fouetté turns is one of the most notoriously difficult in the entire classical repertoire; it takes enormous strength and perfect timing to rotate on one foot over and over while the other leg stays in the air. After thirty fouettés—I couldn't help but count—the Swan Queen stumbled, filling out the rest of the music with a simpler step.

This was the only flub, the only moment of obvious imperfection in a three-hour production. And yet this is the moment that stays with me most. *My brain is broken,* I think, as we file out of our velvet seats—*my perspective permanently skewed.*

I wonder how the dancer, the star of the show, will feel when she gets home. I wonder if she will think about her triumphant pas de deux with Prince Siegfried. If she knows that her final leap into the lake made at least one audience member cry. If she replays the standing ovation she received.

I doubt it.

As we make our way out of the theater, I see little girls in frilly dresses and shiny Mary Janes clinging to their mother's hand as though afraid of all the beauty they've just seen. Some of them are wearing tight ballerina buns. I wonder if they came straight from class this morning, or if they just want to look like dancers all the time.

I see it in their eyes—the yearning to be just like the women they watched onstage. Maybe this will be a passing phase; maybe it will determine the course of their childhoods, their adolescence. The odds are low that it will determine their careers. But it could shape their self-image, their bodies, their relationships for years to come.

And yet: I don't think they will end up with all the same scars.

These girls saw, among the flock of two dozen dainty swans, one who is gender nonconforming. When Ashton Edwards (who uses they/them pronouns) was six, they were crushed to learn that men didn't dance on pointe. A few years ago, Ashton—by then an advanced student at PNB's school—taught themself the basics of pointe work by watching tutorials on YouTube. An apprentice with Pacific Northwest Ballet, Ashton now dances both male and female roles. As a swan in *Swan Lake*—one of the most exaggeratedly feminine roles in the canon—they blended right in.

These girls saw Black dancers wearing brown tights that match their skin, and brown pointe shoes they didn't have to dye themselves.

And, at the height of a Covid surge, they saw dancers onstage in masks: a radical acknowledgment that there is something—health of the individual, and of the group—more important than aesthetic perfection.

When I mentioned the fouetté flub to E, she didn't know what I was talking about.

With ten years of intensive training, plus another decade of sporadic classes and home barre workouts, I am still, and will always be, an "Advanced Beginner." Maybe, at more casual studios, "Beginning Intermediate." I am not trying to be a

dancer; this is some kind of therapy, or recreation. As I dig a
faded leotard out of the dresser in my childhood bedroom; as
I walk to a local studio and say to the receptionist, "Ballet at
seven," I hear my teacher's words, echoing from 2004: "Ballet
is not supposed to be fun." My mom had made the mistake
of saying, "Have fun," as I peeled off my leg warmers and
made my way toward the drafty studio at City Center, and my
teacher overheard. She swiveled around on her toe, graceful as
ever. "It's not supposed to be fun," she said. Her voice rose.
"This is work. This is serious. If you want to say something,
you can say, 'Have a good class.'"

I find a place at the barre, in the corner. I wear a baggy
T-shirt over my ancient leotard. Instead of neatly sewing the
elastics to the soles of my ballet slippers, I have tied them in a
sloppy knot beneath my arch—the kind that would have once
gotten me kicked out of class. I always feel a little ridiculous
as I get ready for ballet, like a kid playing dress-up. I haven't
purchased new dance clothes since 2006; I don't feel entitled
to the accoutrements, the silky skirts and soft leg warmers I
used to love. I make do instead with the last leotards and slippers my mom bought me fifteen years ago. (They have held up
impressively well, considering they cost about twelve dollars.)

Ballet is not fun.

I start giving myself a warm-up: calf stretches at the barre,
a few quick tendus. I can tell, from a glance around the room,
that the majority of my classmates have also had serious
training at some point. I would guess that most of them once
dreamed of being dancers. I don't know for sure, because I
can't bring myself to talk to anyone.

This is work. This is serious.

The teacher demonstrates a simple plié exercise and I take
comfort in the familiar order of the barre. When I run in the

park or work out at the gym, I distract myself with podcasts and pounding music. I check my GPS or the tracker on the machine, calculate my pace and count down the minutes until I can stop. It's medicine, a chore, a means to an end. But it is impossible to do ballet without engaging all of my senses: watching the teacher, listening to the music, feeling the floor. Without pouring all of my mental energy into turning out, pulling up, pointing my feet, straightening my knees. Or in trying to. No human body, let alone mine, can simultaneously do all that.

My teacher was right. Ballet is not fun. It's meditation; it's a physical prayer. It's striving for perfection and then giving in to the moment.

I catch a glimpse of myself in the mirror, and I cringe the way I do when I hear myself speaking French: I know how that verb is supposed to sound, how this step is supposed to look, and I'm momentarily surprised to see that I no longer have the ability to do it. I feel self-conscious when the teacher corrects me—*Why are you wasting your time?* I want to ask. And then I feel defensive: I *know* I'm doing it wrong. The teacher doesn't have to tell me.

I look away from my reflection and think of the second half of Balanchine's dictum: "Don't think, dear. Just do." I arrange my feet in first position and I feel at home in my body and I dance.

Acknowledgments

I am grateful to my agent, the faithful Bridget Wagner Matzie, and to the team at HarperCollins, especially Deb Brody, Jamie Lescht, Kelly Dasta, and the endlessly supportive, instantaneously responsive Emma Peters. Writing is inherently lonely, but I never felt like I was alone on this project.

To the team at Oneworld, especially Cecilia Stein and Rida Vaquas; to Olivia Lo Sardo for the beautiful cover design and to Will Tavlin for careful fact-checking (any errors are mine).

To all those who offered feedback and reassurance on chapters and drafts, and also reassurance on life in general, including Esther Breger, Polly Clayton-Hatfield, Melissa Dahl, Justin Elliott, Katy Fallon, Julia Fisher, Erika Fry, Jeremy Galen, Hannah Gold, Claire Groden, Emily Holleman, Linda Kinstler, Adam Plunkett, Brooke Shuman, Alex Stone, Chris Toumazis, and Genevieve Walker.

To the Zoom writing group that was a lifeline throughout lockdown: Jessica Gross, Lane Florsheim, Anna Van Lenten, Abby Ronner, Jessica Smith.

To my ballet buddies, including Emily Fry, Max Neely-Cohen, Kika Ziesk-Socolov.

To the Hambidge Center and the London Library.

To my parents and their partners.

And to all of the dancers who shared their stories.

Recommendations for Further
Reading and Viewing

In the course of research and writing, I read dozens of memoirs, biographies, and novels set in the ballet world, and watched almost as many ballet-themed films and TV shows.

Here are a few of my favorites (all of which informed my thinking, not all of which made it into this book by name):

To Read

Joan Acocella, *Twenty-Eight Artists and Two Saints*—includes *The New Yorker* critic's essays on dancers and choreographers such as Mikhail Baryshnikov, Vaslav Nijinsky, Frederick Ashton, and Jerome Robbins

Toni Bentley, *Winter Season: A Dancer's Journal*—an impassioned firsthand account of a young dancer's life at Balanchine's New York City Ballet, and the inspiration for many of the ballet memoirs that followed

Misty Copeland, *Life in Motion: An Unlikely Ballerina*—the extraordinary rags-to-riches story of the first Black principal dancer at American Ballet Theatre

Meredith Daneman, *Margot Fonteyn: A Life*—Daneman, a novelist, spent a decade researching this epic account of the ballerina's intimate and professional life

Suzanne Farrell (with Toni Bentley), *Holding On to the Air*—an extraordinary artist's memoir of her creative process, and her side of her controversial relationship with Balanchine

Sophie Flack, *Bunheads*—a former New York City Ballet dancer's coming-of-age novel about a young woman torn between the discipline of dancing and the allure of normal life

Jennifer Homans, *Apollo's Angels: A History of Ballet*—the definitive story of ballet in Europe and America, by a scholar and former professional dancer

Camille Laurens, *Little Dancer Aged Fourteen: The True Story Behind Degas's Masterpiece*—a novelist's meditation on the tragic life of Degas's young muse

Georgina Pazcoguin, *Swan Dive: The Making of a Rogue Ballerina*—a juicy memoir by the first Asian American female soloist at New York City Ballet

Adrienne Sharp, *White Swan, Black Swan*—wistful short stories—some based on historical figures—capture the beauty and sacrifice of life in ballet

Noel Streatfeild, *Ballet Shoes*—the classic 1936 British children's novel—following three orphan sisters dreaming of stardom—was my favorite book when I was ten, and was just as enjoyable when I reread it last year

James Wolcott, *Lucking Out*—a memoir about (among other things) falling in love with ballet in 1970s New York

Fjord Review—like *Pointe* magazine for *n+1* readers—founded a few years ago by an Australian critic

To Watch

George Balanchine's The Nutcracker (1993)—New York City Ballet's *Nutcracker* has been filmed more recently, in 2015, but my favorite version features Wendy Whelan as Coffee and thirteen-year-old Macaulay Culkin as the Nutcracker Prince

Center Stage (2000)—a teen drama about ballet-school rivalries—elevated by performances from American Ballet Theatre stars including Ethan Stiefel and Julie Kent

Dance Academy (2010–2013)—an extremely charming Australian TV show about a group of teens at a fictional ballet boarding school

Breaking Pointe (2012–2013)—a reality TV show set at Salt Lake City's Ballet West—both a soap opera and a showcase for serious dancing

Horizontes (2015)—a rare peek at the Grand Theater of Havana, this documentary features a young student at the Cuban National Ballet School, a star ballerina at the company, and—overseeing it all—ninety-five-year-old Alicia Alonso

Dancer (2016)—a documentary about the troubled Ukrainian ballet prodigy Sergei Polunin, who quit the Royal Ballet School at age twenty-two and then went viral with a dance video to Hozier's pop song "Take Me to Church"

In Balanchine's Classroom (2021)—a documentary featuring emotional interviews with some of Balanchine's most devoted dancers, as well as archival footage of Balanchine at work

Bibliography

Abra, Jock. "The Dancer as Masochist." *Dance Research Journal* 19, no. 2 (Winter 1987–88): 33–39.

Abrams, Abby. "Raising a Ballerina Will Cost You $100,000." FiveThirty Eight, August 20, 2015. https://fivethirtyeight.com/features/high-price -of-ballet-diversity-misty-copeland.

Acocella, Joan. "The Long Goodbye." *The New York Review of Books*, April 7, 1994. https://www.nybooks.com/articles/1994/04/07/the-long -goodbye.

———. *Twenty-Eight Artists and Two Saints: Essays*. New York: Vintage Books, 2008.

Adato, Allison. "Solo in the City." *Los Angeles Times*, December 5, 1999. https://www.latimes.com/archives/la-xpm-1999-dec-05-tm-40787 -story.html.

"Alicia Alonso obituary." *Times*, October 18, 2019. https://www.the times.co.uk/article/alicia-alonso-obituary-t03x56c96.

Alptraum, Lux. "Painful Sex Isn't Normal—Let's Put This Damaging Myth to Bed." *Self*, July 11, 2018. https://www.self.com/story /painful-sex-isnt-normal-myth.

Anderson, Jack. "Alicia Alonso, Star of Cuba's National Ballet, Dies at 98." *New York Times*, October 17, 2019. https://www.nytimes. com/2019/10/17/arts/dance/alicia-alonso-dead.html.

———. "Review: Kirstein Reminisces." *Dance Chronicle* 12, no.1 (1989): 155–61.

Angyal, Chloe. *Turning Pointe: How a New Generation of Dancers Is Saving Ballet from Itself*. New York: Bold Type Books, 2021.

Aronofsky, Darren, dir. *Black Swan*. 2010; Century City, CA: Fox Search-
 light Pictures. https://www.hulu.com/movie/black-swan-ode850bd
 -a343-4dd7-86c4-c008cdaca86f.

Associated Press. "N.Y.C. Ballet's 'Nutcracker' Is a Family Affair."
 November 29, 2000. http://www.lawrence.com/news/2000/nov/29
 /nyc_ballets/.

Balanchine, George. "Mr. B Talks About Ballet: George Balanchine
 Leads America's Dance Boom." *Life*, June 11, 1965.

"Ballet by Numbers." *The Telegraph*, June 29, 2009. https://www
 .telegraph.co.uk/culture/theatre/dance/5686620/Ballet-by-numbers
 .html.

"Ballet Offers Tribute on Moon Venture; SPAC Audience Views Landing." *Glens Falls Times* (Glens Falls, New York), July 21, 1969.

Bamigboye, Baz. "'I Was Barely Eating During *Black Swan*': Natalie
 Portman on the Role That Has Made the Oscar Hers to Lose." *Daily
 Mail*, January 7, 2011. https://www.dailymail.co.uk/tvshowbiz
 /article-1344902/Natalie-Portman-cert-best-actress-Oscar-says-I
 -barely-ate-Black-Swan.html.

Barnes, Clive. "Dance: Miss Farrell in *Bolero*." *New York Times*,
 March 27, 1977. https://www.nytimes.com/1977/03/27/archives
 /dance-miss-farrell-in-bolero.html.

———. "The Dance: School of American Ballet." *New York Times*,
 May 23, 1975. https://www.nytimes.com/1975/05/23/archives/the
 -dance-school-of-american-ballet-3-wellstaged-works-show-student
 .html.

Barry, Ellen. "Greeted as the First Great Millennial Author, and Wary
 of the Attention." *New York Times*, August 31, 2018. https://
 www.nytimes.com/2018/08/31/world/europe/sally-rooney-ireland
 .html.

Baumeister, Roy F. *Masochism and the Self*. New York: Psychology
 Press, 2014. First published 1989 by Lawrence Erlbaum Associates,
 Inc. (New Jersey).

Baumol, William J., Joan Jeffri, and David Throsby. *Making Changes:
 Facilitating the Transition of Dancers to Post-Performance Careers*.
 New York: The aDvANCE Project, 2004.

Becker, Kent G. "Pointe Shoes Part II: Gaynor Minden," *Ballet Focus* (blog), March 18, 2015. https://balletfocus.com/pointe-shoes-part-iigaynor-minden/.

Beetle, Norman, Oliver Bettle, Ursula Neumärker, and Klaus-Jürgen Neumärker. "Body Image and Self-Esteem in Adolescent Ballet Dancers." *Perceptual and Motor Skills* 93, no. 1 (2001): 297–309.

Belle, Anne, and Deborah Dickson, dirs. *Dancing for Mr. B: Six Balanchine Ballerinas.* 1989; New York: Seahorse Films. https://vimeo.com/306729940.

Bentley, Toni.

———. "A Ballerina, Inside Out." *The New York Review of Books,* April 23, 2010. https://www.nybooks.com/daily/2010/04/23/ballerina-inside-out/.

———. "Dancers: The Agony and the Ecstasy." *New York Times,* May 31, 1987. https://www.nytimes.com/1987/05/31/arts/dancers-the-agony-and-the-ecstasy.html.

———. "'Margot Fonteyn': Leaping Beauty." *New York Times,* December 5, 2004. https://www.nytimes.com/2004/12/05/books/review/margot-fonteyn-leaping-beauty.html.

———. *Serenade: A Balanchine Story.* New York: Pantheon, 2022.

———. *The Surrender: An Erotic Memoir.* New York: ReganBooks, 2004.

———. "THiNK 2013: Toni Bentley." November 9, 2013. THiNK conference, Goa, India. 29:42. https://www.youtube.com/watch?v=-jPJiw2czAH8.

———. "The Touch of Class." *Rolling Stone,* September 29, 1983. https://www.tonibentley.com/pdfarticles/rollingstone/DancerDiary_ToniBentley_RollingStones.pdf.

———. *Winter Season: A Dancer's Journal.* Gainesville: University Press of Florida, 2003.

Berger, John. *Ways of Seeing.* London: British Broadcasting Corporation and Penguin Books Ltd., 1972.

Bharadwaj, Shimal. "What Mila Kunis Eats in a Day." *Business Insider,* July 13, 2017. https://www.businessinsider.com/what-mila-kunis-eats-in-a-day-2017-7.

Birnbaum, Robert. "Sigrid Nunez." *Morning News*, March 29, 2007. https://themorningnews.org/article/sigrid-nunez.

Blanshard, Richard, dir. *Living a Ballet Dream: Six Dancers Tell Their Stories*. 2001; Santa Monica, CA: Family Home Entertainment. https://www.youtube.com/watch?v=M-IQQCEW_go&t=128s.

Brady, Joan. *The Unmaking of a Dancer: An Unconventional Life*. New York: Harper & Row, 1982.

Brooks, Katherine. "A Brief but Stunning Visual History of Ballet in the 20th Century." *HuffPost*, October 31, 2014. https://www.huffpost.com/entry/ballet-photos_n_6077576.

Brown, Helen Gurley. *Sex and the Single Girl*. New York: Pocket Books, 1964.

Brown, Ismene. "The Deathless Alicia Alonso, in Person." *The Arts Desk*, October 18, 2019. https://theartsdesk.com/dance/deathless-alicia-alonso-person.

Campbell, Mary. "Ballet's Start Late but Good." *The Arizona Republic* (Phoenix, Arizona), May 23, 1970.

Campoy, Ana. "Ballet: Cuba's Enduring Revolution." Cubans 2001 (student project, University of California, Berkeley, Graduate School of Journalism), last modified April 5, 2002. https://projects.journalism.berkeley.edu/cubans2001/story-ballet.html.

Cardellino, Carly. "The Beauty Secrets of a World-Famous Principal Ballerina." *Cosmopolitan*, November 10, 2014. https://www.cosmopolitan.com/style-beauty/beauty/a31203/beauty-secrets-of-a-principle-ballerina/.

Chalabi, Mona. "The Gender Orgasm Gap." FiveThirtyEight, August 20, 2015. https://fivethirtyeight.com/features/the-gender-orgasm-gap/.

Church, Timothy S., Diana M. Thomas, Catrine Tudor-Locke, Peter T. Katzmarzyk, Conrad P. Earnest, Ruben Q. Rodarte, Corby K. Martin, Steven N. Blair, and Claude Bouchard. "Trends Over 5 Decades in U.S. Occupation-Related Physical Activity and Their Associations with Obesity." *PLOS ONE*. 2011. https://journals.plos.org/plosone/article?id=10.1371/journal.pone.0019657.

Clein, Emmeline. "The Smartest Women I Know Are All Dissociating." *BuzzFeed News*, November 20, 2019. https://www.buzzfeednews

.com/article/emmelineclein/dissociation-feminism-women-fleabag
-twitter.

Conley, Kevin. "Pointe Counterpointe." Onward & Upward with the
Arts. *The New Yorker*, December 1, 2002. https://www.newyorker
.com/magazine/2002/12/09/pointe-counterpointe.

Cooper, Michael. "Breaking the Glass Slipper: Where Are the Female
Choreographers?" *The New York Times*, June 23, 2016. https://www
.nytimes.com/2016/06/26/arts/dance/breaking-the-glass-slipper
-where-are-the-female-choreographers.html.

Copeland, Misty. *Life in Motion: An Unlikely Ballerina*. New York:
Touchstone, 2014.

Cowart, Leigh. *Hurts So Good: The Science and Culture of Pain on
Purpose*. New York: PublicAffairs, 2021.

Croce, Arlene. "Balanchine Said." *The New Yorker*, January 18, 2009.
https://www.newyorker.com/magazine/2009/01/26/balanchine
-said.

Crowley, Chris. "Jia Tolentino Chases Spicy Rigatoni with Karaoke and
Too Much Fireball." The Grub Street Diet. *Grub Street*, August 2,
2019.https://www.grubstreet.com/2019/08/jia-tolentino-grub-street
-diet.html.

Cudnik, Christian. "Carol Sumner." *Ballet Initiative Podcast*, June 13,
2014. Podcast, 1:29:10. https://www.listennotes.com/podcasts/ballet
-initiative/carol-sumner-9bO2BQfnqWX/.

Cusk, Rachel. "Can a Woman Who Is an Artist Ever Just Be an Artist?"
The New York Times Magazine, November 7, 2019. https://www
.nytimes.com/2019/11/07/magazine/women-art-celia-paul-cecily
-brown.html.

Daly, Ann. "The Balanchine Woman: Of Hummingbirds and Channel
Swimmers." *The Drama Review* 31, no. 1 (1987): 8–21. https://doi.org
/10.2307/1145763.

d'Amboise, Jacques. *I Was a Dancer*. New York: Alfred A. Knopf, 2011.

Daneman, Meredith. "The Affair of the Century." *Telegraph*, October 11, 2004. https://www.telegraph.co.uk/culture/4730478/The
-affair-of-the-century.html.

———. *Margot Fonteyn: A Life*. New York: Viking, 2004.

Davies, Dave. "Tracing Ballet's Cultural History Over 400 Years." *Fresh Air*. NPR, December 15, 2011. https://www.npr.org/transcripts /143775428.

Davis, Allison P. "Misty Copeland on Ballet, Race, and Her New Book." *The Cut*, March 5, 2014. https://www.thecut.com/2014/03 /misty-copeland-on-ballet-race-and-her-new-book.html.

Dederer, Claire. "What Do We Do with the Art of Monstrous Men?" *The Paris Review*, November 20, 2017. https://www.theparisreview .org/blog/2017/11/20/art-monstrous-men/.

de Mille, Agnes. *Lizzie Borden: A Dance of Death*. Boston: Atlantic Monthly Press, 1968.

———. *Portrait Gallery: Artists, Impresarios, Intimates*. New York: Houghton Mifflin, 1990.

Dernberger, Brittany N., and Joanna Pepin. "Gender Flexibility, but Not Equality: Young Adults' Division of Labor Preferences." *Sociological Science* 7, no. 2 (2020): 36–56.

Dery, Mark. "Edward Gorey Lives at the Ballet." *The Paris Review*, November 1, 2018. https://www.theparisreview.org/blog/2018/11/01 /edward-gorey-lived-at-the-ballet/.

Deutsch, Helene. *Psychoanalysis of the Sexual Functions of Women*. Edited by Paul Roazen. Translated by Eric Mosbacher. London: Karnac Books, 1991. First published 1925.

Di Orio, Laura. "Pre-Performance Rituals." *Dance Informa Magazine Australia*, December 4, 2012. https://www.danceinforma.com /2012/12/04/pre-performance-rituals/.

Druss, R. G., and A. J. Silverman. "Body Image and Perfectionism of Ballerinas: Comparison and Contrast with Anorexia Nervosa." *General Hospital Psychiatry* 1, no. 2 (1979): 115–21.

Dunning, Jennifer. "Eating Disorders Haunt Ballerinas." *New York Times*, July 16, 1987. https://www.nytimes.com/1997/07/16/arts /eating-disorders-haunt-ballerinas.html.

———. "Pas de Quatre: Hopes of Spring." *New York Times*, May 1, 1998. https://www.nytimes.com/1998/05/01/movies/pas-de-quatre-hopes-of-spring.html.

Dusenberry, Maya. *Doing Harm: The Truth About How Bad Medicine and Lazy Science Leave Women Dismissed, Misdiagnosed, and Sick.* San Francisco: HarperOne, 2018.

Eder, Richard. "Alicia Alonso Takes Cuban Ballet to People." *New York Times*, May 29, 1964. https://www.nytimes.com/1964/05/29/archives/alicia-alonso-takes-cuban-ballet-to-people-52-member-troupe-dances.html.

Ephron, Nora. *I Feel Bad About My Neck: And Other Thoughts on Being a Woman.* New York: Knopf, 2006.

"Eva Alt—Dancer, Social Media Editor, Glossier." The New Jock.

Fairchild, Megan. *The Ballerina Mindset: How to Protect Your Mental Health While Striving for Excellence.* New York: Penguin Books, 2021.

Farrell, Suzanne, with Toni Bentley. *Holding On to the Air.* Gainesville: University Press of Florida, 1990.

Febos, Melissa. *Girlhood.* New York: Bloomsbury, 2021.

Fisher, Barbara. *In Balanchine's Company: A Memoir.* Middletown, CT: Wesleyan University Press, 2006.

Fisher, Lauren Alexis. "Dancers Took Over the Runway at Dior's Spring 2019 Show." *Harper's Bazaar*, September 24, 2018. https://www.harpersbazaar.com/fashion/fashion-week/a23398506/dior-spring-2019-show-paris-fashion-week/.

Flack, Sophie. *Bunheads.* New York: Little Brown, 2011.

Fonteyn, Margot. *A Dancer's World: An Introduction for Parents and Students.* New York: Alfred A. Knopf, 1979.

———. *Margot Fonteyn: Autobiography.* New York: Alfred A. Knopf, 1976.

Foy, Patricia, dir. *The Margot Fonteyn Story.* 1989; London: BBC. https://www.youtube.com/watch?v=95N4J7B2XWI.

Friedman, Danielle. *Let's Get Physical: How Women Discovered Exercise and Reshaped the World.* New York: G. P. Putnam's Sons, 2022.

Fuhrer, Margaret. "A Nonbinary Swan, on Pointe." *New York Times*, April 19, 2022. https://www.nytimes.com/2022/04/19/arts/dance/nonbinary-ballet-dancers-swan-lake.html.

———. "The Secrets of New York City Ballet's Pointe Shoe Room." *Dance Spirit*, March 5, 2018. https://dancespirit.com/the-secrets-of -new-york-city-ballets-pointe-shoe-room/.

Furlan, Julia. "No Contract, No Dancing? City Ballet Fails to Reach Agreement with Dancers." WNYC, April 28, 2011. https://www .wnyc.org/story/127090-no-cotract-no-dancing/.

Gallup Organization. "Personal Weight Situation." 2019. https://news .gallup.com/poll/7264/personal-weight-situation.aspx.

Garber, Megan. "When *Newsweek* 'Struck Terror in the Hearts of Single Women.'" *The Atlantic*, June 2, 2016. https://www.theatlantic .com/entertainment/archive/2016/06/more-likely-to-be-killed-by-a -terrorist-than-to-get-married/485171/.

Gay, Roxane. "Fifty Years Ago, Protestors Took on the Miss American Pageant and Electrified the Feminist Movement." *Smithsonian Magazine*, January 2018. https://www.smithsonianmag.com /history/fifty-years-ago-protestors-took-on-miss-america-pageant -electrified-feminist-movement-180967504/.

George, Nelson, dir. *A Ballerina's Tale*. 2015; New York, NY: Urban Romances. https://www.amazon.com/Ballerinas-Tale-Misty -Copeland/dp/B016L5MRAI.

Gladstone, Valerie. "Still Ignoring Barriers, a Ballerina Returns." *New York Times*, January 25, 1998. https://www.nytimes.com /1998/01/25/arts/dance-still-ignoring-barriers-a-ballerina-returns .html.

Glass, Allison S., Herman S. Bagga, Gregory E. Tasian, Patrick B. Fisher, Charles E. McCulloch, Sarah D. Blaschko, Jack W. McAninch, and Benjamin N. Breyer. "Pubic Hair Grooming Injuries Presenting to U.S. Emergency Departments." *Urology* 80, no. 6 (2012): 1187–91.

Gleick, Elizabeth. "SWF Seeks Anybody." *New York Times*, April 16, 2000. nytimes.com/books/00/04/16/reviews/000416.16gleickt.html.

Glionna, John M. "Trapped in a Dispiriting Dance of Wills." *Los Angeles Times*, August 23, 1998. https://www.latimes.com/archives /la-xpm-1998-aug-23-me-15815-story.html.

Gordon, Suzanne. *Off Balance: The Real World of Ballet*. New York: McGraw-Hill Book Company, 1983.

Gottlieb, Lori. "Marry Him! The Case for Settling for Mr. Good Enough." *The Atlantic,* March 2008. https://www.theatlantic.com /magazine/archive/2008/03/marry-him/306651/.

Gottlieb, Robert. "The Dancer and the Dance." *New York Times,* April 27, 1997. https://www.nytimes.com/1997/04/27/books/the-dancer -and-the-dance.html.

———. *George Balanchine: The Ballet Maker.* New York: Harper Perennial, 2010.

Grigoriadis, Vannesa. "'She Needs to Take Off All Her Clothes While I Am Clothed': Inside the NXIVM Empowerment Sex Cult." *Vanity Fair,* June 19, 2019. https://www.vanityfair.com/news/2019/06/inside -the-end-nxivm-empowerment-sex-cult.

Gross, Jessica. "Finding Comfort in Small Spaces." Longreads, September 2018. https://longreads.com/2018/09/24/finding-comfort-in-small -spaces/.

Gruen, John. *The Private World of Ballet.* New York: Viking, 1975.

Halzack, Sarah. "Alicia Alonso, Indomitable Ballet Star Who Founded National Ballet of Cuba, Dies at 98." *Washington Post,* October 17, 2019. https://www.washingtonpost.com/local/obituaries/alicia-alonso -ballet-star-who-founded-national-ballet-of-cuba-dies-at-98/2019 /10/17/4b5c0d9a-f101-11e9-8693-f487e46784aa_story.html?utm _source=pocket_mylist.

Hamilton, Linda H. *Advice for Dancers: Emotional Counsel and Practical Strategies.* San Francisco: Jossey-Bass Publishers, 1998.

Harss, Marina. "Christine Shevchenko and Devon Teuscher: ABT's Dazzling New Generation of Star Power." *Pointe,* November 28, 2018. https://pointemagazine.com/abt-christine-shevchenko-devon-teuscher/.

Herbenick, Debby, Vanessa Schick, Stephanie A. Sanders, Michael Reece, and J. Dennis Fortenberry. "Pain Experienced During Vaginal and Anal Intercourse with Other-Sex Partners: Findings from a Nationally Representative Probability Study in the United States." *Journal of Sexual Medicine* 12, no. 4 (2015): 1040–51.

Heyward, Anna. "How to Write a Dance." *The Paris Review,* February 4, 2015. https://www.theparisreview.org/blog/2015/02/04/how -to-write-a-dance/.

Hicklin, Aaron. "Misty Copeland: Dancing into History." *The Observer*, March 5, 2017. https://www.theguardian.com/stage/2017/mar/05 /misty-copeland-principal-american-ballet-theatre-life-in-motion.

Hochman, Connie, dir. *In Balanchine's Classroom*. 2021; Ossining, NY: IBC Productions. Film Forum, September 21, 2021.

Hochman, Jerry. "MorDance's *Romeo and Juliet*: When Swords Fly." *CriticalDance*, May 19, 2019. https://criticaldance.org/mordances-romeo-and-juliet-when-swords-fly/.

Hofer, Eileen, dir. *Horizontes*. 2015; Geneva, Switzerland: Intermezzo Films S.A. https://www.amazon.com/Horizontes-Alicia-Alonso/dp /B0786T3141.

Homans, Jennifer. *Apollo's Angels: A History of Ballet*. New York: Random House, 2010.

Hong, Nicole, and Sean Piccoli. "Keith Raniere, Leader of NXIVM Sex Cult, Is Sentenced to 120 Years in Prison." *New York Times*, October 27, 2020. https://www.nytimes.com/2020/10/27/nyregion /nxivm-cult-keith-raniere-sentenced.html.

Howard, Theresa Ruth. "6 Pointe Shoe Manufacturers Commit to Offering More Diverse Shades." *Pointe*, September 30, 2020. https:// www.dancemagazine.com/black-ballet-dancer-pointe-shoes/.

Hytner, Nicholas, dir. *Center Stage*. 2000; Culver City, CA: Columbia Pictures. https://www.hulu.com/movie/center-stage-bdabd7a1-5a42 -41fc-b408-ffcaff94e857.

Illing, Sean. "Proof That Americans Are Lying About Their Sexual Desires." Vox, September 30, 2018. https://www.vox.com/conver sations/2017/6/27/15873072/google-porn-addiction-america -everybody-lies.

Imperial College London. "Ballet Dancers' Brains Adapt to Stop Them Getting in a Spin." *Science Daily*, September 26, 2013. https://www .sciencedaily.com/releases/2013/09/130926204725.htm.

Jacobs, Alexandra. "The Ballerina Who Bent." *Observer*, October 4, 2004. https://observer.com/2004/10/the-ballerina-who-bent/.

Jacobs, Laura. *Celestial Bodies: How to Look at Ballet*. New York: Basic Books, 2018.

Jacques, Adam. "Tamara Rojo: The Ballet-Dancer-Turned-Artistic-Director on Her Burst Appendix, the Bolshoi Acid Attack and Elitism." *The Independent*, July 17, 2013. https://www.independent.co.uk/news /people/profiles/tamara-rojo-the-balletdancerturnedartisticdirector -on-her-burst-appendix-the-bolshoi-acid-attack-and-elitism-8714576 .html.

Jamison, Leslie. *The Empathy Exams*. Minneapolis: Graywolf Press, 2014.

Jennings, Luke. "Sexism in Dance: Where Are All the Female Choreographers?" *The Observer*, April 28, 2013. https://www.theguardian .com/stage/2013/apr/28/women-choreographers-glass-ceiling.

Jonas, Wayne. "Why Is It More Painful to Be a Woman?" *Psychology Today*, August 28, 2018. https://www.psychologytoday.com/us/blog /how-healing-works/201808/why-is-it-more-painful-be-woman.

Jones, Allie. "Wear Spanx, Risk Death—or Worse, Uncontrollable Gas." *The Atlantic*, January 21, 2014. https://www.theatlantic.com/culture /archive/2014/01/wear-spanx-risk-death-or-worse-uncontrollable -gas/357239/.

Kaufman, Sarah L. "'Chocolate Nutcracker': Sweet and Soulful." *Washington Post*, December 20, 2002. https://www.washingtonpost .com/archive/lifestyle/2002/12/20/chocolate-nutcracker-sweet-and -soulful/fode5887-3cad-455f-a7a7-5c2521f713e6/.

———. "Pain, Satin and Paper Towels: What It Takes for Ballerinas to Dance on Their Toes." *Washington Post*, May 26, 2017.

Kelly, Deirdre. *Ballerina: Sex, Scandal, and Suffering Behind the Symbol of Perfection*. Vancouver: Greystone Books, 2012.

———. "These Ad Campaigns Show That Dance Sells." *Dance*, December 31, 2014. https://www.dancemagazine.com/dance-advertisement -campaign/.

Kent, Allegra, with James Camner and Constance Camner. *The Dancers' Body Book*. New York: William Morrow Paperbacks, 1984.

Khakpour, Porochista. *Sick: A Memoir*. New York: Harper Perennial, 2018.

Kiefer, Adam W., Michael A. Riley, Kevin Shockley, Candace A. Sitton, Timothy E. Hewitt, Sarah Cummins-Sebree, and Jacqui G

Haas. "Lower-limb Proprioceptive Awareness in Professional Ballet Dancers." *Journal of Dance Medicine & Science* 17, no. 3 (2013): 126–32.

Kierkegaard, Søren. *The Concept of Anxiety: A Simple Psychologically Oriented Deliberation in View of the Dogmatic Problem of Hereditary Sin*. Translated by Alastair Hannay. New York: Liveright Publishing Corporation, 2014.

Kirkland, Gelsey, and Greg Lawrence. *Dancing on My Grave: An Autobiography*. Garden City, New York: Doubleday & Company, 1986.

———. *The Shape of Love*. New York: Doubleday, 1990.

Kirkup, Sarah. "Balanchine: The Choreographer Who Put the Music First." *Gramophone*. April 3, 2017. https://www.gramophone.co.uk /other/article/balanchine-the-choreographer-who-put-the-music -first.

Kisselgoff, Anna. "Plenty of Pastiche and Pizzazz, but, Sorry, No Popcorn." *New York Times*, January 26, 2004. https://www.nytimes. com/2004/01/26/arts/city-ballet-review-plenty-of-pastiche-and-pizazz-but-sorry-no-popcorn.html.

———. "The Traditional Approach for Afternoon and Evening." *New York Times*, December 11, 2001. https://www.nytimes. com/2001/12/11/arts/ballet-review-the-traditional-approach-for-afternoon-and-evening.html.

Klapper, Melissa R. *Ballet Class: An American History*. New York: Oxford University Press, 2020.

Knapp, Caroline. *Appetites: Why Women Want*. New York: Counterpoint, 2003.

Kourlas, Gia. "Still Dancing, Her Way, from the Soul." *New York Times*, June 2, 2010. https://www.nytimes.com/2010/06/03/arts/dance /03alonso.html.

———. "What Is a Ballet Body?" *New York Times*, March 3, 2021. https://www.nytimes.com/2021/03/03/arts/dance/what-is-a-ballet -body.html.

Kroker, Arthur, and Michael A. Weinstein. *Data Trash: The Theory of the Virtual Class*. New York: St. Martin's Press, 1994.

Laing, Olivia. *The Lonely City: Adventures in the Art of Being Alone.* New York: Picador, 2016.

Langsdorff, Maja. *Ballet—and Then? Biographies of Dancers Who No Longer Dance.* Norderstedt, Germany: Books on Demand GmbH, 2006.

La Rocco, Claudia. "The 'Nutcracker' Test and Other Apprentice Trials." *New York Times*, December 3, 2006. https://www.nytimes.com/2006/12/03/arts/dance/03laro.html.

Laurens, Camille. *Little Dancer Aged Fourteen: The True Story Behind Degas's Masterpiece.* Translated by Willard Wood. New York: Other Press, 2018.

Leder, Drew. *The Absent Body.* Chicago: University of Chicago Press, 1990.

Lloyd, Stephen. *Constant Lambert: Beyond the Rio Grande.* Woodbridge, CT: The Boydell Press, 2014.

Lovatt, Peter. *Dance Psychology: The Science of Dance and Dancers.* Norfolk, VA: Dr. Dance Presents, 2018.

Macaulay, Alastair. "After the Curtain Falls: Talking to Suzanne Farrell, Artist and Muse." *New York Times*, December 19, 2017. https://www.nytimes.com/2017/12/19/arts/dance/suzanne-farrell-ballet-balanchine.html.

———. "Judging the Bodies in Ballet." *New York Times*, December 3, 2010. https://www.nytimes.com/2010/12/04/arts/dance/04ballet.html.

Mangweth-Matzek, Barbara, Claudia Ines Rupp, Armand Hausmann, Georg Kemmler, and Wilfried Biebl. "Menarche, Puberty, and First Sexual Activity in Eating-Disordered Patients as Compared with a Psychiatric and Nonpsychiatric Control Group," *International Journal of Eating Disorders* 40, no. 8 (2007): 705–10.

"Maria Tallchief, 1925–2013." *The Week*, January 8, 2015. https://the week.com/articles/465418/maria-tallchief-19252013.

Martin, John. "The Dance: Debutante." *New York Times*, October 31, 1948. https://timesmachine.nytimes.com/timesmachine/1948/10/31/96603219.pdf?pdf_redirect=true&ip=0.

Mason, Francis. *I Remember Balanchine: Recollections of the Ballet Master by Those Who Knew Him.* New York: Doubleday, 1991.

Massey, Alana. *All the Lives I Want: Essays About My Best Friends Who Happen to Be Famous Strangers.* New York: Grand Central Publishing, 2017.

McLean, Adrienne L. *Dying Swans and Madmen: Ballet, the Body and Narrative Cinema.* New Brunswick, NJ: Rutgers University Press, 2008.

Medeiros, Joao. "How Intel Gave Stephen Hawking a Voice." *Wired*, January 13, 2015. https://www.wired.com/2015/01/intel-gave-stephen -hawking-voice/.

Melendez, Pilar. "NXIVM Trial Opens: Feds Say Founder Keith Raniere Was 'Crime Boss,' Not Guru." *The Daily Beast*, May 7, 2019. https:// www.thedailybeast.com/nxivm-trial-founder-keith-raniere-was -crime-boss-posing-as-guru-feds-say.

Miller, Jess. "Weight Watchers Isn't Fooling Anyone." *Slate*, March 8, 2021. https://slate.com/business/2021/03/weight-watchers-name -change-ww-dieting-culture.html.

Mintz, Laurie. "The Orgasm Gap: Simple Truth and Sexual Solutions." *Psychology Today*, October 4, 2015. https://www.psychologytoday .com/us/blog/stress-and-sex/201510/the-orgasm-gap-simple-truth -sexual-solutions.

Montee, Kristy. "Balanchine's Ballerinas Tell Two Different Stories." *South Florida Sun-Sentinel* (Deerfield Beach), December 23, 1990. https:// www.sun-sentinel.com/news/fl-xpm-1990-12-23-9003040227 -story.html.

"Music: Death of a Swan." *Time*, February 2, 1931. https://content .time.com/time/subscriber/article/0,33009,740938,00.html.

National Eating Disorders Association. "Statistics & Research on Eating Disorders." Accessed March 25, 2022. https://www.national eatingdisorders.org/statistics-research-eating-disorders.

Nguyen, Hoang. "Of the Five Senses, a Majority Would Miss Sight the Most." YouGov America, July 25, 2018. https://today.yougov.com /topics/health/articles-reports/2018/07/25/five-senses-majority -would-miss-sight-most.

Nolan, Megan. *Acts of Desperation*. New York: Little, Brown and Company, 2021.

Nunez, Sigrid. *A Feather on the Breath of God*. New York: Picador, 1995.

———. *The Friend*. New York: Riverhead Books, 2018.

Open Access Government. "Office Workers Spend 75% of Their Waking Hours Sitting Down." August 14, 2019. https://www.open accessgovernment.org/office-workers-sitting-down/71612/.

Orenstein, Peggy. *Cinderella Ate My Daughter: Dispatches from the Front Lines of the New Girlie-Girl Culture*. New York: Harper Paperbacks, 2012.

Orson, Diane. "The Dancer Who Broke Ballet's Height Ceiling." Connecticut Public Radio, March 17, 2017. https://www.ctpublic.org /arts-and-culture/2017-03-17/the-dancer-who-broke-ballets-height -ceiling.

Orth, Maureen. "Private Dancer." *Vanity Fair*, May 1990. https://archive .vanityfair.com/article/1990/5/private-dancer.

Ouellette, Jenny. "Ready, Set, Places: Six Pros Share Their Preshow Rituals." *Dance Spirit*, November 14, 2016. https://dancespirit.com /ready-set-places/.

Palmer, Tony, dir. *Margot*. 2005; West Long Branch, NJ: Kultur Video. https://www.amazon.com/Margot-Fonteyn/dp/B07F1BQQSQ.

Panebianco-Warrens, Clorinda. "Exploring the Dimensions of Flow and the Role of Music in Professional Ballet Dancers." *Muziki* 11, no. 2 (2014): 58–78.

Parker, Janine. "'Flesh and Bone'—Once Again, Ballet as a Crazed Deathmatch." *The Arts Fuse*, November 30, 2015. https://artsfuse .org/137823/fuse-tv-review-flesh-and-bone-once-again-ballet-as-a -crazed-deathmatch/

Pazcoguin, Georgina. *Swan Dive: The Making of a Rogue Ballerina*. New York: Henry Holt, 2021.

Perel, Esther. "You'd Be Perfect for Ralph Lauren." *How's Work?* April 20, 2021. Podcast, 48:51. https://howswork.estherperel.com/episodes /s2-episode-3-youd-be-perfect-for-ralph-lauren.

"Physical Inactivity Poses Greatest Health Risk to Americans, Research Shows." American Psychological Association, 2009. https://www.apa.org/news/press/releases/2009/08/physical-inactivity.

Pogrebin, Robin. "Toning Down Asian Stereotypes to Make 'The Nutcracker' Fit the Times." *New York Times*, November 13, 2018. https://www.nytimes.com/2018/11/13/arts/dance/nutcracker-chinese-tea-stereotypes.html.

Potter, Caroline. "Senses of Motion, Senses of Self: Becoming a Dancer." *Ethnos* 73, no. 4 (2008): 444–65.

Powell, Michael, and Emeric Pressburger, dirs. *The Red Shoes*. 1948; London, UK: Eagle-Lion Studios. https://www.amazon.com/Red-Shoes-Anton-Walbrook/dp/B009B6I0SS.

Price, Brena R., and Terry F. Pettijohn II. "The Effect of Ballet Dance Attire on Body and Self-Perceptions of Female Dancers." *Social Behavior and Personality* 34, no. 8 (2006): 991–98.

Prickard, Angela. *Ballet Body Narratives: Pain, Pleasure and Perfection in Embodied Identity*. Bern, Switzerland: Peter Lang AG, International Academic Publishers, 2015.

Proffitt, Dennis, and Drake Baer. *Perception: How Our Bodies Shape Our Minds*. New York: St. Martin's Press, 2020.

Prose, Francine. *The Lives of the Muses: Nine Women and the Artists They Inspired*. New York: Harper Perennial, 2003.

Radell, Sally A., Daniel D. Adame, and Steven P. Cole. "Effect of Teaching with Mirrors on Body Image and Locus of Control in Women College Ballet Dancers." *Perceptual and Motor Skills* 95 (2002): 1239–47.

Radish, Christina. "Mila Kunis Interview *Black Swan*." Collider, November 23, 2010. https://collider.com/mila-kunis-interview-black-swan/.

Ravaldi, C., A. Vannacci, T. Zucchi, E. Mannucci, P. L. Cabras, and M. Boldrini. "Eating Disorders and Body Image Disturbances Among Ballet Dancers, Gymnasium Users and Body Builders." *Psychopathology* 36 no. 4 (2003): 247–54.

Read, Nick, and Mark Franchetti, dirs. *Bolshoi Babylon*. 2015; London, UK: Red Box Films. https://www.amazon.com/Bolshoi-Babylon-Anastasiya-Meskova/dp/B01LXP6P5I.

Resnick, Brian. "The Silent 'Sixth' Sense." Vox, December 26, 2019. https://www.vox.com/the-highlight/2019/11/22/20920762/proprioception-sixth-sense.

Robb, Alice. "The Afterlife of a Ballerina." *Elle*, October 17, 2016. https://www.elle.com/culture/a39990/alexandra-ansanelli-prima-ballerina-career/.

———. "The 'Flow State': Where Creative Work Thrives." BBC, February 5, 2019. https://www.bbc.com/worklife/article/20190204-how-to-find-your-flow-state-to-be-peak-creative.

Roca, Octavio. "In Defense of 'Story' Ballets: *The Sleeping Beauty* Returns to San Francisco." *San Francisco Chronicle*, March 12, 1995. https://www.sfgate.com/entertainment/article/In-Defense-of-Story-Ballets-The-Sleeping-3041230.php.

Rockwell, John. "Gelsey Kirkland at ABT—Easy Does It." *New York Times*, December 21, 1975. https://www.nytimes.com/1975/12/21/archives/gelsey-kirkland-at-abt-ease-does-it-gelsey-kirkland-at-abt-ease.html.

Roiphe, Katie. *The Power Notebooks*. New York: Free Press, 2020.

Ross, Rick. "Watch Out for Tell-Tale Signs." *The Guardian*, May 27, 2009. https://www.theguardian.com/commentisfree/belief/2009/may/27/cults-definition-religion.

Roupenian, Kristen. "Cat Person." *The New Yorker*, December 4, 2017. https://www.newyorker.com/magazine/2017/12/11/cat-person.

Royal Opera House. *Swan Lake: Corps de Ballet* (The Royal Ballet). https://www.youtube.com/watch?v=TkCijrMgeM8.

Russo, Teresa M., Barbara Woods, Felicia Blum, and Edith Watts. "The Dancers and Degas." Web feature. The Metropolitan Museum of Art, 2007. https://www.academia.edu/26433641/The_Dancers_and_Degas_2007_The_Metropolitan_Museum_of_Art_New_York.

Sack, Robert L., and Warren Miller. "Masochism: A Clinical and Theoretical Overview." *Psychiatry* 38, no. 3 (1975): 244–57.

Sandham, Tricia J. "Former Elite Adolescent Female Dancers Reflect on the Loss of a Professional Dream." Thesis. Saskatoon, Canada: University of Saskatchewan, 2012.

Saul, Emily. "Allison Mack Allegedly Starved 'Dynasty' Star Catherine Oxenberg's Daughter India." *New York Post*, June 7, 2019. https://nypost.com/2019/06/07/allison-mack-allegedly-starved-dynasty-star-catherine-oxenbergs-daughter-india/.

Schneider, Caitlin. "11 Writers Who Started Late." *Mental Floss*, April 16, 2005. https://www.mentalfloss.com/article/63112/11-writers-who-started-late.

Schneider, Harold J., Athena King, Jeffrey Bronson, and Edward Miller. "Stress Injuries and Developmental Change of Lower Extremities in Ballet Dancers." *Radiology* 113, no. 3 (1974): 627–32.

Schwall, Elizabeth B. *Dancing with the Revolution: Power, Politics, and Privilege in Cuba*. Chapel Hill: University of North Carolina Press, 2021.

Shainess, Natalie. *Sweet Suffering: Woman as Victim*. Indianapolis: The Bobbs-Merrill Company, 1984.

Shapton, Leanne. *Swimming Studies*. New York: Blue Rider Press, 2012.

Sharp, Adrienne. *White Swan, Black Swan: Stories*. New York: Random House, 2001.

Shaw, Helen. "Balanchine and Cunningham: The Titans of 20th-century Dance." *New York Times*, May 31, 2019. https://www.nytimes.com/2019/05/31/books/review/balanchine-cunningham-dance.html.

Siegel, Beatrice. *Alicia Alonso: The Story of a Ballerina*. London: Warne, 1979.

Sills, Bettijane, with Elizabeth McPherson. *Broadway, Balanchine & Beyond: A Memoir*. Gainesville: University Press of Florida, 2019.

Silver, Joanna, and Jacqui Farrants. "I Once Stared at Myself in the Mirror for Eleven Hours." *Journal of Health Psychology* 21, no. 11 (2016): 2647–57.

Silverman, Ann B. "Children Commute to Dance in Ballet." *New York Times*, December 5, 1982. https://www.nytimes.com/1982/12/05/archives/children-commute-to-dance-in-ballet.html

Singer, Toba. *Fernando Alonso: The Father of Cuban Ballet*. Gainesville: University Press of Florida, 2013.

"Sitting Disease: How a Sedentary Lifestyle Affects Heart Health." Johns Hopkins Medicine, https://www.hopkinsmedicine.org/health

/wellness-and-prevention/sitting-disease-how-a-sedentary-lifestyle
-affects-heart-health.

Skog, Alan, dir. *New York City Ballet: George Balanchine's* The Nut-cracker. 2011; New York: Live from Lincoln Center.

Smith, Dinitia. "Another Balanchine Disciple Tends the Master's Flame." *New York Times*, March 19, 1996. https://www.nytimes.com /1996/03/19/arts/another-balanchine-disciple-tends-the-master-s -flame.html.

Solnit, Rebecca. "If I Were a Man." *The Guardian,* August 26, 2017, https://www.theguardian.com/lifeandstyle/2017/aug/26/rebecca -solnit-if-i-were-a-man.

Sontag, Susan. "The Dancer and the Dance." *London Review of Books* 9, no. 3 (February 5, 1987). https://www.lrb.co.uk/the-paper/v09/n03 /susan-sontag/dancer-and-the-dance.

———. *Regarding the Pain of Others*. New York: Farrar, Straus and Giroux, 2003.

Stanley, Alessandra. "Martins, Ballet Master, Held on Charge He Beat His Wife." *New York Times*, July 22, 1992. https://www.nytimes .com/1992/07/22/nyregion/martins-ballet-master-held-on-charge -he-beat-his-wife.html.

Sulcas, Roslyn. "Youth's Joy in Movement, Energetic and Unfet-tered." *New York Times*, June 10, 2010. https://www.nytimes.com /2010/06/11/arts/dance/11workshop.html.

Sytsma, Alan. "Ballet Dancer Misty Copeland Is Hooked on Sushi and Seamless." *Grub Street*, September 6, 2013. https://www.grubstreet .com/2013/09/misty-copeland-grub-street-diet.html.

Szalai, Jennifer. "The Complicated Origins of 'Having It All.'" Essay. *The New York Times Magazine*, January 2, 2015. https://www.nytimes .com/2015/01/04/magazine/the-complicated-origins-of-having-it-all .html.

Tajet-Foxell, Britt, and Francis David Rose. "Pain and Pain Tolerance in Professional Ballet Dancers." *British Journal of Sports Medicine* 29, no. 1 (1995): 31–34.

Taper, Bernard. *Balanchine: A Biography*. New York: Harper & Row, 1963.

Teen Vogue. "One Ballet Student's Sacrifice for Her Dreams." *Strictly Ballet*, season 2, episode 1, May 20, 2015. https://www.youtube.com/watch?v=vHfxfocDdBU.

Tennant-Moore, Hannah. "The Vertical Altar." *n+1*, September 9, 2010. https://www.nplusonemag.com/online-only/book-review/vertical-altar/.

Thompson, Derek. "When a Promotion Leads to Divorce." *The Atlantic*, January 14, 2020, https://www.theatlantic.com/ideas/archive/2020/01/whos-afraid-of-ambitious-women/604855/.

Thompson, Jayne. "The Salaries of Ballet Dancers." Chron.com, July 1, 2018. https://work.chron.com/salaries-ballet-dancers-5128.html.

Tishgart, Sierra. "Author Alissa Nutting Prefers Two Hot Dogs on One Bun." *Grub Street*, August 4, 2017. https://www.grubstreet.com/2017/08/alissa-nutting-grub-street-diet.html.

Tuck, Lon. "My Mother, the Prima Ballerina." *Washington Post*, June 17, 1979. https://www.washingtonpost.com/archive/lifestyle/1979/06/17/my-mother-the-prima-ballerina/3dfa35ac-f9c4-4d52-819a-78d3f943cfdo/.

Tucker, Todd. *The Great Starvation Experiment: Ancel Keys and the Men Who Starved for Science*. Minneapolis: University of Minnesota Press, 2007.

Villella, Edward, with Larry Kaplan. *Prodigal Son: Dancing for Balanchine in a World of Pain and Magic*. Pittsburgh: University of Pittsburgh Press, 1992.

Wadler, Joyce. "In Ballet About Dreams, 2 Girls Live Theirs." *New York Times*, December 10, 1999. https://www.nytimes.com/1999/12/10/nyregion/in-ballet-about-dreams-2-girls-live-theirs.html.

Wainwright, Steven P., Clare Williams, and Bryan S. Turner. "Fractured Identities: Injury and the Balletic Body." *Health* 9, no. 1 (2005): 49–66.

Waller-Bridge, Phoebe, writer. *Fleabag*. Season 2, episode 4. Directed by Harry Bradbeer, featuring Phoebe Waller-Bridge, Olivia Colman, and Andrew Scott. Aired May 17, 2019. https://www.amazon.com/gp/video/detail/B0875FRLWQ/ref=atv_dp_season_select_s2.

Watkins, Ali. "Jeffrey Epstein's New York Hunting Ground: Dance Studios." *New York Times*, September 3, 2019. https://www.nytimes.com/2019/09/03/nyregion/jeffrey-epstein-dance-victims.html.

Wingenroth, Lauren. "Over 80% of Ballets Are Still Choreographed by Men." *Dance*, July 24, 2019. https://www.dancemagazine.com /women-ballet-choreographers/.

Winship, Lyndsey. "'You're Never Comfortable as a Dancer': Brilliant Ballerina Beatriz Stix-Brunell's Next Step." *The Guardian*, July 5, 2021. https://www.theguardian.com/stage/2021/jul/05/beatriz-stix-brunell-royal-ballet.

Wolcott, James. *Lucking Out: My Life Getting Down and Semi-Dirty in the Seventies*. New York: Doubleday, 2011.

Woodward, Ian. "Margot Fonteyn: 'I've Never Been a Dedicated Dancer.'" *The Guardian*, February 25, 1970. https://www.theguardian .com/stage/2020/feb/25/margot-fonteyn-interview-nureyev-1970.

Wulff, Helena. *Ballet Across Borders: Career and Culture in the World of Dancers*. Abingdon, UK: Routledge, 1998.

Yakin, Boaz, dir. *Uptown Girls*. 2003; Beverly Hills, CA: MGM. https:// www.amazon.com/Uptown-Girls-Brittany-Murphy/dp/B00101 ZOW2.

Zentner, Marcel, and Tuomas Eorola. "Rhythmic Engagement with Music in Infancy." *PNAS Proceedings of the National Academy of Sciences of the United States of America* 107, no. 13 (2010): 5678–773.

Zimroth, Evan. *Collusion: Memoir of a Young Girl and Her Ballet Master*. New York: HarperFlamingo, 1999.

Index

pain (*cont.*)
   dancing through, 159–61, 163–64,
      167, 174, 175, 176–77, 180–81
   downplaying, 155, 157, 158–59
   enhancing body awareness, 212
   gender discrimination in treatment,
      157
   gendered perception, 155–56
   identity as woman and, 155–57, 159
   masochism, 93–95, 157–58, 165,
      170–72, 174–76
   pointe work, 59, 60, 160–64, 170, 176
   resilience, 179
   SAB, 166–67, 169
   souvenirs, 175–76
   in TV shows and movies, 164–65
Palmer, Tony, 84–85, 86, 88–89
Paltrow, Scot J., 90–91
pandemic. *See* Covid-19 pandemic
Panebianco-Warrens, Clorinda, 54–55
Paris Girls (Meiying painting), 231–32
Paris Opera, 26, 72–74, 115
pas de deux, 76–77
Pas de Quatre, 220
passivity, doctrine of, 77–78, 93, 95
Pauline (SAB classmate), 109
Pavlova, Anna, 141, 159–60
Pazcoguin, Georgina, 217–18
*Perception: How Our Bodies Shape
   Our Minds* (Proffitt and Baer), 208
Perel, Esther, 212
Peter and the Wolf, 132
Petit, Roland, 35
Piano Music for Ballet Class, 50
Piper (former ballet student), 192, 194
Plath, Sylvia, 89, 158
plié, defined, 24n
Plisetskaya, Maya, 25
pointe shoes
   breaking-in process, 57, 134, 161–62
   bunions, 128
   color, 57, 249
   cost, 162
   first fitting, 161
   Gaynors, 162–63
   lifespan, 162, 185–86
   look and structure, 161

   pain, 60, 161, 162–63, 164, 170
   ribbons, 29, 31, 161, 162, 185
   as souvenir/keepsake, 7, 176, 194, 232
pointe work
   in art, 72
   balance, 216
   ballet skirt, 139
   gendered nature of, 76, 77, 161,
     184, 249
   MorDance, 234
   muscles, 45
   pain, 59, 144, 160–64, 170, 176
   as rite of passage, 160–61, 170
Polanski, Roman, 9, 38
Portman, Natalie, 10, 147, 165,
   186–87, 234, 248
post-ballet life, 193–201. *See also
   specific dancers*
   accepting reality, 195–96, 240–41
   avoiding ballet, 194, 241
   continued involvement in ballet,
     193–95, 201, 236
   coping with heartbreak, 193, 195,
     239, 240–41
   depression, 61, 194
   framework for grieving, 195–96
   as imposters in "real world," 194
   new careers, 231–33, 235–38
   new goals, 193, 195
   new identity, 193, 195
   regrets, 239–42, 246–47
   struggle to connect with people, 194
post-wounded women, 158–59
Potter, Caroline, 216–17, 218
The Power Notebooks (Roiphe), 89
Prince, 62
Prodigal Son (Villella memoir), 25, 77
Professional Performing Arts School,
   98, 132, 166
Proffitt, Dennis, 208
proprioception, 222–23
Prose, Francine, 27
Proust, Marcel, 83
Prudden, Bonnie, 214
*The Psychoanalysis of Sexual Functions
   of Women* (Deutsch), 158
pubic grooming injuries, 156

About the Author

Alice Robb has written for *Vanity Fair*, the *Washington Post*, *The Atlantic*, and *The New Republic*, among other publications. Her first book, *Why We Dream*, was recommended by places like *The New Yorker*, the *New York Times*, *Today*, *Vogue*, *Time*, and *The Guardian*, and has been translated into seventeen languages.